c454207600

WN FR
CASTLE UPOI
CITY LIBRARIES

D0551974

Rescues in the Surf

Newcastle Libraries

Lifeboat Tyne at South Shields c1890.

Rescues in the Surf

The Story of the Shields Lifeboats
1789-1939

Stephen Landells

Tyne Bridge Publishing

Acknowledgements

Our grateful thanks to the Duke of Northumberland for kindly writing the foreword.

Tyne Bridge Publishing would also like to thank the National Maritime Museum; North Tyneside Libraries; Port of Tyne Authority; RNLI; South Tyneside Libraries; Swedish National Maritime Museums; Tyne & Wear Archives & Museums; UK Hydrographic Office; John Holness; and all who helped the author with his research, for their generous help with illustrations.

Admiralty charts are ©Crown Copyright and/or database rights. Reproduction by permission of the Controller of Her Majesty's Stationery Office and the UK Hydrographic Office (www.ukho.gov.uk).

Cover image

Detail from a painting, by John Wilson Carmichael, of a rescue at the mouth of the Tyne. So far we havebeen unable to trace the date, origin and whereabouts of this painting,, but the lifeboat is either the Original or the first Northumberland. The print from which the image was reproduced is in the collections of Newcastle Libraries.

The views expressed in this work are those of the author, and in no way reflect the views of Tyne Bridge Publishing or the Council of the City of Newcastle upon Tyne.

©Stephen Landells, 2010

ISBN: 9781857951493

Published in association with Tyne & Wear Archives & Museums

Published by
City of Newcastle upon Tyne
Newcastle Libraries
Tyne Bridge Publishing, 2010
www.newcastle.gov.uk/libraries
www.tynebridgepublishing.co.uk

NEWCASTLE UPON TYNE
CITY LIBRARIES

Class No.

623.829

Acc No.

Issued

All rights reserved. No part of this book may be reproduced, stored or introduced into a retrieval system, or transmitted in any form or by any means (electronic, mechanical, photocopying, recording or other-wise) without the prior permission of the publishers.

Printed by Elanders, North Tyneside

Contents

Tyne & Wear Archives & Museums

This print, of a rescue by lifeboat on Tynemouth Bar, formed part of Henry Greathead's 1802 Parliamentary campaign.

Preface

As a Shields lad I have been aware of the story of Willie Wouldhave, Henry Greathead, and the *Original* and *Tyne* lifeboats, since my childhood. That story kindled a lifelong interest in the lifeboat service and local maritime history.

Once I began to delve into the subject, it soon became apparent that there was a lot more to the story of the Shields lifeboats in respect of the development of this fledgling lifeboat service, the difficulties in maintaining and running the service, the many rescues, and why this service just faded into history. It made a fascinating story, stretching over 150 years.

The aim of this book has been to bring together the numerous and disparate references, source material and my own research into a single and comprehensive study on the Shields Lifeboats and the Tyne Lifeboat Institution. However, I acknowledge that due to the passage of time, and because full records and minutes of the Tyne Lifeboat Institution have either been lost or destroyed, there are gaps in this story that still remain to be filled.

This study begins with the local and economic circumstances that first led to the idea of stationing a boat at the mouth of the Tyne harbour solely for the rescue of shipwrecked mariners, what influenced the design of this boat, and the controversy that ensued over the accolade 'inventor of the lifeboat'.

Subsequent chapters deal with the development of the Tyne Lifeboat Institution, the 1849 lifeboat disaster, and how this led to the re-organisation and reform of the then struggling national lifeboat institution, a great irony considering the role the RNLI played in the demise of the Tyne Lifeboat Institution.

The role that the communities of Tynemouth and South Shields played in the creation of the Volunteer Life Brigades, the forerunners of today's Coastguard Rescue Service, and the pilot community that manned the lifeboats are also examined, together with accounts of some of the more significant rescues carried out by the lifeboat crews. Finally, the factors that led to the operational decline of the Tyne Lifeboat Institution, and the relationship with the RNLI are discussed.

The conclusions reached are based on factual evidence found in these references and on my own assumptions cross-referenced with evidence taken from the remaining written records, maps, paintings of the period and charts. I am, of course, responsible for the content of this book and the views expressed are entirely mine, with any errors being my sole responsibility.

Stephen Landells, July 2010

Foreword by the Duke of Northumberland

My ancestors, the 2nd and 4th Dukes of Northumberland, were heavily involved in the creation of the lifeboat services in the North East and they would be very proud of the way in which those services have evolved to save so many lives over the last 200 years. This wonderfully researched book tells the story of the Tyne Lifeboats, why they began and how they evolved both in design and organisation.

It is hard to appreciate the sheer volume of boat traffic coming in and out of the Tyne in the early years of the lifeboats but the need to save crews and passengers on vessels stuck on the mud banks and struck by north easterly gales was of paramount importance. Protecting the brave lifeboat crews was equally important and the determination to design a safe, stable craft was vital.

In 1790, the first lifeboat was stationed at South Shields, although the resulting choice, following a design competition, was made amid some controversy and over the following years, various designers claimed to have invented the 'modern' lifeboat. The success of this lifeboat led to a second boat being stationed at North Shields, and named *Northumberland*, in recognition of the 2nd Duke who had provided the funds for this boat. The whole process of design, construction and organisation was beset by funding and other problems but nevertheless, a huge amount was achieved as the system evolved, clearly demonstrated by the success of the lifeboat *Tyne* which, serving between 1833 and 1887, is said to have saved 1,024 lives. In 1851, a national competition, backed by the 4th Duke of Northumberland, aimed to produce the best design for a lifeboat as a response to the lifeboat disaster at South Shields in 1849.

Stephen Landells has done a wonderful job in documenting the history and recording the many rescues carried out over this period. It makes one stop and think of the bravery of the early volunteers who rowed out in cold and heavy seas, with bare equipment, leaky waterproofs and no life-jackets!

Duke of Northumberland

Newcastle Libraries

1. The entrance to the Tyne Harbour from Tynemouth, overlooking the Black Middens. Clifford's Fort, and the High and Low Lights can be seen in the middle distance. The first North Shields lifeboat was housed next to the Low Light, with the Original's boathouse located near to where the two ships have been beached on the South Shields shore to the left of the picture.

Tyne & Wear Archives & Museums

2. The Wreck by John Scott. The location of this wreck is on the Black Middens with the Tynemouth Lighthouse in the background.

Trinity Towers Lookout

Lifeboat Memorial

South Shields Volunteer Life Brigade Watch House

Herd Sand

South Beach Boathouses

Tynemouth Ba

South Pier

North Pier

3. This photograph shows the locations of many sites referred to in this book. After the construction of the piers, removal of the Herd Sands, and the riverside development, the view of the harbour entrance and shoreline has changed greatly since the days of Fairles, Wouldhave and Greathead.

Original's Boathouse

Tyne Sailors' Home

Coble Landing

Lawe House

Low Light Boathouse

Tynemouth RNLI Station

Pilot Jetty Boathouse

East Fish Quay Boathouses

The Groyne

Mussel Scarp Sands

Tynemouth Volunteer Life Brigade Watch House

Tynemouth RNLI No. 2 Boathouse

Black Middens Rocks

Tynemouth RNLI No. 1 Boathouse

Prior's Haven

Airfotos

4. The model submitted by Greathead to the Parliamentary committee 1802.

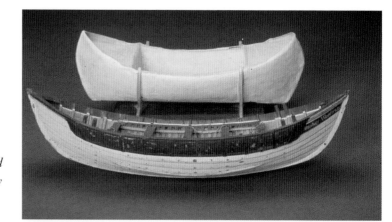

5. Wouldhave's tin model and the Greathead-built Bawdsey lifeboat of 1801.

6. A model by George Farrow of the South Shields lifeboat Original. The model is located at Trinity House, Newcastle.

7. A model of the Tyne as originally built in 1833, Trinity House, Newcastle..

Tyne & Wear Archives & Museums

8. The Invention of the Lifeboat by the Newcastle painter, Ralph Hedley.

This painting was displayed at the Royal Academy in 1897. Willie Wouldhave is in his cottage working on the tin model that he submitted to the Lawe House Committee. It is on display in South Shields Museum.

9. *The entrance to the Tyne, by J.W. Carmichael. The North Shields lifeboat house is next to the Low Lighthouse.*

10. *Shipwrecks off the Tyne c1825-1850. Unknown Artist.*

Tyne & Wear Archives & Museums

11. *The Entrance to the Tyne, by John Scott (detail). This view, from the Coble Landing South Shields shows, on the left, the North Shields lifeboat house to the seaward of the Lowlight, the Herd Sand Beacon on the right, and a brig in The Narrows.*

Tyne & Wear Archives & Museums

12. *Launching the Lifeboat, by Luke Clennell, 1810.*

13. Samuel Malcolm 1842-1935. Founder Member of South Shields Volunteer Life Brigade and Vice President of the Tyne Lifeboat Society.

14. The Wreck off the South Pier by J. McLea, showing the South Shields Volunteer Life Brigade Watch House and the South Beach Lifeboat House, 1897.

Tyne & Wear Archives & Museums

15. The tug William towing the brig Brotherly Love across Tynemouth Bar with the North Pier construction works in the background, 1875, by John Scott.

Tyne & Wear Archives & Museums

16. Shipwreck off Tynemouth, by Charles George Jefferson.

17. A Wreck off the South Pier, by John Scott. The ship is the Fowlis.

18. Going to the Wreck, by Joseph Garbut, 1875.

Tyne & Wear Archives & Museums

19. The Northumberland at the opening of Tyne Dock, 1857, by John Scott.

Lifeboat, South Shields

52280.

Author's collection

20. The Tyne and her original shelter, from a postcard.

Author's collection

21. A model of the second Northumberland lifeboat made by North Shields shipwright Robin Thompson, Tynemouth Volunteer Life Brigade.

Author's collection

22. The Bedford, awaiting restoration, at Eyemouth Harbour.

IN MEMORY OF THE BRAVE AND SKILFUL PILOTS WHO
ACTED AS COXSWAINS OF THE TYNE LIFE BOATS AND
WHO WITH THEIR CREWS WERE THE MEANS OF RESCUING
MANY THOUSANDS OF SHIPWRECKED SAILORS
FROM A WATERY GRAVE.

George Smith, died March 16th 1848, Aged 58.	Joseph Smith, died July 17th 1873, Aged 74.
John Milburn, died April 29th 1864 Aged 67.	Gilbert Young, died March 29th 1884, Aged 76.
Jacob Harrison, died October 31st 1867 Aged 75.	Matthew J. Lawson, died Nov 6th 1889 Aged 81.
Jacob Burn, died August 9th 1871, Aged 73.	Andrew Harrison, died Apl 6th 1890, Aged 72.
William O. Thurlbeck, died March 1st 1896, Aged 47.	

ALSO IN MEMORY OF THE PILOTS WHO LOST THEIR
LIVES BY THE CAPSIZING OF THE LIFE BOAT
"PROVIDENCE" WHEN ATTEMPTING TO RESCUE THE CREW
OF THE "BETSY" ON DECEMBER 4TH 1849.

Lancelot Burn, Cox.	John Marshall,	Ralph Shotton,
John Burn,	Thomas Marshall,	William Smith,
John Burn, Junr	James Matson,	George Tindle,
John Bone,	John Phillips,	George Tinmouth,
John Donkin,	Ralph Phillips,	James Wright,
Robert Donkin,	William Purvis,	John Wright.
	James Young,	Henry Young.

ALSO IN MEMORY OF JAMES WATSON, AND JOHN
WHEATLEY, OF NORTH SHIELDS, WHO LOST THEIR
LIVES BY BEING WASHED OVERBOARD FROM THE
LIFE BOAT "NORTHUMBERLAND", WHEN ATTEMPTING
TO RESCUE THE CREW OF THE BRIG "GLEANER" OF
BLYTH, ON DECEMBER 18TH 1872.

This Tablet was erected by the Trustees of the
Tyne Life Boat Institution, August 1896.

WILLIAM CAY. CHAIRMAN

This brass plaque in St Stephen's, the Pilots' Church, in Mile End Road,
South Shields commemorates the wreck of the Betsy, 1849.

Newcastle Libraries

THE HARBOUR OF SHIELDS IN A GALE.

The rescue of a Crew in the Life-boat.

The North Shields Lifeboat returning to its station at the Low Lighthouse. Although no boathouse is shown, there is a canopy located on what became the site of the boathouse.

1 For those in peril on the sea

The towns on either side of the Tyne entrance, South Shields, North Shields and Tynemouth hold a unique position in the establishment and development of maritime rescue in this country.

In 1790 the first purpose-designed lifeboat was launched in South Shields, as was the first ship's lifeboat designed and built in 1827. The first Volunteer Life Brigade was established at Tynemouth in December 1864 soon followed, in January 1866, with a Brigade at South Shields: these became the forerunners of today's Coastguard Rescue Team service. It was also at North Shields, in 1905, that the RNLI chose to station its first petrol engined lifeboat.

To lifeboat enthusiasts, Willie Wouldhave and Henry Greathead are synonymous with the design and construction of the first purpose-built lifeboat in the United Kingdom. However, claims by both men and their supporters that promoted each of them as the 'inventor' of the lifeboat created a controversy that sidelined those who were the main driving force behind the creation of a lifeboat service at the mouth of the River Tyne.

The entrance to the Tyne today, with its two piers, dredged channel, quays, and at South Shields, roads, housing, a hotel, promenade and car parks on land that has been reclaimed from what was the tidal Herd Sands, gives no clues about the conditions that would have existed when the idea for a lifeboat was first conceived. The north side of the river along the cliffs of Tynemouth had the treacherous Black Middens rocks and Mussel Scarp sands, revealed at half-tide. On the south side, there are the Herd Sands which extended more than half a mile from land to its furthest point and more than a mile to the south to Trow Rocks. Between the two, guarding the entrance into the river, there was the notorious Tynemouth Bar.

A chart of the river made by John Fryer of Newcastle in 1782, showed the minimum depth of water on the bar at low water at 7ft., and at high water, a similar depth of water covered the Herd Sands. The entrance, known as The Narrows, was 420ft. wide at low water, and before 1863, when the first dredging works on the river commenced, it was not unknown for people to wade across this narrow stretch of the river between North and South Shields at low water spring tides.

The river mouth was totally exposed to the full force of north-easterly to south-easterly gales, and even in ideal conditions, ships had to contend with crossing the Bar. No vessel drawing more than 20ft. could enter or leave the river, even at high-water springs, and when the wind was from a seaward quarter the available depth was diminished according to the troughing of the waves. Vessels drawing between 17 and

18ft. were often delayed, sometimes for up to two or three months after loading, owing to a succession of on-shore winds which prevented them from sailing on the high spring tides. When favourable conditions prevailed it was not uncommon for wind-bound fleets of 300 ships to leave the river on a single tide.

Even in ideal conditions, the Tyne was a difficult river to navigate. Most ships entering the river were travelling 'light', coming to the Tyne to pick up a cargo of coal, having discharged their ballast out at sea to avoid harbour ballast charges. A master trying to enter the river when running before an easterly gale, compounded by the strong cross-tidal current, towards a lee shore and having to aim for a narrow river entrance with rocks to the north, sandbanks to the south, and a sand bar across the entrance would not have much margin for error.

Indeed, at the mercy of a gale and tides, a captain had little control over the destiny of his ship and crew, with ships successfully entering the river in such conditions more by luck than judgement.

By the latter part of the 18th century, the Tyne was becoming the foremost port in the country through the export of local coal to the south coast and Europe. The number of ships using the river was increasing and both North and South Shields were burgeoning ports. At its peak, 5,000 ships used the port each year; 80 per cent were small brigs and snows of up to 250 tons on coastal voyages.

The increase in traffic using the port led to a corresponding increase in the loss of ships, their cargo and crew, which was of commercial concern to their owners and insurers.

It was these events that led to the birth of the first purpose-designed lifeboat in the country.

Port of Tyne Authority Archive

John Fryer's Chart of the Tyne Entrance, 1782, showing the Herd Sand, the Black Middens, the Narrows and the Tynemouth Bar spanning the river entrance.

2 The first steps

Before the events at the mouth of the Tyne that heralded the first purpose-designed lifeboat and the establishment of a lifeboat station at South Shields, there had been only two known attempts to set up life-saving organisations in the United Kingdom.

In Europe, the Dutch Government's attempts in 1769 to establish lifeboat stations proved unsuccessful due to problems in securing regular crews for the boats. In the early 1800s the Dutch Monarchy placed six Greathead-type lifeboats around the coast, but these fell into disrepair and disuse due to poor organisation.

The first record of a lifesaving service in England originated at Bamburgh Castle in the late 18th century, when a Trustee of the local Bishop Crewe Charity, Archdeacon John Sharp, turned his attention to those shipwrecked on the local coastline and nearby Farne Islands.

In the 1750s, Sharp reconstructed part of Bamburgh Castle as a beacon for mariners, and pressed Trinity House to build lighthouses on the Farne Islands. In a document entitled 'An Account of the Signals made Use of at Bamburgh Castle', publicised on Christmas Eve 1771, Sharp advocated measures such as beach patrols on horseback during storms, signals flown from the castle, premiums to local boatmen for going off to vessels in distress, and the provision of accommodation in the castle for shipwrecked mariners.

In 1788, Sharp contacted Lionel Lukin, a London coachbuilder who, in 1785, had modified and patented a Norway Yawl by adding internal air cases, cork gunwales and a heavy keel, all to provide stability and buoyancy. Lukin called it the 'Unimmergible Boat.' Lukin's intentions were to produce a stable workboat rather than a boat specifically to save lives at sea. Sharp, in April 1789, a month after the wreck of the *Adventure,* sent Lukin a Northumbrian coble to be modified in a similar way to the yawl.

Unfortunately, there are no records or evidence as to when the coble was returned or whether it was actually used for lifesaving, although records indicate that Sharp's other initiatives were being continued. Whilst one of Lukin's letters of 1806 states that, '*Of the success of this boat, after it had received my alterations, I had very satisfactory accounts having been informed that by the use of it many lives were saved in the course of the first year,*' there is no conclusive evidence that Sharp's coble was used for lifesaving at Bamburgh. With Archdeacon Sharp's death in 1793, the impetus behind the boat may have been lost, but it certainly cannot be disputed that his work had spread along the North East coast and to the maritime community on the Tyne.

In the North West, Liverpool had developed into the premier transatlantic port, and the appointment of William Hutchinson as Dock Master and Water Bailiff in 1759 began a series of events that would further develop the port and, through Hutchinson's humanitarian efforts, establish the country's first organised lifeboat service.

The approach to the port, through a narrow channel off Formby, was difficult to navigate with many sandbanks and strong tidal currents, and even though beacons marked this channel, a pilotage service was established in 1765.

In the 1770s the Liverpool Docks Board established a lifeboat station at Formby Point. The precise date remains uncertain as previous minute books were destroyed in a fire. However, it was likely to have been before 1776, as a minute of the Liverpool Common Council of 5 March 1777 indicates that a boat and house had been in existence long enough for them to be in need of repair. In 1781, charts of the Mersey approaches indicate the position of the boathouse at Formby Point. A salaried crew and boat keeper were maintained.

Surviving records do not indicate what type of boat was stationed at Formby, although it may have been a local type, a Mersey Gig, a two- or three-masted, sprit-sail rigged boat, requiring a crew of three or four, capable of being rowed or sailed. This type of boat was used for pilotage.

The Formby boat was the only lifeboat serving the port of Liverpool until 1803. In 1801, the Dock Committee, possibly as a result of Greathead's campaign for recognition, requested details of the construction, expense and management of the North Shields lifeboat. It was not until 1802 that an order was placed with Greathead for a boat that was subsequently stationed at Hoylake.

The fact that the Dock Committee expressed interest in the lifeboats then stationed at the mouth of the Tyne may indicate that the Formby boat had not been specifically designed as a lifeboat, but been adapted for that purpose from a boat of tried and tested local design.

3 A lifeboat service on the Tyne

The Coal Trade and the Gentlemen of the Lawe House

As with the port of Liverpool, the rapid expansion of the coal trade from the Tyne during the latter part of the 18th century, the commencement of Baltic trading links and the inability of ships to navigate the Tyne up to Newcastle, led to South Shields developing into a maritime centre of some importance.

Newcastle Corporation controlled all aspects of river affairs in terms of harbour dues and improvements but shipowners were becoming increasingly frustrated at the intransigence of the Corporation to improve the navigable condition of the river and, as a result, were concentrating their activities and operations downstream.

The Corporation, as conservators of the River Tyne, held the view that maintaining its condition meant simply preventing it from getting worse.

By 1740, it was recorded that both South Shields and North Shields had eight ships and the same number of owners. Ten years later, this had increased to 600 vessels of just over 200 tons each, excluding those ships registered at Newcastle. South Shields, as a maritime centre was at its height during the wars with the French in the latter part of the 18th century. Ships were supplied to the Government as transports and when France declared their support for the American Independence movement, many colliers were armed for their own protection with other shipowners fitting their ships out as privateers.

The increase in profits created by the war resulted in an increase in the number of ships owned on the river, but shipowners also had to deal with the problems created by the navy Press Gangs who favoured the experienced seamen found on the Tyne. Indeed, Peggy's Hole, a natural deep pool off North Shields and immediately upstream of the Narrows, was so named after the navy sloop *Peggy*, which anchored there in 1755 to press local seamen.

To protect their interests and investments, the Shields shipowners formed themselves into mutual protection societies and marine insurance clubs. The first was established in North Shields in 1778, followed by numerous others set up during the French wars. A particularly powerful group, known as 'The Coal Trade', controlled almost all matters concerning the shipping on the Tyne. A branch or Committee of 'The Trade' had its headquarters in the Lawe House at South Shields, which overlooked the mouth of the Tyne and the treacherous Herd Sands and Black Middens rocks. It was this Committee, 'The Gentlemen of the Lawe House,' that heralded the beginnings of an organised lifeboat service on the Tyne.

South Tyneside Libraries

The Lawe House, c1885.

The Lawe House lifeboat competition

The wreck of the collier brig *Adventure* on the Herd Sands in March 1789 was the catalyst that led to the provision of a lifeboat at the mouth of the Tyne. Having watched the crew perish in the surf as the brig broke up 300 yards offshore and in sight of the many spectators, The Gentlemen of the Lawe House were of the opinion that the *Adventure's* crew may have been able to be saved if a rescue boat capable of operating in heavy surf had been stationed at the mouth of the Tyne.

A Committee was formed to pursue the matter. It was chaired by 28-year-old Nicholas Fairles, and had as members, Henry Heath, Cuthbert Marshall, William Masterman, Michael Rockwood and Joseph William Roxby. Fairles, a Justice of the Peace, was a prominent citizen of the town with wealth accrued from many family business interests. The other Committee members had varied business interests as shipowners and later in marine insurance.

With little or no boat design and building expertise, the Committee, two months after the wreck of the *Adventure,* placed a very small advert in the *Newcastle Courant* on 2 May 1779:

A reward of two guineas will be given to any person producing a plan (which shall be approved of by the Committee appointed for that purpose, as the best) of a boat, capable of containing 24 persons, and calculated to go through a very shoal, heavy, broken sea. The intention of it being to preserve the lives of seamen, from ships coming ashore, in hard gales of wind. Plans will be received on any day, at the Law-House, South Shields, and the Committee will meet at three o'clock on the 10th of June, to determine who shall be entitled to the reward. The Committee will be obliged to any Gentleman favouring them with his hints, or sending a plan to that day.

Even though this short deadline of less than five weeks was extended to 22 July, the response was disappointing. While much information was received by letter, only two models were submitted, these by 41-year-old Willie Wouldhave and 32-year-old Henry Greathead who had submitted his model within the original deadline. Hodgson, in The Borough of South Shields, published in 1903, states that a third model was submitted by Michael Rockwood, a member of the judging Committee, that embodied most of the points of the Norway Yawl, a boat in which he had been saved at Memel in the Baltic but this is the only reference to this model.

At the same time as the *Newcastle Courant* advert was placed, Trinity House undertook a number of measures to improve safety at the mouth of the Tyne. On 4 May 1789, and following a visit by Master of Brethren of Trinity House, a buoy was placed

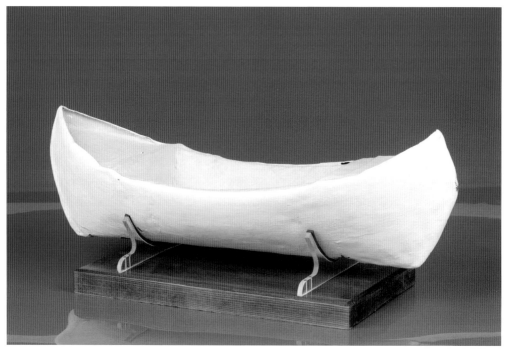

Tyne & Wear Archives & Museums

Wouldhave's tin model on display at South Shields Museum.

on the Herd Sands. Two weeks later, the Brethren also agreed to lay navigation buoys at the harbour entrance and in September of the same year a beacon was placed on a sand spit that ran off the Herd Sand, and a stone with a metal ring was placed on the Black Middens for ships in difficulties to make safe to.

Greathead's model, in the opinion of the Committee, did not meet their requirements for a boat that could operate in the local conditions prevalent at the mouth of the Tyne. This model, a flat-bottomed, shallow draught barge with semi-circular ends, little sheer and no inherent buoyancy, resembled that of the troop carrying barges that Greathead had no doubt seen and used during his time as a ship's carpenter both in the merchant marine and when serving in the Royal Navy during the American War of Independence.

Wouldhave's model, on display at South Shields Museum, and built in tinplate, is 57cm in length and 23cm in breadth, weighing 3.2kg with cork infill. The boat was to be built in copper sheeting, with a flat keel, high peaked identical ends, and a lack of rake in its stern and stem lines. Air cells of square copper boxes would provide buoyancy. The boat did, however, have the characteristic fore and end boxes that gave it a self-righting capability, a design not adopted in lifeboats until the early 1850s.

Wouldhave's inspiration for his self-righting design came from his observations of a woman at Field House well, on the Lawe at South Shields, who asked him to help her lift her skeel, or tub, of water onto her head. He noticed that the float to prevent water from splashing out of the skeel was half of a circular wooden dish – a quarter of a spheroid – and that whatever position it was placed in it always returned hollow side up.

Wouldhave's entry was certainly advanced for its time and radical in its design, the use of copper and its self–righting capability. It is likely that these innovative properties influenced the Committee in rejecting this design as unsuitable for local conditions. The sea conditions at the mouth of the Tyne and on the tidal Herd Sands during an onshore gale would create a substantial amount of surf, and the essential qualities of a boat to operate in such conditions are an inherent stability where it would be difficult to capsize, good manoeuvrability and responsiveness to steering, with an ability to ride over the breaking waves. A self-righting boat capsizing in the surf and shallow waters of the Herd Sands would have little chance in righting while being buffeted by the oncoming breaking seas and with insufficient depth to right.

According to W.A. Hails, in his pamphlet, 'An Enquiry concerning the Invention of the Lifeboat', the Lawe House Committee tested both models in water. Greathead's boat capsized and stayed bottom up, and Wouldhave's model stayed upright. Hails also states that a third contender, a local shipwright called Hope was to enter the competition, but on hearing that Wouldhave was also entering a model, withdrew in the knowledge that Wouldhave's submission was far superior.

At Fairles's suggestion, Wouldhave was offered one guinea for his trouble, which he declined, although subsequent financial accounts show that it was paid to him. His model was left with the Committee to assist them in their work.

With no outright submission that satisfied the Committee's requirements, they took it upon themselves to produce a boat design. Hails, as outlined in his pamphlet, wrote to Fairles seeking his views on the true events after the competition. Fairles's response, in letters dated 4 and 9 February 1806, clearly outlines the important role that both Fairles and the judging Committee played following consideration of the submissions.

In his replies, Fairles stated that the Committee decided to combine their knowledge and experience with information they had received from competition entries to produce a boat design.

As part of this process, Michael Rockwood recounted his experiences of being rescued by a boat that resembled a Norway Yawl, when shipwrecked at Memel, East Prussia, now Klaipeda in Lithuania. However, the Committee considered that such a boat, with a relatively deep draught, would not be suitable in the surf conditions encountered at the harbour entrance in and around the Herd Sand and Black Middens. They did agree that a boat should have each end elevated and alike, as described by Michael Rockwood and the bottom should be something between a coble and yawl and large enough to enable two people to row abreast.

The Committee also took into account written submissions. Before any models had been received, the use of cork in the boat had been recommended in a letter received from a Mr Hays, of Alnmouth, a matter the Committee had also been considering following a suggestion by Fairles.

Following their consideration of the models, letters and no doubt advice from local pilots and fishermen, the Committee finally agreed on a number of design principles for a boat; it must be buoyant with a shallow draught, have elevated ends to divide the water with the least possible resistance and to prevent water entering the boat when rowing through breaking surf, and that each end of the boat must be similar to enable it to leave a wreck without having to turn beam on to seas.

It would appear that the Committee's original remit had been to secure a completed model or sound design principles upon which to award the prize and then proceed with its construction. They had no intentions of establishing the design principles, a task that was now forced upon them.

As outlined in Fairles's letters to Hails, following the Committee's agreement of design principles, the momentum to secure a boat ceased, and it was not until Fairles and Rockwood met, by accident, that they discussed what should be done to progress the matter. Perhaps if they had not met the impetus for a boat may have been lost.

At this meeting with Rockwood, Fairles took the initiative, suggesting that a clay model be made based on the Committee's design principles. The model was adopted by the Committee and given to Greathead, who was appointed to build the boat and keep an account of expenses. The Committee instructed that Greathead should make no charge or profit, but would be compensated by the Committee for the work.

A paragraph in the *Newcastle Courant* refers to the boat being built in Greathead's yard in September 1789, with construction of a boathouse commencing on 14 September. This was also designed to give shelter and accommodation to shipwrecked sailors; on 31 October 1789, two sloops, the *Kinghorn* and *Wright's John* were wrecked on the Herd Sand and their crews sheltered in the new boathouse.

Greathead's contribution to the design of the boat was his suggestion for it to have a rockered or curved keel to give better manoeuvrability. However, credit must be given to his boatbuilding skills in transforming a clay model and the Lawe House Committee's ideas into an actual boat.

The resultant boat, which did not adopt Wouldhave's self-righting principle, was 28ft. 6in. long by 9ft. 6in. beam and 3ft. 2in. depth amidships, as subsequently described by Greathead in his own written specification of the boat he supplied for customers.

The hull was clinker built with cork buoyancy fendering fastened with metal strips

Author's collection

A Perspective View of Mr. H. Greatheads Life-Boat going out to assist a Ship in Distress.

A print of the Original published at the time of Greathead's Parliamentary campaign, 1802.

onto the midships gunwale. It rowed ten oars, double banked, and was steered by a sweep oar from the stern, together with a steering oar at the bow, and had a crew of 12. For close quarters manoeuvring, the coxswain based in the stern was assisted by a second coxswain, sometimes called the bowman, who was stationed in the bow and operated a second steering oar.

While dimensions of the *Original* seemingly differ, the *Zetland* at Redcar, the ninth boat to be built by Greathead is 31ft. by 10ft. 6in., and a line drawing of a Greathead boat prepared for the Swedish Navy, in May 1807, illustrates a boat with a length of 29ft. 6in. and a beam of 10ft. 5in.

The variations in the dimensions of Greathead's boats would probably have been due to the availability of one-piece good quality grown timber for the keel, rather than from a lack of proper scaled working drawings. The boat builders had to rely on their skills and the materials available to them to construct a boat based on the principle of the beam measuring one third of the length of the boat, and the depth measuring one-third of the length of the beam.

The boat, which was not named, became known as the *Original*, and was kept on a carriage in a lifeboat house located at the end of what was Pilot Street, where River Drive and the Harbour View housing development is today.

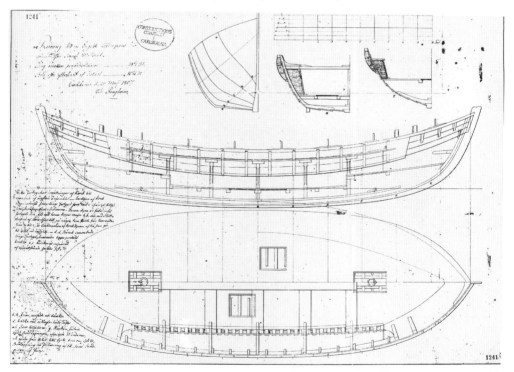

Sjöhistoriska museet Stockholm

1816 drawing of a Greathead Lifeboat prepared for the Swedish Navy. This drawing appeared in England in W. Falconer's 'A New Universal Dictionary of the Marine', 1815.

The total cost of the boat and boathouse was met by the Coal Trade:

	£ s d
Mr Wouldhave, for his model	1. 1. 0
Mr Greathead's bills	74.9. 3
John Bage, House, etc	58.10. 7
Advertisements	1. 11. 6
12 cork jackets	11.11. 6
Getting boat to the house	0. 11. 0
Ropes for straps and grommets	0. 5. 0
Expenses to Newcastle	0. 10. 0
Rope to Mr Green	1. 4. 5
Total	£149. 13. 9

The boat first launched on service on 30 January 1790 when a vessel came ashore on the Herd Sand. The *Newcastle Courant* reported on 6 February 1790:

We hear from Shields that the boat lately built by Greathead for the purpose of preserving the crews of ships coming on the Herd Sand was first tried on Saturday, and far exceeds the expectations of those who had the most sanguine hopes of its utility, for going off three times to a vessel there on shore through a very heavy sea, she scarce shipped any water. We have the satisfaction to add, that the sailors present were entirely ready in offering themselves upon the occasion.

The local pilots living in South Shields formed the crew of the *Original* and Trinity House, who managed and employed them, subsequently inserted into the pilots' licences a clause that they should man the boat whenever required. This was a condition that never required any enforcement.

Greathead, in his own publication 'The Report of the Evidence, and other Proceedings in Parliament respecting the Invention of the Lifeboat' (4 June 1803) provided instructions for managing the lifeboat. As 13 years had elapsed between the first launch of the *Original* and these instructions, Greathead would have drawn upon his own experiences as a crew member, seeing the lifeboat in operation, and, no doubt, talking to the *Original's* crew and local pilots when writing this document.

This document described how the *Original* performed but also provided a platform for Greathead to market his lifeboat building business.

Greathead outlined the two sizes of boat he built, one to row with ten oars, the other with eight; the style depending on geographical location, local conditions and the number of men available to crew the boat.

Two men stationed in the bow and stern would operate the long sweep oars to steer the lifeboat. The rowers faced the steersman. The other made sure that his sweep oar was kept out of the water, except when manoeuvring in close quarters. The crew rowed double banked, with their oars slung over an iron thole with a grommet.This meant they could row either way without turning the lifeboat, with the sweep oarsmen reversing their roles. This design meant that the lifeboat did not have to turn around and face any beam seas while in broken water.

Greathead also provided instructions on launching the lifeboat, recommending a launching point that would enable the boat to head straight into the sea, the steersman keeping his eye fixed on the waves and the boat launching without shipping any water.

Upon reaching a wreck, he described how the lifeboat crew must take care in the breaking seas near the stranded vessel to avoid the boat being damaged by striking the wreck. If the wind blew toward the land, while returning from the wreck, the boat would come on shore without any effort other than steering.

The boats were painted white on the outside to assist visibility, and the bottom was initially varnished but it could be painted afterwards if preferred. The oars were made of fir. Greathead had discovered that a rove ash oar was too pliant but a stronger, heavier oar exhausted the rowers too quickly.

Greathead also described how his lifeboat could be launched. The boat could be transported on a carriage from its boathouse to the point of land nearest the wreck, or where they would be able to head to the sea most directly. The rollers of the carriage were concave so they would roll over spars or oars laid lengthways on the sand if it was too soft to bear the weight of the boat.

Greathead also advocated that the crew should be trained and gain experience and confidence by taking the boat out in rough weather. He concluded that it would be prudent to post his instructions for the benefit of those pilots who manned the lifeboat.

With regard to the launching the lifeboat by carriage, Wouldhave criticised Greathead's design, commenting that the small diameter wheels would become bogged down in the sand thus preventing the launch of the lifeboat.

Robert Anderson, Secretary of the Tyne Lifeboat Institution, in his submissions to the 1851 Northumberland Lifeboat Design Competition Committee, stated that the *Original* was very nearly the same shape of the Tyne Lifeboat Institution boats stationed at North and South Shields, but was only 28ft. long, 9ft. 4in. broad, and 3ft. 1in. or 2in. deep, amidships. She had no air cases, but only a belt of cork outside, which did not go to the ends, and she was packed with cork inside and along each side and under the thwarts. When she filled with water the crew had to return frequently to bale it out with buckets. The old *Northumberland* boat, built at the expense of the Duke of Northumberland a year or two later, was similar in design and size to the South Shields boat. These were the only lifeboats at the port for many years.

A lifeboat station at North Shields

In 1797, the success of the *Original*, which saved 200 lives in the first seven years of service, led Nicholas Fairles and the South Shields Committee to consider the urgent need of stationing a lifeboat at North Shields, as several ships had come ashore and required assistance within a short period of time.

However, there was a severe shortage of funds, not only for paying the crews of the *Original* for their services, but also to build a second boat and boathouse. The financial problems were such that members of the lifeboat crew were sometimes not rewarded unless the owner of the rescued ship paid the appropriate fee.

Fairles, on behalf of the South Shields Lifeboat Committee, in a letter published in the *Newcastle Courant* on 23 December 1797, appealed to the public, and more specifically local coal owners, merchants and Mutual Insurance Clubs, for funds.

The appeal set out to achieve five aims, the continued maintenance and operation of the South Shields station; the establishment of a station at North Shields; the provision of temporary accommodation and clothing for those survivors brought ashore; the creation of a degree of rivalry between crews in getting their boats launched first, therefore improving the standard of operational readiness; and the ability for both boats to assist each other when on service.

The four Committee members who were signatories of the appeal letter, Nicholas Fairles, Michael Rockwood, Henry Heath and Joseph William Roxby had been members of the Lawe House Competition Committee in 1789.

While the appeal letter resulted in some public support, it did not elicit the positive response that had been hoped for, a somewhat surprising result in view of the exploits of the *Original*, and the increasing number of shipowners on the river.

However, it was the involvement of Hugh Percy, the 2nd Duke of Northumberland, that secured the construction of a second lifeboat. The House of Percy, whose ancestral seat was Alnwick Castle, also had a property, used during the summer months, at North Shields, opposite the ferry landing. This became a sailors' home, and was later converted into apartments.

In late November 1797, a matter of weeks before the South Shields Committee's appeal, the Duke witnessed the *Original* rescuing the crew of the *Planter*, which had run ashore onto the Herd Sand. The *Original* launched twice more that day, rescuing the crews of the *Beaver* of North Shields and the brig *Mary* of Newcastle.

After enquiring about the Shields lifeboat, the Duke met Nicholas Fairles at South Shields, inspected the lifeboat and met the crews who had been involved in the rescues the day before. On the basis of his discussions with Fairles, the Duke offered to fund a boat if Fairles could secure a crew.

The leading citizen of North Shields, a John Walker, was a member of a subscription coffee house on Dockwray Square, an area of North Shields that overlooks the river entrance. It was to Walker, on 30 January 1798, that the Duke of Northumberland's offer was given, and Walker and the gentlemen of the Dockwray Coffee House formed a Committee to establish a station and secure the construction of a boat.

A public meeting was held at the George Tavern on 8 February, with Henry Greathead in attendance. Walker's proposal for Greathead to build a lifeboat was agreed and sent to the Duke for approval. Greathead did suggested two improvements to the design of the boat; the coppering of the boat's bottom and an increase in cork buoyancy. The cost of the boat, incorporating these improvements, Greathead estimated at between £130 and £140 – significantly more than the cost of the *Original*.

The boat was two feet longer and wider than the *Original* and the final cost was £159 4s 0d.

She was named *Northumberland,* after her patron, and was completed during the summer of 1798. She was kept next to the Low Light House and launched directly over the sands and into the river at Peggy's Hole. Painted white, she pulled 12 oars, double banked and performed her first rescue on 16 November that year, rescuing the crew of the sloop *Edinburgh*, which had gone ashore onto the Herd Sand.

A boathouse was constructed on the same site sometime before 1803.

4 Willie Wouldhave, lifeboat designer

Willie Wouldhave is usually held to have been born in Liddell Street, North Shields in 1751, the date recorded on his tombstone. However, research undertaken by Thomas Pyke, a former librarian at South Shields during the late 19th century, found that 'William, son of Thomas Wouldhave, a rope maker', was baptised at All Saints Church, Newcastle on 16 August 1748.

Wouldhave, who served an apprenticeship as a house painter, was known to be 'distinguished for his eccentricity of manners, versatility of mind, and a peculiarly inventive genius.' Wouldhave suggested improvements to the building of docks and salvaged a ship that had sunk at the harbour mouth. He also constructed curious mechanical instruments.

At one time he was appointed sexton of St Hilda's Church, but resigned almost immediately. Subsequently appointed Parish Clerk in December 1804, he held this post until December 1819, supplementing his income by teaching singing to the children of the Charity School. As Parish Clerk, Wouldhave witnessed many marriages, duly signing the Marriage Register, as illustrated here.

South Tyneside Libraries

No contemporary portrait of Wouldhave is known to exist. However, a local sculptor, Rowe, assisted by descriptions by people who knew Wouldhave, and by sittings with his daughter who greatly resembled her father, carved a two-ft. high bust that is now displayed in South Shields Museum.

were married in this *Church* by *Banns* with (_____ *Parents* _____ this *Thirteenth* _____ *October* in the Year One thousand eight hundred and *thirteen* By me *Will.ⁿ Meningham Int Cu* This Marriage was solemnized between us { *Ramus Hamichis* *Margaret Roseberry* } In the Presence of { *M.ⁿ Ridley* *William Wouldhave* }

No.57.

South Tyneside Libraries

Willie Wouldhave's cottage on Nelson Bank, South Shields.

Wouldhave died aged 73, poor and neglected, in a cottage on Nelson's Bank, East Holborn near to the Mill Dam, South Shields, on 28 September 1821. He was buried in St Hilda's Churchyard. The tombstone now in existence was erected in October 1921, the 100th anniversary of his death. It was funded by public subscription following the decay of the original headstone, which is now displayed inside St Hilda's Church. Successive road widening schemes that encroached into the churchyard, led to the relocation of his grave.

Wouldhave left a wife, Hannah, who died on 28 March 1824, aged 73 years. His daughter, also named Hannah, was a seamstress, and when discovered living in poverty, was given an annual pension by the Tyne Lifeboat Institution. She died in 1858 aged 73 years.

Wouldhave did attempt to enforce his claim as the inventor of the lifeboat, but owing to his poverty, his uncouth manner, and the apparent violence of his language towards those who opposed him, his attempts failed. However in July 1802, he did enlist the help of W.A. Hails, a Shieldsman, to promote his claim in response to Greathead's Parliamentary award. The outcome of this belated attempt against Greathead, who now had Parliamentary approval and the support of local people of status and influence within the rigid class structure of Georgian society, was a case of too little, too late.

Arbeia Society TWAM

South Tyneside Libraries

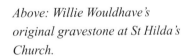

*Above: Willie Wouldhave's
original gravestone at St Hilda's
Church.*

Left: the replacement.

Author's collection

5 Henry Greathead, lifeboat builder

Author's collection

Henry Greathead, and his twin brother John, were born in Richmond, North Yorkshire on 27 January 1757. His connection with South Shields went back to 1763, when his father was transferred from Richmond to hold the post of Supervisor of the Salt Duties.

Following a shipwright's apprenticeship, Greathead, at the age of 20, went to sea as a ship's carpenter, first in the merchant navy for a year, and then with the Royal Navy. He served for five years, before coming ashore in 1783, two years before he set up his boatbuilding business in South Shields.

Greathead lived in Wellington Street, in South Shields. Hodgson, in his history 'The Borough of South Shields' records that '*with the exception of the newly built property in the Market Place and the aristocratic dwellings in and around Wellington Street, the town was still confined to the long tortuous line of streets alongside the river.*' It would seem that Greathead, albeit from relatively humble beginnings, considered himself a gentleman and a local man of some substance, and having a large property, a status to maintain, and a growing family to support, required a source and level of income to maintain his standing in local society.

As a businessman, Greathead realised that as a lifeboat builder there was an opportunity to promote his boatbuilding business, and embarked on a campaign to secure orders for his yard.

In 1798, the year he had completed the second lifeboat, *Northumberland,* for North Shields, he sent a model of the *Original* to Sir John Swinburne, MP and High Sheriff of Northumberland, and to the Duke of Northumberland, to whom Swinburne was related through marriage. Greathead corresponded with Swinburne, a known humanitarian, who suggested improvements to the design. At the same time Greathead supplied stories of the exploits of the *Original* to the local and national press.

In April 1800, Greathead secured orders to construct lifeboats for St Andrews and Lowestoft, which gave him the impetus to expand his boatbuilding business by proclaiming himself the inventor of the lifeboat. In May 1801 he placed this claim before the Newcastle Literary and Philosophical Society, with Sir John Swinburne, as President, endorsing the claim and awarding Greathead the sum of five guineas. Greathead was also introduced to Rowland Burdon, MP for Sunderland, also a member of the Society, who later provided the means for him to present his claim to Parliament and members of the Government in February 1802.

In October 1801, Greathead sought the help of the Gentlemen of the Lawe House. Fairles, in his letter to W.H. Hails dated 4 February 1806, stated that he was surprised that Greathead had approached both himself and members of the Lawe House Committee to sign a certificate testifying that he was the inventor of the boat. Fairles refused this request as he could not consider Greathead the inventor and commented that Greathead should show his original model to see if it indeed resembled the *Original*.

Following a suggestion by Fairles, a revised certificate was agreed, dated 29 October 1801, stating that Greathead did submit to the Committee a model of a boat for the purpose of lifesaving and from his design and explanations he was selected to build the first boat, the curved keel, which was not on his model submission but a later recommendation from Greathead.

Only three members of the original Lifeboat Competition Committee, Heath, Masterman and Roxby, signed the certificate, together with 20 Lawe House members. Significantly, it was not signed by Nicholas Fairles, the chairman of the Committee, and certainly did not go as far as Greathead would have liked. If any other certificate had been obtained by Greathead, Nicholas Fairles stated that this was unknown to him. Rowland Burdon, MP wrote to Fairles asking why he had not signed Greathead's certificate. Fairles responded that he could only state the truth and facts of the matter and nothing else.

Undaunted, Greathead continued his campaign. In November 1801, this was assisted by a letter to Swinburne from Thomas Hinderwell, a leading citizen and shipowner of Scarborough, extolling the virtues of the lifeboat that had been built in Scarborough from plans supplied by Greathead. Hinderwell's text was used in a submission to the Royal Humane Society in December 1801, which awarded Greathead their Honorary Medallion, and then to secure an order through Trinity House to supply a lifeboat for Ramsgate. In January 1802, the Society of Arts offered Greathead the choice of a medal or financial award. Greathead, in choosing the money, revealed his true intent, but in fact received both a gold medal and 50 guineas.

Greathead's campaign was now in full flow, and his courting of local gentlemen of

Tyne & Wear Archives & Museums

LIFE-BOAT.

Ye sea-built castles! wonders of the deep!
Ye storm-engendering clouds! where thunders sleep,
Whose dreadful waking, and tremendous roar
Shakes Ocean's empire to his utmost shore!
Whose wrath around, when hostile fleets surround,
Sinks them down-storming thro' the vast profound;
Then bursts the savage shout of conq'ering joy,
For your accomplish'd purpose—to destroy!
Strike your proud flags! your tops in homage wave,
To one small boat, whose purpose is to SAVE!

THE building of a Boat for the *saving* of Lives, from Ships driven on the Shores of this Kingdom, was *originally* suggested by the Subscribers to the News-room, at the *Law House*, South Shields, in March, 1789, who, from Situation, were the more immediate Spectators, of the Destruction inevitably attending Vessels and their Crews coming on the Sand, at the South Entrance of Tynemouth Haven; and the *first* Boat for that Purpose, with a House for its Preservation (which serves as a *Depôt* for Ships' Materials saved) were built at the Expence of the Ship-Owners of the Port; and on the 30th of January, 1790, its Utility was first experienced, which exceeded the most sanguine Expectations—so much so, that the Cork Jackets then bought for the Persons going off in her, are now never used. Since that Time, the DUKE OF NORTHUMBERLAND built another Life Boat, to be kept at North Shields, and which, for distinctions' sake, is called the

NORTHUMBERLAND LIFE-BOAT.

By these two Boats, some Hundreds of valuable Lives have been saved at Shields, during the last eleven Years; and the laudable Example is now generally following. Mr Henry Greathead, of South Shields, the Builder, having executed several Orders, not only from different Parts of this Kingdom, but for Foreign Ports: and it is hoped, the Entrance of every Harbour, and every Road-stead, on the Shores of the United Kingdom will shortly be provided with a similar Boat.

The Boat is about thirty Feet long over all, and ten Feet broad, built in the flaunching Manner represented in the Cut, and decked at the Floor Heads, rows with twelve oars, fixed with Grummets or Iron Pins, is steered by one, and covered with Cork on the outside two or three Strokes down from the Gunwale, will carry thirty People well, and live in a most tremendous broken-headed Sea.

Mr H. Greathead has been presented by the Royal Humane Society, with a handsome Medallion, accompanied with a Letter from Dr Hawes. On one Side is a Boy blowing a nearly-exhausted Torch; Motto, *Lateat scintillula forsan.*—Around, under his Feet, *Soc. Lond. in Resuscitat. inter mortrorum inst. MDCCLXXIV.*—On the reverse, *Do. Greathead cives ob servatos,* 1801.—Around *Hoc. prætium cive cervato tulit.*

The following Letter, received by Mr GREATHEAD, is an additional Testimony of its Utility.

SIR,   *Scarborough,* 17th *Nov.* 1801.

THE life-boat of Scarborough, which was built *without the least deviation* from the *moulds* and *plan,* which you sent here at my request, has even exceeded the most sanguine expectations, and I have now received *experimental conviction* of its great ability in cases of shipwreck, and of its perfect safety in the most agitated sea. Local prejudices will ever exist against *novel inventions,* however excellent may be the principles of their construction, and there were some at this place who disputed the performance of the life-boat, until a circumstance lately happened which brought it to the test of experience, and removed every shadow of objection, even from the most prejudiced minds.

On Monday the 2d of November, we were visited with a most tremendous storm, and I scarcely ever remember seeing a more mountainous sea. The Aurora of Newcastle, in approaching the harbour, was driven ashore to the southward, and as she was in the most imminent danger, the life-boat was immediately launched to her assistance. The place where the ship lay was exposed to the whole force of the sea, and was surrounded with broken water, which dashed over the decks with considerable violence. In such a perilous situation, the life-boat adventured, and proceeded through *the breach of the sea, rising on the summit of the waves without shipping any water,* excepting a little from the spray. On going upon the *lee quarter* of the vessel they were endangered by the *main boom,* which had broken loose, and was driving about with great force; this necessitated them to go *along-side,* and they instantly took out four of the crew, but the sea which broke over the decks having nearly filled her with water, they were induced to put off for a moment, when seeing three boys (the remainder of the crew) clinging to the rigging, and in danger of perishing, they immediately returned and took them into the boat, and brought the whole to land in safety. By the means of that life-boat, built from your plan, and the exertion of the boatmen, seven men and boys were thus saved to their country and their friends, and preserved from the inevitable destruction which otherwise awaited them. The boat was not the least affected by the water which broke into her when alongside the vessel, and indeed the boatmen thought it rendered her more *steady* in the sea. I must also add, that it was the general opinion that no other boat of the *common construction* could have possibly performed this service, and the fishermen, though very adventurous, declared they would not have made the attempt in their own boats. We have appointed a crew of fishermen to manage the boat under the direction of the committee, and the men are so much satisfied with the performance of the boat, and so confident in her safety, that they are emboldened to adventure upon the most dangerous occasion. I have been thus circumstantial, to show the great utility of the life-boat, and I should think it would be rendering an essential service to the community, if any recommendation of mine should contribute to bring this valuable invention into more general use. I remain,

To Mr Henry Greathead, South Shields,   Sir,

The inventor of the life-boat.   Your most obedient Servant,

                                                                                    THO. HINDERWELL.

T. Appley, Printer, North Shields.

influence paid off on 25 February 1802, when Rowland Burdon MP, to whom Greathead had been introduced nine months previously, put before Parliament a petition stating that following a series of shipwrecks in 1789 on the sands and rocks at the Tyne harbour entrance, and with no means of saving the lives of the crews, a number of local gentlemen advertised for plans and models of a boat suitable for this purpose. The petition then informed Parliament how Greathead had submitted a model, how his ideas were approved by the Committee, and how he was commissioned to build the boat, which carried out its first rescue in January 1790, and had, since that date, saved no fewer than 200 lives. According to Burdon, Greathead had been:

> ... instrumental in saving the lives of so many persons; and the utility of the Boat being now established...and that the Petitioner having derived little or no pecuniary advantage whatever from the invention...he humbly hopes that this Honourable House will take his case into consideration, and grant your petitioner such reward, as to this Honourable House shall seem meet.

The petition was somewhat economical with the truth and does not make reference to the role that Nicholas Fairles and the Lawe House Committee played or to the fact that Greathead's competition model was considered totally unsuitable. Greathead is also disingenuous in stating that he 'derived little or no pecuniary advantage from the invention.' Previously he had described himself as the inventor of the lifeboat but his failure to obtain the full endorsement of the Lawe House Committee must have influenced this change in approach. The timing of the Parliamentary Petition, 11 years after the launch of the *Original*, is also likely to have been influenced by the fact that the patent on Lukin's Unimmergible Boat, granted in 1785, expired in 1802.

The petition was referred to the Parliamentary Committee of Supply, which was given powers to send for persons, papers and records to assist them in their task. The Committee, which included Rowland Burdon and MPs from the north-east and coastal counties, met on 26 February. The Committee agreed that they should investigate the utility of the lifeboat, the originality of the invention and whether he had received any remuneration.

In addition to Greathead himself, the Committee questioned eight witnesses who had been recommended by the petitioners. These were Ralph Hillery, a seaman with 45 years' experience; Captain William Carter of South Shields; Richard Wilson, shipowner of Scarborough; Captain Gilfred Lawson Reed, an Elder Brother of Trinity House, and responsible for the management of Lowestoft Lifeboat; Thomas Hinderwell of Scarborough, shipowner; Samuel Plumb of Lower Shadwell, shipmas-

Left, One of Greathead's Parliamentary Submissions, Thomas Hinderwell's letter.

ter, but formerly of South Shields; Sir Cuthbert Heron of South Shields; and William Masterman, shipowner of South Shields, but no Nicholas Fairles.

For Greathead and his supporters to assemble such a group, from different parts of the country, must have entailed financial outlay and organisation. During the subsequent debate on Greathead's petition, it transpired that Greathead's stay in London had cost between £100 and £200. This begs the question as to whether Greathead's backers had a financial stake in Greathead's boatbuilding business with Greathead playing a high-risk strategy to secure a positive financial outcome that would enable him to develop his business as a specialist lifeboat builder.

The witnesses, some of whom had either served in the *Northumberland* lifeboat at North Shields, or had seen the Shields and Scarborough lifeboats in action, extolled the virtues of the

Author's collection

THE

REPORT

OF THE

EVIDENCE, AND OTHER PROCEEDINGS IN PARLIAMENT,

RESPECTING

THE INVENTION OF THE

LIFE - BOAT.

ALSO

Several other AUTHENTIC DOCUMENTS Illustrating the ORIGIN, PRINCIPLES, and CONSTRUCTION of the LIFE-BOAT, and its PERFECT SECURITY in the most turbulent Sea.

With several PRACTICAL DIRECTIONS for the MANAGEMENT of LIFE-BOATS.

BY

HENRY GREATHEAD, OF SOUTH SHIELDS.

LONDON:

Printed by Luke Hanfard, Great Turnſtile, Lincoln's-Inn Fields.

1803.

Greathead-built boats in terms of their design, construction and operation. The Committee pursued a particular line of questioning in examining whether there were any similarities between the lifeboat and a Norway yawl, seemingly to establish whether Michael Rockwood's reference to the Memel boat that had rescued him, rather than Greathead's input, had influenced the design of the boat. The witnesses were of the opinion that the Norway yawl, designed for sailing, did not have the curvature of keel, the rake of stem and stern, and a shallow draught to enable it to work in surf, that were prevalent in the lifeboat.

The presence of Sir Cuthbert Heron, Baronet, who had witnessed the wreck of the *Adventure* and William Masterman, a member of the original Lawe House Committee, provided the element of social status and credibility before the Parliamentary Committee, in corroborating the statements of the local Shieldsmen. Both Heron and Masterman, a signatory of the October 1801 certificate, stated that Greathead's model plan had been approved by the Lawe House Committee in 1789.

A further certificate, dated February 1802, was also submitted to the Parliamentary

Committee, having been signed by 23 resident gentlemen and shipowners of South and North Shields. This included three of the five original Lawe House Committee members, William Masterman, Henry Heath, Joseph Roxby, but again, Nicholas Fairles and Michael Rockwood did not sign the certificate (Rockwood may have died by this time). This certificate stated that Greathead had invented and constructed the North and South Shields lifeboats, which, in the previous 11 years had saved between 200 and 300 lives, and advocated that Greathead be rewarded for his humanitarian efforts.

By far the most contentious of testimonies was that from Greathead himself, who stated, in front of the Parliamentary Committee that he was the inventor of the lifeboat. Under examination by the Committee, Greathead gave a quite one-sided account that totally ignored the true facts and events that led to the construction of the *Original.* He stated that the idea for a lifeboat came to him as a result of the loss of several ships at Shields, particularly the *Adventure*, on the Herd Sands with the loss of all her crew in 1789, when no boat had been able to go to her relief. A premium was offered by the shipowners and inhabitants of South Shields for the construction of a boat specifically for saving shipwrecked mariners. He offered a model, which was approved and he was employed to build a boat from it. That model was similar to the model put before the Committee. As the Lawe House Committee had rejected Greathead's competition model, the model placed before the Parliamentary Committee was that of the *Original.*

There was no mention of the role of Nicholas Fairles and the Lawe House Committee in driving forward the idea for a boat to rescue shipwrecked seamen, nor Fairles's and Rockwood's clay model, and no direct reference to Willie Wouldhave and his model. Greathead went further in distorting the facts to his advantage, by taking credit for Wouldhave's observations at the Field House Well, which he no doubt could have heard when Wouldhave presented his design to the Lawe House Committee.

Greathead then stated that he had built lifeboats for North Shields, Oporto, Lowestoft, Woodbridge, Ramsgate, Montrose and St Andrews, and was currently building boats for Liverpool and Memel. The profit derived from a boat varied from £10 to £15 above the price of materials and labour. A ten-oared boat cost £165.

The Committee's report was completed on 31 March and the findings were debated in Parliament on 2 June. During this period, further awards were made to Greathead with 100 guineas received from Trinity House on 4 March 1802. Lloyds of London awarded a further 100 guineas, in addition to establishing a fund of £2,000 to encourage the construction of lifeboats around the coast.

At the start of the debate Rowland Burdon moved that Parliament should award £1,000 to Greathead in recognition of his work on the lifeboat. Other MPs moved that the sum should be increased to £2,000 because of the number of seamen saved by the lifeboat. The Chancellor of the Exchequer was opposed to such a large amount on the grounds that it would enable Greathead to set himself up as a lifeboat builder and benefit from the financial rewards of building such boats.

One of the MPs stated that the fees and expenses incurred by Greathead in prosecuting his petition amounted to £200. The Chancellor queried this, suggesting that the sum was more likely £100, and added that during Greathead's stay in London he had been introduced to several bodies that could benefit his business. The Chancellor concluded that he had no objection to the sum of £1,200 being made to cover expenses and fees.

On 9 June 1802 the Parliamentary Committee resolved to award Greathead £1,200 as a reward for his invention of the lifeboat.

Within a period of 13 months, Greathead's campaign to be recognised as the inventor of the lifeboat was successful in securing the endorsement of Parliament, Trinity House and Lloyds. Before October 1801, when Greathead began his campaign, he had built only five lifeboats, but during 1802 his boatbuilding yard built ten boats, with 14 built in 1803. The purchase of these boats was assisted by the funds set up by Lloyds of London in March 1802. Construction output began to diminish soon after with only four boats built in 1805, two in 1806, one in 1807, three in 1808 and two in 1810. In total, Greathead built 44 boats, 42 of these in the ten-year period from 1800 to 1810. Eleven were for stations abroad.

Greathead's lifeboats were not universally accepted around the coast; the boats at Penzance and Lowestoft were unpopular with crews as they were considered unsuitable for local conditions. In retrospect, this is understandable, as the South Shields boats had been specifically designed to operate in surf and from a short distance from the shore; in the case of the *Original*, within a 1.5 mile radius of the Tyne entrance, where the majority of wreck services occurred. These boats were not designed to be rowed over longer distances. With lifeboat design in its infancy, this fact possibly illustrates Greathead's lack of design expertise and understanding.

Records indicate that Greathead was one of the crew of the *Northumberland* lifeboat that launched to the brig *Bee,* which had run aground on the Spanish Battery rocks on 5 December 1803.

With the national economy declining, the continuing Napoleonic wars and the lack of sponsors and investors, the number of lifeboats built declined during the latter half of the 1810s, and Greathead and his family moved to London to promote his lifeboat building business.

Letters held in the Bodleian Library, Oxford, dated 1817 and 1818, indicate that even in his final years, he was still trying to make a living from building lifeboats, petitioning the navy to carry a 25ft. version of his design as a ship's boat and producing a sailing version of the lifeboat. But despite the financial rewards bestowed upon him, Greathead was declared bankrupt in 1807, his name appearing in the *London Gazette* amongst the list of bankrupts, and again in November 1810. In 1811, he again petitioned Parliament, who awarded him a further £650 in 1812 on account of the expenses incurred in bringing forward his earlier petition. This finance was to no avail, as in October 1813, Henry Greathead was imprisoned for debt.

Research by descendants of Greathead has established that he died on November 21, 1818, aged 63, four years after the death of his wife Catherine on 12 March 1814. Both were buried at St Anne's Church in Limehouse, London. His place of residence was given as Stepney.

Henry Greathead's father, John, became Supervisor of Salt Duties at South Shields in 1763, when Henry was six years old. On 17 March 1786, aged 29, Henry Greathead married Catherine Wood of Norwich, the daughter of a collector of salt duties for the eastern district of Yorkshire. They had six children.

Their daughter, Mary Ann Greathead, married a local pilot, William Grey Pearson on September 11, 1810, and her sons Charles and James Pearson, both pilots, were crew members of the Tyne Lifeboat Institution boats. Tyne Lifeboat Institution accounts for 1841 show that a pension was paid to Mary Ann Pearson.

The campaign by W.A. Hails

W. A. Hails, a shipwright, mathematician, marine draughtsman and resident of the close-knit seafaring community of South Shields had helped to launch the *Original* on service. In 1806, he wrote 'An Enquiry Concerning the Invention of the Lifeboat'. This pamphlet, a treatise in support of Wouldhave as the inventor of the lifeboat, put forward a series of arguments dismissing Greathead's dubiously established claim but strongly advocating Wouldhave as sole inventor, while acknowledging the role played by Nicholas Fairles and the Lawe House Committee.

Hails first arrived in South Shields in 1790. After a two-year absence, he returned, and remained until August 1798. He did not remember anyone who stated that Greathead was the inventor of the lifeboat, until soon after Greathead's Parliamentary reward. The only dispute, in the public eye, he recalled was between the Lawe House Committee and Wouldhave. Hails was motivated to publish this work solely on the grounds of setting the record straight as Wouldhave did not have the financial or social standing to respond to Greathead's campaign. More pointedly, Hails believed that Greathead was so taken up with his boat's excellence that he gave no credit to the draughtsman who had drawn up the detailed plans and had somewhat conveniently forgotten that this boat bore no resemblance to his own model submission.

Hails' involvement began in July 1802, a month after Parliament had recognised

Greathead as the inventor of the lifeboat. Wouldhave asked Hails to be the bearer of a letter to the Newcastle Literary and Philosophical Society, which had, in May 1801, awarded Greathead £5 in recognition of his invention of the lifeboat. A copy of this letter is now in the collections of Tyne & Wear Archives & Museums.

Wouldhave stated that, despite Greathead, by a '*strange kind of patronage*', receiving premiums from Parliament and a number of societies, it was he and not Greathead who was the inventor of the lifeboat. Although the Lawe House Committee had rewarded him for his model submission, he accused the Committee of an undeserved persecution and injustice in taking his ideas and incorporating them into the design of the *Original*.

Wouldhave continued that the rewards had been pocketed by the builder, Greathead, and not the inventor. Despite being poor, he requested the society to be '*convinced by argument rather than by riches, and assured by demonstration and not fair speeches*', a reference no doubt to Greathead's supporters in Parliament.

Wouldhave offered to display his original plan and challenged the society to compare this against the lifeboats built by Greathead. If they were not then satisfied that he was the inventor of every good feature of the boat, he would drop the matter.

He also questioned Greathead's assertion regarding the proposal to use cork in his plan and the comparisons between Greathead's model and a Norway Yawl, challenging Greathead to produce his model submission, which Wouldhave described as a butcher's tray, rounded at each end in the form of a sailor's cupboard.

Wouldhave commented that after his plan (model) had been in the Lawe Committee room for about five weeks, the Committee offered him a guinea on the grounds that his entry had come second. Wouldhave asked who was first and there was no reply. Wouldhave returned the guinea to a Mr Teasdale and requested that it might be posted to his account as he was determined not to pocket it.

He concluded his letter by inform-

Author's collection

AN

ENQUIRY

CONCERNINING

THE INVENTION OF

THE LIFE BOAT.

INCLUDING

REMARKS ON Mr. GREATHEAD's REPORT

OF THE EVIDENCE AND OTHER PROCEEDINGS IN
PARLIAMENT RESPECTING IT:

WITH

A DESCRIPTION OF THE BOAT,

PRINCIPLES OF THE CONSTRUCTION, &c. &c.

To which are added,

Authentic Documents,

NEVER BEFORE PUBLISHED,

Which effectually set aside Mr. Greathead's Claim to the Invention.

By W. A. HAILS,

Mathematician.—Author of " Nugæ Poeticæ."

Non illi, imperium pelagi, sævumque tridentem;
Sed mihi forte datum.   VIRGIL.

GATESHEAD:

PRINTED AND SOLD BY J. MARSHALL:

SOLD ALSO BY THE BOOKSELLERS IN NEWCASTLE AND ITS
VICINITY; AND BY LONGMAN, HURST, REES,
AND ORME, LONDON.

1806.

ing the Society that there were hundreds of people in South Shields who knew him to be the inventor of the lifeboat and that his own poverty had prevented him from being able to challenge Greathead's actions.

At this same time another letter appeared in the *Monthly Magazine*, challenging Greathead's claim. Hails replied to the *Monthly Magazine*, outlining the series of events that led to the building of the *Original*.

Hails failed to induce a response from Greathead, despite further letters to the *Monthly Magazine* in September and October 1802, although Hails states that he considered that Greathead's 1803 publication 'The Report of the Evidence and Other Proceedings in Parliament respecting the Invention of the Lifeboat', was a direct result of bringing this matter into the public domain.

Hails examined and disputed Greathead's published claims, but also quoted from Nicholas Fairles's letter of 4 February 1806, where Fairles stated that he could not consider Greathead to be the inventor of the lifeboat, but did attribute to him his contribution of the curved keel design of the *Original*. Of more significance was Fairles's admission that,

> *Had I paid proper attention to the request of the Literary and Philosophical Society of Newcastle (of which I was an Honorary Member) in furnishing that society with an account of the construction and advantages derived from the lifeboat, you would not at this time have had occasion for any information from me, and the public would have been in possession of the truth long ago.*

Hails also disagreed with a number the points in Fairles's letter and wrote to him to that effect, receiving a response on 9 February. Fairles confirmed that Wouldhave's model did not find favour with either himself or the Committee, and had little bearing on the ideas that the Committee subsequently agreed upon and that ultimately resulted in the *Original*.

Hails disputed Nicholas Fairles's account, arguing that Wouldhave's model satisfied the majority of the Committee's objectives, in being buoyant, able to divide the water with least possible resistance, having similar ends to avoid the necessity of turning, elevation of the ends to prevent broken water from entering in great quantities, and unable to be 'overset'.

However, Hails questioned the conduct and competence of the Lawe House Committee in dismissing Wouldhave's design and arguing that Wouldhave's model had not been fully examined by the Committee as a result of Wouldhave's lowly social status.

Wouldhave's view, as quoted by Hails, was that his model was presented to show a general outline of the form and the essential properties of a boat, with Wouldhave expecting that some alterations might be made without affecting the fundamental principles of his design. Hails suggested that if he had been chairman of the Lawe House Committee, he would have given the resultant boat more rake than in Wouldhave's model, for appearance rather than for the practical need of 'dividing the water', the boat's superior buoyancy and its capacity of 'floating only in the proper position' fulfilling this function. Hails concluded, after comparing Wouldhave's model with the *Original*, that the reasons that convinced him that Wouldhave should be recognised as the inventor of the lifeboat were:

The (*Original*) lifeboat has familiar ends.

The lifeboat has great elevation of the ends, as does Wouldhave's model.

The lifeboat is rendered buoyant by cork, a principal part of which is placed along the sides within the boat. Wouldhave's model proposes cork along the sides and inboard, in boxes at each end.

The stems of the lifeboat have very much rake, which differs from Wouldhave's model. However, Hails continued that if the angle between the keel and stem on Wouldhave's model was cut away by an elliptical curve, the curved keel and the raking stems of the lifeboat would result.

Hails concluded that Greathead should be recognised as the builder of the lifeboat, and Nicholas Fairles as responsible for the final design of the lifeboat. However, he maintained that full recognition as the inventor of the lifeboat should be given to Wouldhave for the design principles he proposed in his model and that, in his opinion, had been incorporated in the *Original*.

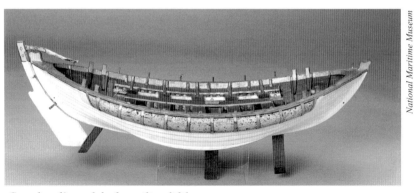

National Maritime Museum

Greathead's model of a sailing lifeboat.

6 Design and invention

Can the design of the *Original* be seen as unique and innovative? Or was it an amalgam of a number of ideas that took their inspiration from the design and form of boats that were in general use on the River Tyne during the latter part of the 18th century, and from the sea-going experience of local pilots and seamen who had sailed to Europe, the Americas and Africa?

The Lawe House Committee's initial brief was for a boat capable of containing 24 people to go through a very shoal-heavy, broken sea. Other than this, it would appear that the Committee had no pre-determined ideas as to the form or design of the boat, although they did dismiss Greathead's model and found Wouldhave's 'concept' model of a self-righting boat made of copper too radical. The Committee did advertise for plans of the complete article. With the result of the competition being inconclusive, the Committee then combined to produce a design in response to their original brief. It is likely that they consulted local pilots, fishermen, and mariners familiar with the tidal and sea conditions at the mouth of the Tyne.

The Committee was essentially looking for a boat that could be launched into breaking seas, was manoeuvrable but stable and able to withstand going to ground when operating in the heavy surf conditions experienced on the Black Middens and Herd Sand.

The Northumbrian coble, still in use to this day, was at the time of the Lawe House competition, a very distinctive boat used for fishing, piloting and foying. Clinker built, this boat was designed to be launched and recovered, stern to shore, through heavy surf if conditions dictated. The coble is characterised by a pronounced forward sheer, a curved raking stem, a deep rounded forefoot, and wide rounded beam. The forward flare gave the necessary lift and buoyancy in heavy seas and surf, and buoyancy when heeling, and the high bow prevented water breaking inboard when putting to sea or making for shore. Cobles varied in length from ten to 40ft., having a length/beam ratio of 4:1.

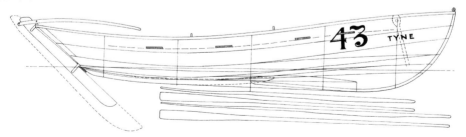

J. Holness

The pilot coble Tyne, illustrating the flared bow of this type of boat.

The double-ended coble or mule, was decked and had a full-length keel. The advantage of the mule over the traditional coble design was that they could run more safely in a following sea, but lacking any aft buoyancy, they could be more difficult to beach. Pilots and fishermen who worked from rivers and harbours and off flat beaches favoured them.

The Tyne Keel was used to transport coal up and down the Tyne from the riverside coal staithes, downstream to sea-going collier brigs. These vessels were double ended and wide beamed, with a rounded section  amidships, designed to be used in the shallow waters of the river, either sailed or rowed. Most keels were in the region of 42ft. long with a beam of between 16 and 17ft., a ratio of 1:2.5.

Following consideration of Wouldhave's and Greathead's submissions, the Committee agreed that the boat should be buoyant, well formed and alike at each as described by Michael Rockwood from his experiences in being rescued at Memel. The bottom should be something between the coble and yawl, wide enough for two people to row abreast, proportional in length, with greatly elevated ends.

The resultant design, as modelled in clay by Fairles and Rockwood, incorporates the flared bow feature of the coble, the double-ended nature of the mule, the wide beam of the keel, and the strong clinker construction of the coble and keel.

The length/beam ratio used for all of the Tyne lifeboats was 3:1. The depth was one third of the beam, which was one third of the length, design principles which were maintained for the construction of all of the Tyne lifeboats.

Greathead's suggested use of the curved 'rockered' keel would have increased the turning ability of the boat. As Hails suggests, somewhat speculatively in his pamphlet supporting Wouldhave, a curved keel was a feature common on the West Indian

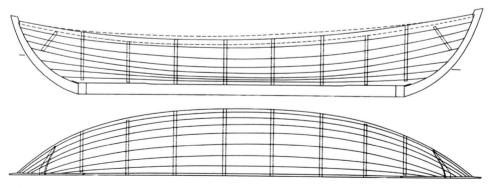

Author's Collection

A Shetland Sixern

NOTE:
1. LINES ARE INSIDE OF PLANKING
2. CHINE (PLANK) SHAPES ARE ONLY APPROXIMATE
3. STRINGERS SHOWN ON 00 TO K ARE FOR BUILDING FRAME ONLY.
4. FR SECTIONS TO AID IN SHAPING FRAMES.
5. DETAILS TO BE BASED ON SWEDISH LIFEBOAT PLAN.

GREATHEAD LIFEBOAT
SCALE: 3/16" = 1'-0" (1:64)

DRAWING IN PREPARATION - FEBRUARY 2007 - BY GRAHAM GREATHEAD - BASED ON SECTION-LINES FROM THE SWEDISH LIFEBOAT DRAWING IN ADRIAN G. OSLER'S BOOK "Mr Greathead's Lifeboats", AND OUTPUT FROM THE "HULL" PGM OF CARLSON DESIGN CORP OF TULSA, OK

A drawing of a Greathead Lifeboat by Graham Greathead, Hermanus, South Africa, 2006. The flat-bottomed midships sections enabled the boat to maintain an upright position when coming ashore through surf and hitting the beach.

'Moses' boats (Greathead had travelled through this area during his time as a ship's carpenter) and on the fast whaling boats used on the arctic whaling ships that frequented the Tyne.

Comparisons have also been made between the lines of the *Original* and subsequent 'North-Country' type lifeboats with those of the Scandinavian-influenced designs of the Shetland Sixerns, and the Greenland Pinnace. The Sixern is characterised by a double-ended hull, bold sheer, rounded shallow mid-section bilge and clinker construction, albeit with a straight keel. These boats, also known as a 'Norway Yawl' had excellent sea-keeping qualities, the larger types were used for fishing up to 40 miles offshore and able to deal with the large Atlantic and North Sea swells and following seas.

Whatever the comparisons, the design of the *Original,* as driven by Nicholas Fairles and Michael Rockwood, and interpreted and constructed by Greathead's draughtsmen and carpenters, drew on a number of mainly local influences.

The prevailing sea conditions at the mouth of the Tyne required a strong, stable and manoeuvrable surf boat. The shape and form of this boat was a distillation of the designs of the local cobles and keels, the knowledge and expertise of the local pilots and fishermen who used these boats daily, in all kinds of weather and tidal conditions, and the local boat building techniques of the day.

What resulted was a unique boat, making best use of the technology and expertise of the time, that was entirely suited for the local sea conditions at the mouth of the Tyne in which it was designed to operate.

Who then invented the lifeboat?

Can one person be recognised as having invented the lifeboat? Contrary to the claims of both Greathead and his sponsors, and Hails, on behalf of Wouldhave, no single individual can lay claim to the title 'Inventor of the Lifeboat'.

Greathead's model was unanimously dismissed by the competition committee and Wouldhave's idea of a self-righting boat, built in copper with a straight keel, was considered to be too radical, and not suited to the shallow surf conditions of the Herd Sands.

None of Wouldhave's ideas were incorporated in the *Original* and it was not until 60 years later, following the Northumberland Competition in 1851, that a self-righting lifeboat design was adopted. The comparisons between this winning entry, with the fore and aft high end boxes that give the self-righting ability, and Wouldhave's model are self-evident.

For Wouldhave to be the inventor of the lifeboat, the *Original* would ultimately have been self-righting. Greathead's design was flat-bottomed, with semi-circular

RNLI

Wouldhave's tin model and the Greathead-built Bawdsey lifeboat of 1801.

ends and little sheer, features which were not incorporated in the boat he subsequently built. On this basis neither Wouldhave nor Greathead could be given the accolade of 'Inventor of the Lifeboat' despite the local and national recognition to the contrary.

Wouldhave may have designed a self-righting lifeboat, but he certainly did not design the *Original*.

Little recognition has been given to the influential role that Nicholas Fairles played in chairing the Lawe House Committee. Following the inconclusive competition, it was Fairles, together with Michael Rockwood, who took the initiative and distilled the ideas of the Committee into a clay model.

Greathead, with his boatbuilding skills, was then approached and turned this model into a working lifeboat, his only contribution to the design of the boat being the introduction of a rockered keel.

Without the drive and commitment of Nicholas Fairles, the idea to build and operate a purpose-designed lifeboat may have been forgotten until such time as another shipwreck provoked the conscience of a community to do something about helping those who were dying along our coasts.

South Tyneside Libraries

This photograph illustrates the differences in design between Wouldhave's tin model of his self-righting lifeboat and the non self-righting design of the Tyne.

7 Expansion and disaster

The beginnings of an organised lifeboat service

Independent lifeboat committees had been operating their boats on the Tyne for 34 and 26 years before the foundation of a national lifeboat service, the Royal National Institution for the Preservation of Life from Shipwreck (RNIPLS) in March 1824. It was not until six months after this date that the Newcastle Association for the Preservation of Life from Shipwreck was formed at a meeting at Trinity House, Newcastle.

The first President was William Clark, with William Chapman, Treasurer, and Richard Plummer, Secretary. The Association was responsible for 'the providing of lifeboats, Manby's rocket apparatus, Dennett's rocket apparatus, rope ladders, and other means to be used under experienced hands for the rescue of life'.

As part of this fledgling national lifeboat organisation, the North and South Shields Lifeboat Committees, the Crewe Trustees, Newcastle Trinity House, and other local lifeboat stations, such as Boulmer and Blyth, co-operated under the Presidency of the 3rd Duke of Northumberland, while maintaining their independence. Rocket apparatus was provided at North and South Shields, Blyth and other local ports. The pilots and fishermen of the Tyne undertook regular training drills, and on 18 June, 1834, a comparison between the relative merits of Manby's and Dennett's rockets apparatus took place on the Herd Sands at South Shields. Dennett's apparatus was eventually adopted by the Government, which formed the basis for Coastguard rescue equipment that was used by the Volunteer Life Brigades.

This Association operated until around 1845, when the various local lifeboat Committees expressed a wish to reorganize and decided to leave.

Difficulties in funding

During the 1790s, funding to operate the lifeboat was provided mainly by the coal trade, local shipowners and marine insurance underwriters, with contributions depending on the financial circumstances of the wealthy individuals who supported the lifeboat. In 1795, due to a lack of funds, Trinity House stepped in with financial assistance, and it would appear that around this time the involvement of the coal trade group of businessmen waned.

In 1797, Nicholas Fairles and the Lawe House Committee appealed to the public and local businessmen for further funds, but with the economy and shipping along the coast suffering due to the war with France, this had limited success.

The frequency of service launches and the requirement to reward the crews after each service effectively reduced the funds available to maintain the lifeboats.

These problems continued for a number of years, and on the 29th November 1808, Nicholas Fairles called and presided over a public meeting in South Shields that agreed to establish a fund for the continued operation and maintenance of the lifeboat.

Fairles and the Committee considered that the town, having been the first to provide a properly designed lifeboat, had a responsibility to continue this service, and recommended the establishment of the South Shields Lifeboat Institution with subscriptions and donations sought from the local population, public bodies and individuals.

It was agreed that ship owners should subscribe 10s 6d per ship to this fund. In return, they would not be charged if the lifeboat was launched to assist or rescue the crews from their ships. A similar fund was established for the North Shields lifeboat.

For non-subscribers, there would be a charge of five guineas for the boat to launch, over and above the reward given to the crews. If further assistance from the lifeboats was required, the Committee would claim an appropriate fee.

It was also recommended that the lifeboat would launch to all strangers and foreigners if assistance was required. A journal of the services performed by the lifeboat would be kept that included the names of the ships and number of men rescued.

The Committee gave themselves the task of managing the fund, rewarding the crews, keeping the boat in repair and ready for service, appointing a keyholder to the boathouse and ensuring that equipment was available so the boat would be always ready.

This phrase 'Always Ready', in Fairles's rules and regulations was to become the motto of the lifeboat service and Volunteer Life Brigades in years to come.

Those appointed to the Committee were mainly local shipowners: Sir Cuthbert Heron, Bart.; Nicholas Fairles, Esq.; John Roxby; John Salmon; George Marshall; James Kristen; Robert B. Robby; Thomas Forrest; Edward Harder; Matthew Warble; Edward Prussic; Thomas Forsythia; John Thompson of West House; George M. Cleugh; Thomas Bell; Charles Maguay; Richard Fell; John Thompson of Hill House; and John Hardy, jun.

A further meeting of the Committee was held on 6 December at South Shields Town Hall to discuss how to bring into effect the new resolutions.

Under the chairmanship of Nicholas Fairles, the Committee wrote to the Lord Bishop of Durham, the Lord Lieutenant of the County, the members and Corporation of Newcastle, the Master and Brethren of the Trinity House, Newcastle, the Coal Exchange, London, and to the different subscription rooms in neighbouring towns, requesting their assistance in establishing a fund.

The boat was to be put in a state fit for service immediately, and three keys provided for the boat and boat house; one to be kept by Mr Salmon (one of the Committee) one

South Tyneside Libraries

NORTHUMBERLAND
Life Boat.

WHEREAS the BOAT HOUSE DOOR, has of late been repeatedly broken open, and the Boat taken away, without the sanction of the Committee, at same time leaving the House open, and thereby exposing the Boat's Stores to pilferage, in order to put a stop to such Outrageous proceedings, the Committee are determined to punish any Person or Persons found guilty of such Conduct in future.

The Committee also determine, that the Crew who may go off with the Boat, shall on their return moor the Boat, and at a proper Time of the Tide, assist in getting her into the House, and in order to have the Exepence of the Boat going off amicably settled, Persons liable to pay, are requested not to settle with any Person, without a written Order for the same, signed by two of the acting Committee.

A KEY of the BOAT HOUSE DOOR is lodged with the TIDE SURVEYORS, at the CUSTOM HOUSE WATCH HOUSE, and the Boat will be in constant readiness, to go off in all cases of Danger, to save the Lives of Shipwrecked Mariners, and for no Purpose whatever.

SHIP-OWNERS are respectfully reminded, that any Ship which has not contributed TEN SHILLINGS AND SIXPENCE to the Fund of the Life Boat, since such Ship became their Property, are liable to pay the whole Expence of the Boat going off (about EIGHT POUNDS) should such Assistance be necessary.

Donations and Subscriptions

will be received by Mr JAMES BURNE, Treasurer; also by the acting COMMITTEE at NORTH SHIELDS; or at the CUSTOM-HOUSE, NEWCASTLE.

JOHN HUTCHINSON
WILLIAM REAY
MILES HANN
ROBERT YOUNG
} ACTING COMMITTEE.

North Shields, March 12, 1823.

This public notice dated March 1823, a year before the founding of the RNLI, illustrates the problems experienced by the North Shields Lifeboat Committee in running and maintaining an efficient and effective lifeboat service.

by Mr Greathead, and the other lodged in the pilots' office. Mr Greathead, or the Deputy Master of the Pilots' Office would manage the assistance given to ships in distress should no member of the Committee be available.

It was also recommended that the boat be kept afloat and properly moored opposite to the boat house during winter months. The crew should be paid a proper gratuity for going off to ships in distress, and it was the crew's responsibility to put the lifeboat back on its moorings after each mission.

The Committee asked local boatbuilders and rivermen not to impede launching by placing or storing timber or boats in front of the boat house doors. The Committee also sought suggestions for improvements to the safety of the lifeboat.

There must have been a number of underlying problems in the running of the South Shields lifeboat for Nicholas Fairles to have had to call a meeting and establish rules and regulations 18 years after the first launch of the *Original*.

It is interesting to note that the *Original* was apparently in an unseaworthy condition, evidenced by the phrase *'the boat be immediately put in a state fit for service'*. If *'the boat be kept afloat, and properly moored, opposite to the present Boat House, for the winter months'*, it could be launched and got away more speedily than if it had to be manhandled out of the boathouse.

In effect, these rules established a commercial lifeboat service, whose crew members were paid for their efforts. As the boat would launch to a ship in distress without knowing its home port, charges would have to be sought retrospectively in some cases. This issue came to a head 32 years later with the *Friendship* scandal.

Nicholas Fairles died on 23 June 1832, following an assault by two miners.

In March 1832, local miners began a strike against the coal owners' somewhat dubious methods of measuring their productivity. Following the eviction of a number of mining families from their houses, riots ensued. The strike lasted till September, with the coal owners bringing in outside labour to keep the mines in production. Seventy-one-year-old Fairles, then a senior magistrate in South Shields, had been heavily involved in enforcing the law against the striking miners, and when riding to Jarrow Colliery, where trouble was expected, he was set upon at Tyne Dock by two striking miners who had been drinking in a nearby public house.

One of the miners, William Jobling, stopped Fairles and, taking hold of the horse's bridle, asked him for money so that he could get a drink. Fairles refused, stating that he would have given him something if he had been sober. While Fairles and Jobling were talking, a second miner, William Armstrong, came from behind and struck Fairles on the back of his head with a heavy stick, knocking him to the ground and beating him on the head. Jobling did not participate in the attack, but held the horse. Jobling was arrested that evening, but Armstrong escaped to London on a collier and then to Australia.

Fairles was taken to his home, attended by the local doctor, but died of his injuries on 23 June.

The Coroner's inquest, held at the Golden Lion Hotel, in South Shields, resulted in a verdict of murder against Jobling and Armstrong, and Jobling was committed for trial at Durham Assizes. Despite Jobling having only held the horse during the assault, as Fairles confirmed before he died, he was found guilty of murder and sentenced to death by hanging. The judge directed that the body be hung in irons at the scene of the murder.

Jobling was hanged at Durham on 3 August. His body was cut down, coated with pitch, and then dressed in the clothes he wore when the crime was committed. It was taken to Jarrow Slake, escorted by a troop and company of soldiers, and then encased in iron bars, and hung from a gibbet, just above the high water mark. Although guarded day and night by the police, the body was stolen during the night of 31 August and privately buried.

The *Friendship* scandal and amalgamation of the local Lifeboat Committees, 1840

The 1808 rules and regulations worked well until December 19, 1839, when the brig *Friendship* of Blyth, was lost at the mouth of the Tyne. The lifeboat rescued her crew, but her owner declined to make the usual contribution to the fund or pay for the crew's services of 10s 6d per lifeboatman. The case was taken to North Shields Court, where the owner was ordered to pay £20, which he declined to do. There was no legal means to enforce payment.

This led to local shipowners and businessmen meeting on 15 April 1840 to establish the 'means for raising a general and permanent contribution towards the more effectual maintenance of the lifeboat establishment of the Port of Newcastle'. It was agreed that every vessel using the Tyne should voluntarily contribute to a lifeboat fund based on vessel tonnage. Those vessels under 100 tons would contribute one shilling, 100 to 300 tons, two shillings, and over 300 tons, three shillings per annum, to be paid at the Customs Houses at South Shields, North Shields or Newcastle.

Those owners who declined to contribute were to pay for the use of the boat and the services of men as previously, i.e.10s 6d a man. Foreigners and strangers who had subscribed during the previous year or at their last visit to the river, would also benefit.

At the same time the management of the South and North Shields boats was consolidated into the Tyne Lifeboat Institution, with a Committee of 23 members, nine from each harbour borough and the remainder from Trinity House.

Pilots and lifeboatmen also augmented their income with salvage work, with cases ending in dispute in the Magistrates' Court. One such instance followed the wreck of the Russo-Finnish brigantine, *Frederika,* in a strong north-easterly wind and heavy sea, on the morning of 14 November 1841. In ballast from London, and with no pilot onboard, the captain crossed the bar too far to the south and grounded on the Herd Sand. The captain and crew were taken off by the *Northumberland* lifeboat, after which the crew of the lifeboat, with additional hands, boarded the ship, set sail and anchored in a location on the edge of the Herd Sand known as The Wheel, waited for the tide to flood, and were towed back into the river by the steamboat *Freedom.*

The captain had made an offer of £36, £2 for each pilot involved in the salvage. The local pilots and lifeboatmen, Jacob Harrison and John Hutchinson disputed this, as did John Bone who stated that they had been offered £50. The case was heard in the Magistrates' Court, where the brigantine was valued between £500 and £600. The presiding Magistrates questioned a Lloyds Agent and two seamen who stated that the services rendered were not as high as outlined and undertaken by the 18 pilots. However, the Magistrates awarded a sum of £45, or £2 10s per man.

In 1843, the crew of one of the South Shields lifeboats sued the owners of the Dutch vessel, *Zealander* of Middleburg, for salvage. At the subsequent hearing, the lifeboat crew had required the captain to sign an agreement to pay them £200 salvage before they would assist in refloating the vessel. The newly formed Lifeboat Committee decided that such salvage work did not fall within the remit of the Institution, and prohibited the use of lifeboats for salvage purposes.

This decision led to a number of pilots purchasing the old *Northumberland* lifeboat, which they then used as a salvage boat. Pilots also used other boats built on similar lines to the lifeboats, such as the *William Wake* built in 1859, for the same purpose.

The 1849 lifeboat disaster

On December 4 1849, the brig *Betsy,* of Littlehampton, was driven onto the Herd Sands. The *Providence* launched to her assistance from the Coble Landing boathouse at South Shields, and when alongside, capsized with the loss of 20 of its crew of 24 pilots.

While this was a devastating blow to the close-knit seafaring community of South Shields, this disaster also had significant national ramifications that led to the rejuvenation and re-organisation of the Royal National Institution for the Preservation of Life from Shipwreck, which at that time was nearing bankruptcy. An influx of funds to the national institution, riding on the back of public sympathy following the disaster, led to the 1851 National Lifeboat Competition and the development and construction of new lifeboat designs that used the best technology of the day.

The significance of this event and the re-organisation of the RNLI that followed would not be lost in terms of the role the RNLI played in the demise of the Tyne Lifeboat Society some 50 years later.

On the morning of Tuesday 4 December, an east-north-easterly onshore gale, with snow and sleet showers, had been blowing since the Sunday before, and combined with a strong ebb tide, was making conditions on Tynemouth Bar difficult. Just before 9am, the brig *Betsy*, laden with a cargo of salt, was entering the Tyne towed by a steamship. To cross over the Bar, the master of the steamship lengthened the towing cable which resulted in the *Betsy* drifting onto and, with the falling tide, grounding, on the Herd Sand. Attempts by the crew to refloat her proved unsuccessful and the *Providence* launched from the Coble Landing soon after.

With the prevailing sea conditions driving the brig further onto the sands, the *Betsy* was now lying approximately a half mile offshore, on the low water tide line, at a point where the South Pier is today, her bow facing east and port beam facing the on-coming swells. With a three-knot tide running at quarter ebb, the depth of water on the Herd Sands was falling and the breaking surf increasing.

The *Providence,* the largest and latest of the Tyne boats, was seven years old, 34ft. in length, pulling 14 oars. She launched with a crew of 24, eight more than her usual

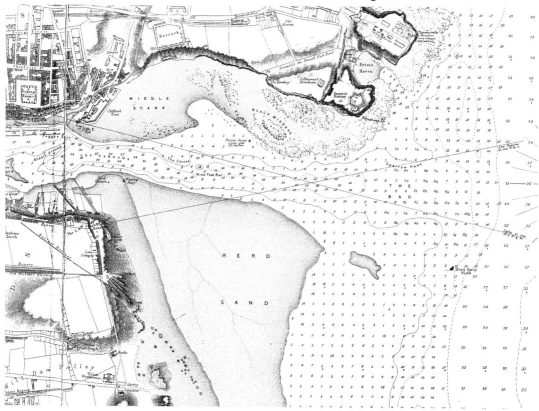

1849 Admiralty Chart of the Tyne Entrance.

complement. No fewer than 29 pilots had boarded the lifeboat, five having to be ordered ashore. She reached the *Betsy* in a matter of minutes, after the crew rowed a distance of about three-quarters of a mile from the Coble Landing boathouse, with the assistance of the ebb tide, but against the incoming beam swells and surf that was breaking on the exposed northern extent of the Herd Sand, that defined the southern edge of the river channel.

Launcelot Burn, the coxswain, and John Milburn, the second coxswain, were both in the stern, side by side, each with a steering oar, with two other steersmen in the bow. On their first approach, no ropes had been prepared on the *Betsy*, so the lifeboat hailed the crew and gave instructions to have two ropes ready and then stood off whilst the ropes were prepared. This necessitated a second approach to get alongside the starboard, leeside of the *Betsy*. Upon approaching the brig, a rope was thrown from her quarter into the lifeboat's bow. An eddy caused by the 3-knot tide running past the stern of the *Betsy* pivoted the *Providence* on its bow, with the stern now facing east and the starboard side of the lifeboat alongside the brig. With the bow rope secure, John Milburn called for a rope from the bow of the ship and got hold of it, as did John Marshall, who hauled through the stern ring, having about four fathoms in hand. The lifeboat's oars were laid inboard on its starboard side with some of the port side oars in the water to keep the lifeboat against the ship.

While the rope was being hauled through the stern ring of the lifeboat and the crew of the *Betsy* had just been given instructions to board, a terrific sea swept around the bow of the brig, striking the *Providence* under her starboard quarter. This threw the stern of the lifeboat into the air, and her crew, the stowed oars and open water ballast fell down into her bow. The rope in the stern of the lifeboat did not hold, she was driven astern of the *Betsy* and into the oncoming ebb tide that filled the boat and capsized her.

None of the lifeboat crew were wearing their cork lifejackets. One of the lifeboatmen, John Harrison, caught a rope and climbed onto the *Betsy*, while three others, John Milburn, George Marshall and George Ayre, managed to get onto the upturned hull. The remaining crew were either trapped underneath the lifeboat or struggling in the water being knocked against the oars that had fallen out of the boat when she capsized.

Upon seeing the disaster, the *Tyne,* under the command of the pilot master, launched and picked up the three survivors clinging to the keel of the *Providence*. The lifeboat finally came ashore at the southern end of the Herd Sand, towards Trow Rocks, over half a mile from where the boat capsized.

The *Tyne* was beached and, after a number of attempts, the crew, together with pilots and locals who had made their way to the beach, managed to right the *Providence,* but found none of the crew underneath.

At North Shields, the *Northumberland* had been delayed in launching, as the boat-house key was missing. The crew had to smash down the boathouse door to launch. The *Northumberland* rescued the crew of the *Betsy* and John Harrison. Two hours after the disaster, the body of Launcelot Burn was found near to Trow Rocks. Twenty pilots lost their lives.

Launcelot Burn left a widow and two children.
John Burn left a widow and four children.
John Burn Junr. Unmarried.
John Bone left a widow and five children.
John Donkin, married no children.
Robert Donkin, left a widow and two children.
John Marshall left a widow and three children.
Thomas Marshall left a widow and six children.
James Matson, married no children.
Ralph Phillips left a widow and one child.
John Phillips, unmarried.
William Purvis left a widow and five children.
Ralph Shotton left a widow and four children.
William Smith left a widow and three children.
George Tinmouth left a widow and two children.
George Tindle left a widow and one child.
James Joseph Wright left a widow and eight children.
John Wright, married.
Henry Young, married no children.
James Young, married no children.

Two years later, on December 23, 1851, one of the survivors, George Marshall, died of tuberculosis, at the age of 25, leaving a wife and young child.

In June 1851, the National Lifeboat Institution awarded Silver medals to four Tyne Pilots, including a posthumous medal to John Burn snr, who drowned in the disaster and John Milburn, who survived.

The inquest and recriminations

An inquest was held at 11am the following day into the death of Launcelot Burn, the only lifeboatman recovered from the disaster. The Coroner, J.M. Favell, instructed the jury, mainly comprising of local seafarers, that three issues required to be examined:

Why and how did the disaster happen?
Was the boat seaworthy and did its design and construction enable it to be termed a

lifeboat?

Was the disaster caused by the state of the boat, the mismanagement or carelessness of its crew, or *'some casual circumstances'*?

The Coroner informed the jury that the accident would be reported both nationally and worldwide, and that it was the jury's duty to state in their verdict, the causes of the disaster.

Three witnesses were called, the first being the mate of the *Betsy*, John Wheldon. He described how the brig ran aground, the ship's head lying out to sea facing east south east, and when the lifeboat came alongside, two ropes, one forward and one aft were thrown to the lifeboat. The lifeboatmen, who were holding the ropes, then told the crew to get into the boat, and as he was climbing over the rails, a large sea came around the bow of the brig and struck the lifeboat under its counter, the lifeboat's bow to the ship's bow. The sea came between the ship and the port side of the lifeboat, capsizing it to starboard. The tide was about quarter ebb at the time when the accident happened.

The second witness was John Milburn, a surviving member and second coxswain of the *Providence*, a pilot for 35 years, and a lifeboatman for 30 years since he was 18. Milburn described the events of the previous day and was of the opinion that if the boat had been made fast, the accident would not have happened.

Milburn described the features of the *Providence,* that having been out in her on numerous occasions, she was a safe boat, and he had been out in her in far worse weather, encountering heavier seas than the day of the disaster. He had also examined the boat after it was recovered, and found nothing wrong with her. He considered that the accident was caused by the tide operating at one end and the sea at the other end of the ship. The crew were not wearing any life preservers, as they were stiff and cumbersome and prevented a man from being as active as he might be. There were two-dozen life preservers in the boathouse, but they were looked upon as lumber. The crew were not lashed in, but there were sliplines fore and aft all the way round the interior of the boat, and on each side amidships. There were slip buoys under the thwarts ready for unlashing for persons overboard, and two grapnel lines to use in case they could not get near to a vessel. She was air-boxed at either end with a central well, and two water ballast pumps.

Milburn was of the opinion that had another lifeboat been afloat, Tindle and the two Burns might have been saved, but none of the other crew surfaced from under the boat. If there had been lines along the boat's waterline, John Burn may have been saved.

Milburn then criticised the workmen who had been boring into the Herd Sand for a foundation for a pier. A number of iron rods were sticking up in different places, and had it not been for one of them that was in their way, they could have got to the ship on the first attempt. There was a rod about 20 yards to the south of where the *Betsy* lay, and it took great concentration to keep clear of it. Everybody's mind was taken up with the rods when they first got near to the wreck. It did not prevent them getting alongside the second time, but it would have been a lot easier if the rods had not been there.

He thought the pier works were being carried out by the Corporation of Newcastle. The rods were right in the track of the lifeboat going from South Shields to rescue a vessel on the Herd Sand, and likewise in the way of pilot cobles going out to vessels. They were covered at high water, but appeared at half ebb. The rods were dangerous and should be marked by buoys.

The third and final witness was William Thompson, a lad belonging to the *Betsy*. He stated that the rope which John Marshall had supposed had not been made fast on the brig had indeed been fastened to one of the brig's timber by him, and that at the time of the accident, if it was hanging slack, it had not been pulled taut by the lifeboat's crew.

The Coroner then sent two pilots to inspect the *Providence* to see if the aircases were in proper order. They returned, stating that they had found about a gallon of water in them, which was not unexpected because the boat had received several hard knocks in rough seas.

The foreman of the jury stated that, two or three weeks earlier, he had experienced problems with the iron rods on the Herd Sand when going out to a ship.

Following their deliberation, the jury was unanimous in returning the verdict,

That Launcelot Burn was drowned by the lifeboat upsetting when alongside the Betsy and that the iron rods set up on the Herd Sand are in a very dangerous position and likely to cause great loss of life by being in the direct road of lifeboats passing from South Shields across the Herd Sand and likewise the pilot cobles.

The verdict, obtained the next day, echoed the concerns of John Milburn, placing the sole cause of the disaster on the iron rods associated with the construction of the South Pier. With feelings running high, such a verdict, decided by local seamen and pilots, is not that surprising.

However, the testimonies of the *Betsy*'s crew and John Milburn conflict. The position of the lifeboat relative to the *Betsy*, and how the lifeboat capsized, differed with Milburn stating that the lifeboat's stern was to the bow of the *Betsy*, while Wheldon stated the bows of each craft were together, although because the lifeboat was double-ended, Wheldon may have been mistaken.

The issue of whether the bow rope from the *Betsy* was safely and securely attached to the lifeboat, a matter which the Coroner had instructed the jury to consider, in terms of the mismanagement or carelessness of the lifeboat crew, was either never addressed or summarily dismissed.

It is also surprising that the master of the *Betsy,* out of a crew of three, or the remaining two surviving lifeboat crew did not give evidence at the Inquest. If they had not sufficiently recovered from their ordeal, the Coroner could have simply adjourned the inquest until such time as they could appear as witnesses.

In these circumstances it was convenient to blame the disaster on the iron rods, even though, as Milburn stated in his evidence, the reason the first approach was aborted was that no ropes were ready, and the rods did not puncture the lifeboat.

The iron rods in question formed part of what became abortive pier foundation works undertaken by the Corporation of Newcastle. These rods were located to the north of today's South Pier.

On 7 December the *South Shields Gazette* launched a scathing attack on the Newcastle Corporation, stating that the accident would not have occurred, but for the mismanagement and neglect of the Corporation, which was responsible for the management and improvement of the navigable river channel and harbour approaches.

The *Gazette* alleged that a number of iron rods had been left sticking up on the Herd Sand, without so much as a buoy to mark the place. The rods were covered at high water, and only partially visible at half-ebb. In such circumstances, the lifeboat would either have reached the *Betsy* on the first approach, or would have come alongside her in a better position.

The *Gazette* report argued that the disaster would not have happened if the attention of the men in the lifeboat not been distracted by one of these dangerous rods planted right in their course as they approached the *Besty*. Had they not seen the rod, the likelihood was that they would have run right against it, and lost their lives that way.

This article was also written at a time when the shipowners of Shields were in dispute with the Newcastle Corporation over harbour dues not being spent on river and harbour improvements, but on projects within Newcastle.

Using the lifeboat disaster as a medium to pursue another agenda, the article concluded that this issue was yet another instance of entrusting the management of the river to a body that resided eight miles inland and had no professional knowledge of nautical matters. Had the Commission had local representation, the danger to the local pilots from these iron rods would have been removed.

This article produced an immediate response from R.H. Mitchell, Superintendent of the Borings on the Herd Sand, in a letter to W.A. Brooks, the River Engineer, as reported in the Corporation of Newcastle Council minutes, and published in the *Newcastle Journal* on 15 December 1849.

Mitchell stated that the iron rods were necessary to carry on boring operations, but as a precaution against danger he personally visited the Pilot Office to give notice that these rods were to be put in the Herd Sand, and to inform the pilots of the various positions of the rods at different times.

All the iron rods that formed the scaffolding to take the borings from had been removed on the Saturday before the gale of 4 December when the crew of the lifeboat were lost. The only marks left were bench marks, to find the positions of the borings. There were only two of them, one a boring rod, stuck in the sand about 2ft., the other a pipe standing up about 6ft., and buoys were attached to each, with enough rope to show at high water.

According to Mitchell these bench marks were not on the course the *Providence* took to reach the *Betsy*. His own observations placed the nearest bench mark a hundred yards to seaward, or eastward, of the brig at low water.

Mitchell concluded that he had eight witnesses to prove the removal of the iron rods on the previous Saturday – the men who removed them – and that had the staging still been in place, it may have been the means of saving some of the gallant crew.

Robert Anderson, Thomas Salmon and Solomon Sutherland, Honorary Secretaries of the Tyne Lifeboat Institution, confirmed the events surrounding the disaster in a letter to the *Shields Gazette* on 14 December 1849, which also launched the public appeal fund. In this letter, which was reproduced in submissions to the Northumberland Competition Committee in 1851, they also refer to the iron rods being on the sands 20 yards to the south of the *Betsy*, and which resulted in the lifeboat having to swing round to avoid them, so the lifeboat's stern was against the brig's bow and to seaward, despite John Milburn's evidence to the contrary.

The politics surrounding the conduct of the Newcastle Corporation in their failure properly to manage and improve the river became inextricably linked with the recriminations following the disaster.

With hindsight, the disaster would appear to have caused by the unfortunate timing of a large wave hitting the *Providence* just as the slack on the bow rope from the *Betsy* was being hauled into the lifeboat and made secure. The open water ballast tank would have also contributed to the momentum of the boat capsizing. Anderson informed the 1851 Committee that the water ballast tank had been closed and improved since the accident, giving a greater stability to the boat.

However, the courage, bravery and determination of the South Shields pilots was illustrated by the launch of the *Providence* on 28 December 1849, John Milburn in command, during one of the worst gales in living memory when the Leith steamer *Brilliant* was in difficulties off the Tyne Bar. The body of one of the lifeboat crew lost three weeks earlier was brought ashore as the lifeboat launched.

Appeal fund

Within two weeks of the disaster, public meetings had been held in South Shields, North Shields and Newcastle, to start an appeal on behalf of the 18 widows and 46 children of the drowned lifeboatmen. Forty of the children were under the age of ten years.

Queen Victoria sent 100 guineas with similar amounts from the Corporation of Newcastle, Trinity House, Newcastle, and the Dean and Chapter of Durham. Trinity House in London sent £200; the public meeting in South Shields raised £460. When the report of the disaster was read out on the Glasgow Exchange, over 100 guineas was subscribed in five minutes. In total, the appeal fund reached £3,011 8s 6d.

A report in the *South Shields Gazette* dated 8 February 1850 informed that at a meeting of the Widows and Orphans Fund Committee, it was determined that dependants would receive – widows, six shillings a week; girls, until 14 years of age, two shillings a week; boys, to 12 years of age, two shillings a week.

The disaster is commemorated by a brass plaque unveiled in 1896 in St Stephen's, the Pilots' Church, in Mile End Road, South Shields.

The names of the 20 crew of the *Providence* are among the 778 names of lifeboatmen who did not return from answering the call to save lives at sea that are recorded on the RNLI Memorial, unveiled in September 2009, outside their headquarters in Poole.

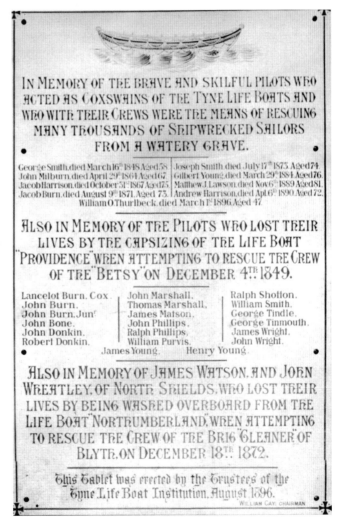

Author's collection

IN MEMORY OF THE BRAVE AND SKILFUL PILOTS WHO ACTED AS COXSWAINS OF THE TYNE LIFE BOATS AND WHO WITH THEIR CREWS WERE THE MEANS OF RESCUING MANY THOUSANDS OF SHIPWRECKED SAILORS FROM A WATERY GRAVE.

George Smith, died March 16ᵗʰ 1848 Aged 58. John Milburn, died April 29ᵗʰ 1864 Aged 67. Jacob Harrison, died October 31ˢᵗ 1867 Aged 75. Jacob Burn, died August 9ᵗʰ 1871, Aged 73. Joseph Smith, died July 17ᵗʰ 1875 Aged 74. Gilbert Young, died March 29ᵗʰ 1884 Aged 76. Matthew J. Lawson, died Nov 6ᵗʰ 1889 Aged 81. Andrew Harrison, died Apl 6ᵗʰ 1890 Aged 72. William O. Thurlbeck, died March 1ˢᵗ 1896 Aged 47.

ALSO IN MEMORY OF THE PILOTS WHO LOST THEIR LIVES BY THE CAPSIZING OF THE LIFE BOAT "PROVIDENCE" WHEN ATTEMPTING TO RESCUE THE CREW OF THE "BETSY" ON DECEMBER 4ᵀᴴ 1849.

Lancelot Burn, Cox. John Burn. John Burn, Junᵣ John Bone. John Donkin. Robert Donkin. John Marshall. Thomas Marshall. James Matson. John Phillips. Ralph Phillips. William Purvis. Ralph Shotton. William Smith. George Tindle. George Tinmouth. James Wright. John Wright. James Young. Henry Young.

ALSO IN MEMORY OF JAMES WATSON. AND JOHN WHEATLEY. OF NORTH SHIELDS, WHO LOST THEIR LIVES BY BEING WASHED OVERBOARD FROM THE LIFE BOAT NORTHUMBERLAND, WHEN ATTEMPTING TO RESCUE THE CREW OF THE BRIG 'GLEANER' OF BLYTH, ON DECEMBER 18ᵀᴴ 1872.

This Tablet was erected by the Trustees of the Tyne Life Boat Institution. August 1896.

WILLIAM CAY, CHAIRMAN

8 The lifeboat design competitions

The 1841 local lifeboat competition

The difficulty of securing a regular and constant source of funding to maintain the operational effectiveness of the lifeboats raised questions about their condition and seaworthiness in 1840. In an article dated 7 November 1840 in the *Port of Tyne Pilot*, the Committee of Management of the Northumberland lifeboat informed the public that the *Northumberland*, the property of the Duke of Northumberland, had been thoroughly examined, completely stripped, and fully repaired. The apparatus for emptying water had been adopted, with modifications made to her height above water. The boat was now perfectly watertight.

Despite this assurance, the newly formed Tyne Lifeboat Institution had to address the concerns of the lifeboat crews regarding the state and condition of the North Shields lifeboat.

On 29 October 1841, the *Port of Tyne Pilot* and *Northumberland and Durham Advertiser* newspaper, based in South Shields, highlighted the concerns of local pilots and lifeboat crews over the condition of the *Northumberland.* The paper had previously reported the poor state of this lifeboat in December 1839. Since then repeated complaints had been made about the seaworthiness of the boat being so poor that it was now putting the lives of its crew at risk. When rescuing the 11 crew of the Russo-Finnish vessel *Frederika*, which had ran aground on the Herd Sand, the *Northumberland* nearly sank as it was it was filled with water and only reached the shore with great difficulty.

Two of the *Northumberland*'s crew contacted the newspaper stating that if something was not done about getting her thoroughly repaired, or getting an entirely new boat, men would not be found to man her. The pilots of North Shields were ready to contribute £1 each towards the cost of a new boat and the public would no doubt contribute as well. The *Port of Tyne Pilot* supported the claims of the two lifeboat crew members and stated that it was a disgrace to the port that the *Northumberland* lifeboat was in such a poor condition. The newspaper believed that there was a Lifeboat Fund available for the purpose of procuring a new boat, but if not, a public fund should be established.

The same edition also reported on the South Shields lifeboat, *Tyne*, stating that in the past week the boat had launched on two occasions. She rescued nine people from the *Fox* of London, and on the following day, she saved 13 from the *William Wallace* of South Shields, both vessels wrecked on the Herd Sands.

In the report, the newspaper commented on the seaworthiness of the eight-year-old

Tyne. A reporter had overheard one of her crew, John Bone (who was to lose his life in the 1849 lifeboat disaster), stating that although she was an excellent boat, if a heavy sea were to fall upon her, she would probably be lost with all hands. She would be much better if she was fitted with air-boxes. The newspaper urged the South Shields Lifeboat Committee to improve the seaworthiness of the lifeboat.

The condition of the 43-year-old *Northumberland* provoked a written response from William Reay, a Trustee of the Lifeboat Committee, who claimed that during the previous winter the *Northumberland* had been thoroughly stripped and surveyed by two professional men who found her timbers in perfect condition. All necessary repairs had been made by the North Shields boatbuilder, Mr Pletts.

William Reay challenged the newspaper's informant to explain how, at her last launch, 21 men felt able to crowd themselves into a boat they stated was unseaworthy, instead of the normal complement of 14.

These remarks provoked a strong and united response from the Coxswain, Gilbert Young, and crew of the North Shields lifeboat, published in the *Port of Tyne Pilot* on 12 November 1841. They stated that the *Northumberland*, the oldest lifeboat in use, was small, unseaworthy, and not fit to be called a lifeboat. Young referred to a recent rescue when, had another sea struck the lifeboat when returning from a foreign vessel wrecked on the Herd Sand, she would have foundered, causing the deaths of the lifeboat men and rescued seamen, 31 men in total.

Young also raised the issue of the size of the boat. It was not unknown for the *Northumberland* to have to make two trips to bring a single ship's crew ashore. If one of her Majesty's cutters was to come ashore, or if the South Shields boat was unavailable, the *Northumberland* would not be able to give any assistance.

In a direct response to William Reay, Gilbert Young stated that 14 men formed the normal crew of the boat, but that because of her condition, 20 men were required to row the *Northumberland* against

Chris Lambert

The grave of Gilbert Young, coxswain of the North Shields Lifeboat, Northumberland, during the 1860s and 1870s. Preston Cemetery, North Shields.

the wind and sea. He concluded that she was a disgrace to the port.

With the *Northumberland*, now 43 years old, coming to the end of her operational life, a replacement boat seemed to be a distant prospect for the North Shields crew. A new boat had been built for the South Shields station nine years previously to replace the *Original*, albeit three years after her wreck. Conscious of the delay of the Lifeboat Trustees in building a replacement for the *Original*, the pilots in bringing the condition of the North Shields lifeboat into the public domain, put pressure on the Trustees to re-solve the issue. As in 1789, it was decided to hold a competition for the design of a new boat.

On 7 November 1841, Robert Anderson, a shipbroker and agent for the Marquis of Londonderry, the local coal baron, who also held the post of Honorary Secretary of the Tyne Lifeboat Institution, placed an advert in the *Port of Tyne Pilot* offering a pre-mium of £10 for the design of a new lifeboat. Plans and models were to be submitted for judging no later than 14 December, and a contract to build the winning entry would be considered by the Trustees.

The fact that Anderson's response came seven days after the date of Gilbert Young's open letter indicates the seriousness of this matter and the Trustees' concerns to re-solve the situation. The short period of five weeks for boatbuilders to submit their de-signs underlines the urgency of the situation.

The winner of the premium was George Farrow, a native of South Shields and a for-mer apprentice to Henry Greathead. Another entrant was William Greener, of Aston New Town, Birmingham. The prominent feature of each of these designs was a closed tank for water ballast.

On 10 and 17 June 1842, Robert Anderson placed a further advertisement in the *Port of Tyne Pilot*, requesting the submission of tenders from local boatbuilders. The design drawings and specifications of the new lifeboat were available for inspection by prospective tenderers from 13 June, with final submissions to be made by 21 June.

However, it was not until 16 December 1843 that the *Newcastle Journal* reported that the Trustees for the Port of Newcastle Lifeboat Fund sought final tenders for a new lifeboat that included Farrow's water ballast design. The result was the launch of the second *Northumberland* in 1844.

The first *Northumberland* was kept in reserve at the Coble Landing South Shields, until sold out of service to local pilots, renamed the *Noble Institution*, and used as a salvage boat. Remaining service records indicate that this boat was launched on a number of occasions on wreck services.

The 1850 Local Lifeboat Competition

Following the capsize of the *Providence*, and despite the inquest into the disaster finding the lifeboat seaworthy, the Tyne Lifeboat Institution, together with the Wear Lifeboat Committee, ran another design competition offering three prizes for improved lifeboats.

Upwards of 50 models were submitted. The result was announced on 19 March, 1850, the winning models being exhibited at Trinity House in

National Maritime Museum

Farrow's 1850 Competition model.

Newcastle, where the second and third prize models are still kept. The first prize of £30 was awarded to George Farrow of South Shields, the second of £20 to John Lister of Sunderland, and the third of £10 to John Tindle of North Shields.

Farrow, born in 1786, was a local boat builder who had been an apprentice in Henry Greathead's yard during the early 1800s. He died in 1880 aged 94.

The Lifeboat Committee stated that Farrow's boat,

> *... fitted with airboxes was such as to leave the centre of the boat much more commodious than in any former plan, and should the boat be capsized, she will right herself immediately, either in smooth or broken water, with a full complement of men, and when filled will discharge the water from her platform in 8 seconds. She is fitted with a self-ballasting bottom for admitting the water into the centre of the boat by a simple contrivance.*

However, Farrow's winning design using Wouldhave's self-righting principles was not adopted by the Tyne Lifeboat Institution, which never built a self-righting lifeboat. Lister's boat rowed ten oars, had four thwarts, with three scuppers on each side. Tindle's boat also rowed ten oars, but had six thwarts, with a central open draining well with six drainage holes.

The 1851 National Lifeboat Competition

The fortunes of the National Institution at this time were at a low ebb. Political and financial support for the organisation had began to decline from the 1830s and by the time of the 1849 disaster, donations received during that financial year totalled only £354. The founder had died in poverty, and the chairman and secretary were approaching their 80th birthdays.

Author's collection

The second (right) and third (left) prize winning models in the 1850 Local Lifeboat Competition, Trinity House, Newcastle.

As a consequence of the disaster, and riding on the back of public sympathy following it, the 4th Duke of Northumberland, the recently appointed President of the National Lifeboat Institution, set about reforming the National Institution, and consulted with the Chairman and Vice Chairman in May 1850 regarding a competition for a better design of lifeboat.

The 4th Duke, Algernon was born in 1792, and entered the Royal Navy as a 13-year-old midshipman, in 1805. He succeeded his father, who had funded the first lifeboat at North Shields, in 1847.

A notice to boatbuilders was placed in *The Times*, the *Shipping Gazette*, the *United Service Gazette*, and copied into several local newspapers in October 1850 offering a prize of 100 guineas for the best model of a lifeboat to be submitted to the Admiralty by February 1851. The notice also stated the main defects in existing lifeboats that they could not self-right; could not free themselves quickly of water; and that they were too heavy for transporting along beaches. The matters of form, construction, and fittings would be left to the skill of the builder.

As in 1789, a disaster had resulted in a competition for a new lifeboat design. Whereas the Lawe House Committee were looking for design ideas for the first lifeboat best suited to local conditions, the 1851 Competition Committee had the benefit of 62 years of lifeboat evolution based on Greathead boats, Costain's boats at Liverpool, William Plenty, George Palmer and the Norfolk and Suffolk beach boats.

Two hundred and eighty models and plans were submitted. The Committee undertook a general review of the models, grouping them according to their characteristic features. There was a group in the form of pontoons; catamarans or rafts formed a second group; a third group was described as having a troopship or steamer's paddle-box boat; boats in the fourth group were based on the north-country coble; and lastly, a group of ordinary boats in everyday use, but modified according to the nature of the coast they were intended for.

After the models were examined to establish their abilities for pulling and sailing, buoyancy, ability to discharge water, and their dimensions, the models were tested on the Thames to assess their stability and were brought before the Committee. At this stage, as there were many boats with similar characteristics, it was difficult to assess the relative merits of each design. The Committee agreed a number of features that they considered comprised the essential qualities of a lifeboat, and points were awarded on the basis of the 15 design characteristics:

Qualities as a rowing boat in all weathers	20 points
Qualities as a sailing boat	18 points
Qualities as a sea-boat; as stability, safety, buoyancy forward for launching through surf etc.	10 points
Small internal capacity for water up to the level of thwarts	9 points
Means of freeing boat of water readily	8 points
Extra buoyancy; its nature, amount, distribution and mode of application	7 points
Power of self-righting	6 points
Suitability for beaching	4 points
Room for, and power of, carrying passengers	3 points
Moderate rate of transport along shore	3 points
Protection from injury to the bottom	3 points
Ballast, as iron 1, water 2, cork 3	3 points
Access to stem or stern	3 points
Timber heads, for securing warps to	2 points
Fenders, life-lines	1 point
	Total 100 points

The competition came about as a result of the capsize of a non-self-righting lifeboat, and the original competition notice referred to the need for a design for a self-righting lifeboat. However the Committee considered that the essential quality was a good rowing boat, able to get off the beach in any weather, with the maximum 20 points awarded for this quality. The power of self-righting was allocated just six points – seventh out of the 15 criteria. The means to free a boat of water, a factor in the capsize of the *Providence*, was fifth in priority, with eight points.

The competition was won by James Beeching of Great Yarmouth, with 84 points, whose self-righting design exhibited the same principles as Wouldhave's 1789 model, with high air boxes at the bow and stern. Beeching's design was modified by the RNIPLS and adopted nationally as their standard self-righting lifeboat.

The model submitted by George Farrow, which the judging Committee considered to be self-righting, scored 72 points out of 100, coming sixth in the competition. The design had also been successful in local competitions held in 1842 at South Shields and 1850 in Newcastle, and exhibited the basic principles of the Tyne lifeboats, but now included Wouldhave's self-righting capability. As the 1851 competition awarded

Author's collection

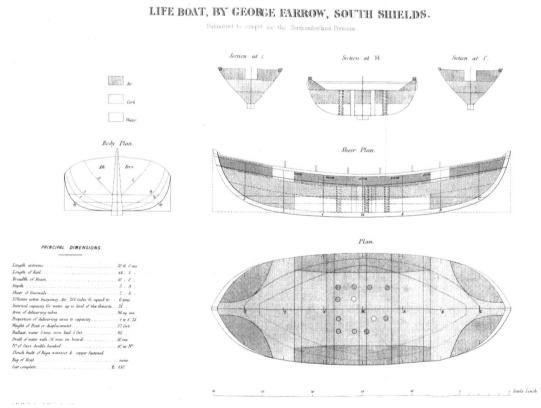

George Farrow 1851 National Competition design.

18 points for sailing qualities, the fact that this entry still scored so highly illustrates the sea keeping qualities of Farrow's non-sailing design.

The North East was well represented in the competition. In addition to George Farrow, there were a further ten entries. South Shields entries came from Robert Blair, a sea pilot; Benjamin Birch, a boatbuilder; and John Scott, a maritime artist. From North Shields there were Dowey; Fry; and Thomas Anderson, a boatbuilder, who had built the second *Northumberland*. From Sunderland came John Lister, who came second in the local 1850 competition; and Thomas Wake and Sons. Newcastle entries came from Atkinson and R. Taylor. Their designs were variations on the form of the lifeboats used on the Tyne

Taylor was awarded 65 points; Benjamin Birch, Robert Blair and Thomas Wake were all awarded 63 points.

The Committee Report remarked that the group of lifeboats from Shields, the Tyne, Sunderland, Hartlepool and Whitby resembled flat-bottomed troopships, or paddle box steamers, and that the model submitted by George Farrow was a typical example of this class. It had 'small internal capacity, water ballast in the bottom to be admitted when afloat, raised air-cases in the bow and stern sheets, clear access to the extremities, ample room for carrying passengers, and she would right herself in the event of being upset, all of which are good qualities'.

Author's collection

John Scott's 1851 national competition entry, Tyne and Wear Museums.

The dispute between Greener and Farrow, which had began in 1842, as to their respective claims of inventing water ballasting in a lifeboat continued at the 1851 competition. The judging Committee offered no opinion but remarked that this mode of ballasting was common to many of the lifeboat models sent from different parts of England.

In respect of the Shields boats, the Committee commented that:

their advantages, beyond great stability, were not easy to be discovered; if the lifeboats were towed out to the site of the wreck by a steam tug, as at Liverpool, (and which, in a port like Shields abounding with steam-tugs, might have been expected) it would be easier to understand, but for a boat that has to pull out of a river, and often against a strong wind and tide, it is difficult to comprehend why such a form as that given to Beeching's boat should not be preferred.

The Committee did acknowledge that despite their decision, the boats stationed at North and South Shields have done good service, and had been instrumental in saving hundreds of lives.

The comments of the Committee are consistent with their objective for a design for an all-purpose standard design lifeboat. Their criticisms of the Shields type of lifeboat are possibly justified as they were relatively heavy boats and difficult to launch. However, these boats were specifically designed to operate within a limited radius of no more than a mile from their boathouses, having great stability and manoeuvrability to operate safely in and around the surf on the Herd Sand and Black Middens, where the majority of ship groundings occurred.

George Farrow, being one of Greathead's apprentices, would have been well versed in the design and construction of the local lifeboats. He was vocal in supporting Willie Wouldhave's claim of identifying the essential principles of lifeboat

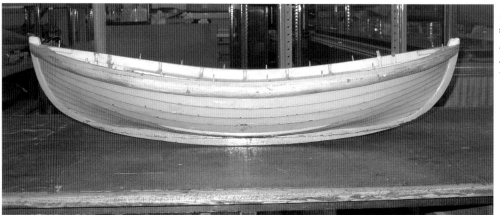

Author's collection

This George Farrow lifeboat model is similar in design to that presented to the 1851 National Competition Committee, Tyne and Wear Museums.

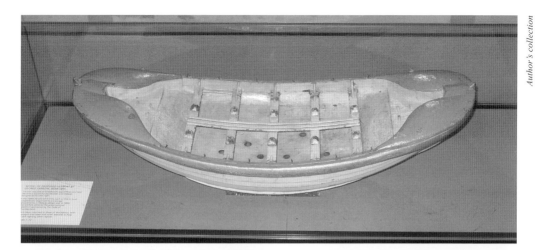

Author's collection

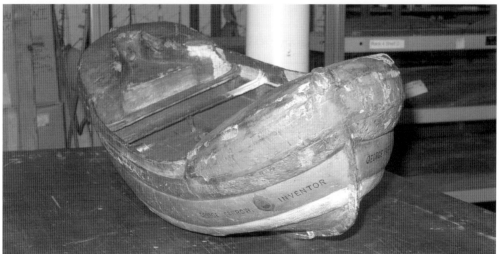

Tyne & Wear Archives & Museums

Model of George Farrow's self righting lifeboat design.

design, namely, the ability to self-right, extra internal buoyancy, sheer of gunwale and the double stem, and his lifeboat designs were based upon the principles of the *Original,* the boats being double-ended and following the one-third proportions rule prevalent in all of the Shields lifeboats.

However, Farrow did also design self-righting lifeboats in the 1850 local competition and the 1851 national competition, based on a variation of these principles. His innovative idea of water ballast in a lifeboat was first introduced at the 1841 competition, and adopted in the construction of the local institution boats built after 1844.

The Tyne Lifeboat Institution stuck rigidly to the design principles first used in the *Original,* but with some modifications regarding water ballasting and the use of cork and air cases. Despite the local and national lifeboat competitions, it is difficult to understand why the Tyne Lifeboat Institution failed to develop or adopt these new ideas in lifeboat design, as promoted in both Farrow's and Beeching's national competition models.

The construction of the piers and removal of the Herd Sand and Bar would soon remove the sea conditions that influenced the design of the first surf lifeboats. As the Royal National Lifeboat Institution later recognised, the Tyne would soon require a lifeboat with better endurance to operate outside the piers and over longer distances.

Author's collection

A model by George Farrow of the South Shields lifeboat Original, Trinity House, Newcastle.

9 The lifeboats

Throughout its operational existence of 147 years, the Tyne Lifeboat Institution and the local lifeboat Committees that preceded it built and operated ten lifeboats.

Original and *Northumberland*

The *Original* and *Northumberland* were the only two Greathead-built lifeboats that served on the Tyne. The *Original* was 28ft. 6in. long by 9ft. 6in. beam and 3ft. 2in. depth amidships. The hull was clinker built with cork buoyancy fendering fastened with metal strips onto the midships gunwale. It rowed ten oars, double banked, and was steered by a sweep oar from the stern, together with a steering oar at the bow, and had a crew of 12.

The *Northumberland* was 30ft. in length, painted white with a coppered bottom, and also pulled ten oars, double banked. In 1840, her deck was raised to allow self-draining tubes to be fitted.

These boats would have looked exactly the same as the *Zetland,* now on display at the Redcar Lifeboat Museum, with the exception that the original cork fendering amidships proved to be vulnerable and was replaced by timber on the *Zetland*. On later Tyne boats, a semi-circular profiled cork and canvas fender ran along the whole length of the gunwale.

Tyne

It was not until three years after the *Original* was wrecked on service that South Shields had a replacement lifeboat. 1833 saw the launch of the *Tyne,* a clinker-built boat, 32ft. by 10ft., with ten oars rowed double-banked. In a 54-year career, she saved 1,024 lives.

The delay in replacing the *Original* was due to difficulties in securing funds for a new boat. It led to the Newcastle Shipwreck Association requesting the National Lifeboat Institution to place a boat at Tynemouth Haven in 1832. The boat was stationed there for ten years.

Following the wreck of the *Electra* in March 1845, the *Tyne,* although severely damaged, was towed back to South Shields by the *Providence*. There she was substantially rebuilt to reflect the features and design of the second *Northumberland* and *Providence*. These design features were subsequently incorporated into all later boats. The *Tyne* had her deck raised to enable airtight compartments and a water ballast tank to be fitted underneath, an improved self draining system, and larger cork fenders fitted around the gunwales.

The *Tyne* spent the latter part of her career at the South Beach boathouse and performed her last service in December 1884. She was replaced by the *Willie Wouldhave* in September 1887. The *Tyne* was kept in reserve at the Coble Landing, before being given to South Shields Council. In 1894 she was put on permanent display at the Pier Head in South Shields.

South Tyneside Libraries

The Tyne after the October 1941 air raid.

During an air raid on the night of Thursday 2 October 1941, the *Tyne* and its shelter were severely damaged. For the second time during that week the Luftwaffe had carried out a raid on South Shields causing significant damage throughout the town, including a hit on a public air raid shelter with many fatalities. The air raid took place between 9pm and midnight. Three

Author's collection

The restored Tyne returning to the Pier Head in 1946.

South Tyneside Libraries

The Tyne on the Coble Landing boathouse slipway, 1858, with the pilot crew dressed in their working uniform, Coxswain Andrew Harrison in his distinctive top hat in the stern, and his grandson Jacob Harrison, second to the left of his grandfather. The Providence can be seen in the lifeboat house. To the right of the boathouse and coble, there is a boat with the lines of a lifeboat. This could be the first Northumberland lifeboat, which was sold to local pilots, re-named the Noble Institution and used as a salvage boat, and, on a number of occasions, on ac-tual rescues.

Luftwaffe aircraft were shot down by RAF Beaufighter night fighters, of which a Heinkel 111 bomber came down off the coast and a Dornier 17, three miles off Tynemouth. The Canadian pilot of the Beaufighter observed the crew of four parachuting from the plane.

The port side, midships section of the *Tyne* was completely destroyed when the shelter roof fell onto the boat. It was not until late 1945 that the boat and shelter were repaired. The *Tyne* was returned to the Pier Head in January 1946. The works were undertaken by Robson's boat builders of South Shields. A report in the *South Shields Gazette* of 8 January, 1946 stated that the whole side had to be replaced, and the boat was generally overhauled. There were no original building plans and the boat builders had to study the design as they cut away the damaged part to rebuild the boat with new hardwood planks.

During subsequent years, Robson's repainted and carried out minor repairs to the *Tyne*. This boatyard had also built, in 1830, Cromer's second lifeboat, based on the 'North-Country' design. Some 160 years later, during the late 1980s-90s, Robson's were repairing and refitting many RNLI boats as well as fitting out two Arun class boats, in 1989, 52-42, *Murray Lornie*, and 52-45, *Mabel Williams* in 1990.

Northumberland

A second lifeboat for the North Shields station, also named *Northumberland* was built in 1844, by Thomas Anderson of North Shields. She was 33ft. in length by 11ft. in width and rowed ten oars. The most radical departure from earlier boats was the introduction of water ballast and a raised platform and drainage holes. This boat was sold out of service in 1884.

Providence

The *Providence,* built in 1845 by Woodhouse of South Shields at a cost of £234, was a larger boat, at 34ft. by 10ft. 10in., a depth of 3ft. 4in., and pulling 14 oars. She was capable of carrying between 50 and 60 people. The deck was 20in. above the keel. Her carriage cost £60.

The boat was double-ended with a belt of cork, 18in. broad, and 3.5in. thick in the middle, around her outside, below the gunwales. It acted as a fender in addition to giving buoyancy. She was fitted with 224 cubic feet of air-cases, 15in. in height, and located in the ends, the bottom and sides, and up to the thwarts. A water ballast tank was contained in an open central well, 12in. deep by 6ft. square that could hold up nearly one ton of water. It was filled by opening two valves when the boat was afloat, the valves dropping and closing themselves when the tank was full. She had open tubes through her bottom that, in the case of her being filled, emptied her, with 29 men on board, in four minutes, leaving two or three inches of water upon her deck.

The *Providence* was sold out of service in 1872 and used as a water boat on the river until she was broken up in 1899.

The Floating Fire Engine

The Tyne Lifeboat Institution also maintained and manned a floating fire engine, moored near to the Coble Landing. This was built in 1841 at a cost of £653 10s 6d. There are no records as to whether the floating fire engine was ever used although remaining records indicate that it was still in existence in 1866. A superintendent was in charge of its maintenance and operation.

Prior

In 1855, a second lifeboat, to be stationed on the north side of the Tyne entrance, was built by Mr Dowey of North Shields. The *South Shields Gazette* dated 16 February 1855 reported her successful trials among the breakers outside the harbour. The boat was constructed on the same design as the South Shields lifeboat. It was 28ft. long and pulled ten oars.

This boat is thought to have been the *Prior*, which was transferred to the South Beach boathouse after the RNLI re-established a station at Tynemouth Haven in 1862. Surviving records indicate that the last service call of the *Prior* was on November 24, 1868, when she launched, with 16 crew, to the Tyne Improvement Commission Hopper Barge No. 25. There are no accounts of what happened to this boat or when she was taken out of service, although it can be surmised that with the construction of the *Tom Perry* and *Willie Wouldhave* in 1872 and 1876 respectively, the *Prior* came out of service sometime during that period.

Tom Perry

The *Tom Perry,* 33ft. by 11ft, depth of 3ft. 6in., pulled 12 oars and was completed in June 1872, as a replacement for the *Providence.* She was built by James Jackson of South Shields, and cost £200, being funded from a gift of £600 to the Tyne Lifeboat Institution by Mrs. T. Perry of Harton Village, South Shields, in memory of her husband.

Miss Moore, daughter of the Mayor of South Shields, undertook the naming ceremony at the Coble Landing. This was followed by a display of The *Tom Perry's* abilities including a demonstration of her self-draining capacity when boys from the training ship *Wellesley* filled the lifeboat with water.

South Tyneside Libraries

The Tom Perry with the training ship Wellesley, North Shields, in the background.

The 66-year-old *Tom Perry* was sold in February 1938 to a Mr Devlin, a local salvage diver, for use as a diving boat moored at Howden Dock. The boat came to a sad end being left to rot as a derelict on the tidal mud banks of the river.

Willie Wouldhave

The *Willie Wouldhave*, built in 1876, was originally stationed at the South Beach boathouse. No records of her dimensions exist, however, she is thought to have been around 30ft. in length and 10ft. wide. She was transferred to North Shields in 1882, to replace the *Northumberland*, but she proved unpopular with her crew, returning to the south of the river in January 1884. The *Willie Wouldhave* and South Beach boathouse were destroyed in an arson attack in March 1947.

James Young

The *James Young* was built for the North Shields station, to replace the smaller and unpopular *Willie Wouldhave*, by James Jackson at his boatbuilding yard on the Lawe

South Tyneside Libraries

The Willie Wouldhave, South Beach Station.

Tyne & Wear Archives & Museums

A model of the 1876 built Willie Wouldhave, currently on display in South Shields Museum. The internal layout of this boat differs little from that of the Tyne, built in 1833 and refitted in 1845.

at South Shields. She was 32ft. in length with a beam of 11ft., pulling 12 oars and was completed in January 1884, at a cost of £260. The *James Young*, was named after the then Chairman of the Tyne Lifeboat Institution Trustees who had defrayed the cost of the boat.

The James Young after the April 1941 air raid.

The 57-year-old *James Young*, together with the Tynemouth RNLI boat, *John Pyemont*, were destroyed in their boathouses during an air raid on 10 April 1941, six months before the *Tyne* was similarly damaged. As a result, the station was closed, heralding the end of 143 years of service from the North Shields lifeboat station.

Graham Farr Collection (RNLI)

Bedford

In 1886, the Tyne Lifeboat Institution took delivery of the last boat to be built for the organisation, the *Bedford*. Built by L.B. Lambert of South Shields, she was named on Tuesday, 21 December 1886, by Miss Mary Hall. Built on similar lines to the *Tom Perry* she was 33ft. 2in. in length, 10ft. 8in. in width, 3ft. 6in. in depth, pulling 12 oars. The boat, which cost £330, and a new boathouse, were funded from a bequest of £1,000 from a Miss Bedford of Pershore, Worcestershire, in memory of her brother, an engineer killed in the construction of the Tyne Piers.

Following the formal ceremony, the boat was filled to the gunwales with water, with the crew standing on her thwarts. On the word of Superintendent Coxswain, Andrew Harrison, the cork plugs were removed and the boat emptied herself in 52 seconds.

J. Gregory of South Shields, an agricultural implement maker, built the launching carriage. It measured 29ft. in length and 7ft. in width, weighed 4 tons, and had 4 wheels that fitted onto the timber slipway.

The Trustees of the late Miss Bedford also funded the 31ft. self-righting lifeboat that was based at the RNLI's Holy Island No. 2 Station in1891. Also named *Bedford*, the boat had a very short operational life being declared 'obsolete' and subsequently condemned and sold in 1900.

By 1935, the RNLI had been operating a motor lifeboat from its station at North Shields Fish Quay for 30 years, and over that period of time had developed a number of different types of motor lifeboat, with twin engines, below deck cabins, on deck crew protection and radio telecommunications to suit specific operational requirements.

The Tyne Lifeboat Institution, however, still maintained that their rowing surf lifeboats were best suited to the conditions experienced at the mouth of the river, despite the completion of the piers, removal of the Herd Sand and dredging of the river channel.

For a number of years the Trustees had refused to countenance the change to engine power, however, at the Annual Meeting of the Tyne Lifeboat Society, held at the Royal Hotel, South Shields on 21 March 1935, a question was raised by one of the members, Mr A.L. Mann of Newcastle, as outlined in a report of the proceedings in the *South Shields Gazette*. Speaking at the luncheon after the meeting Mr Mann stated that:

A practice once a year is not in my mind sufficient to keep the men who man the boat in a state of physical fitness. I think the time is rapidly approaching when a

South Tyneside Libraries

The Bedford on her slipway at the Coble Landing, 1886.

Graham Farr Collection (RNLI)

The engine and fuel tank in the Bedford.

motor should be installed in one or more of the boats. Sentiment is the only thing that is standing in the way of the motorisation of the lifeboat. It is a pity, because we ought to be able to give a first class service and immediate service. On a recent occasion our fellows had not sufficient strength to pull the boat where it was wanted. I am glad to hear from our Chairman that the whole question of motorisation of one or more of the lifeboats will not be postponed much longer.

Alderman Sykes, President of the Society, assured members that the Committee would be acting on this matter soon. A Mr George Baird, of North Shields, stated that he had examined the National Lifeboat at the north side, and felt that there would be little difficulty in converting one of the boats into a motor lifeboat. It would be less expensive and more effective to convert a small draught boat as it had been proved that small craft could often get to a ship when bigger lifeboats were unable to do so.

The Committee of Trustees decided that only one boat would be motorised, and Bairds of North Shields began fitting a petrol engine to the *Bedford* in August 1935. The conversion required the reconstruction of the stern for a rudder and tiller to be fixed, and a gunmetal frame for the propeller. A Garner petrol engine was fitted in the stern of the boat with the fuel tank located on the port side. However, the conversion significantly affected the *Bedford's* stability and sea-keeping qualities.

The *Bedford* was transferred from the Coble Landing boathouse to the Pilot Jetty boathouse on 11 April 1936, replacing the *Tom Perry*. John Whale, a former pilot and superintendent coxswain of the *Bedford* and *Willie Wouldhave*, now in his 70s, oversaw the transfer.

The *Shields Gazette* reported that John Whale's pride in the newly equipped boat seemed at least equal to his regret at losing the 63 year old *Tom Perry*, in which he had gone many times to the rescue of wrecked and endangered seamen. The article continued that in the days of bigger vessels, the South Shields lifeboats were called out less frequently. The last occasion a lifeboat was launched was to go to the assistance of a small vessel, which had grounded on the Black Middens, about three years previously. On the 10 March 1933, the *Tom Perry* launched to the *Ellind,* but her services were not required. It was not necessary to take off the crew and the vessel floated off on the tide, without assistance.

The newspaper commented that the lack of regular crews did not indicate anything haphazard in the organisation. Captain Arthur Surtees, Secretary of the Society told the *Gazette* that 'there is never any trouble about getting volunteers. Men are only too pleased to go if they are required.'

When, in 1935, the Society finally decided to embrace modern technology and motorise the 49 year-old old *Bedford,* this was more as a reaction to manpower problems

Graham Farr Collection (RNLI)

Superintendent Coxswain John Whale and the Bedford following her conversion into a motor lifeboat.

than a response to changes in operational conditions.

While the approach the RNLI took in 1904 with the conversion of an existing boat was understandable, the conversion of the *Bedford* in the context of the advances in motor lifeboat design undertaken by the RNLI during the 1920s and 1930s, did not result in a better lifeboat, and illustrates a somewhat conservative and unimaginative attitude together with an unwillingness to change, possibly influenced by the lack of sufficient financial resources to do so.

The RNLI's smallest single screw motor lifeboats, the 32ft. surf light motor cost £3,200 in 1935, with the slightly larger 35ft. 6in. non-self-righting Liverpool class boat and the 35ft. 6in. self-righting lifeboat both costing around £3,400.

The finances of the Tyne Lifeboat Society had been structured in such a way that there were no significant cash reserves to purchase a purpose-built motor lifeboat, hence the conversion of the *Bedford*. Even if finance had been available, and a modern motor lifeboat constructed, it begs the question as to what effective purpose this could have served with the presence of the RNLI's motor lifeboat at North Shields.

The *Bedford* stayed in the Pilot Jetty boathouse until October 1968 when, after an offer to maintain and display the boat had been declined by South Shields Borough Council, her future was assured when she was removed for display to the Exeter Maritime Museum. The *Bedford* is now on display at Eyemouth.

South Tyneside Libraries

The Tyne Lifeboat Society fleet in the early 1900s. From left to right, the Bedford, Willie Wouldhave (in background), Tom Perry and James Young.

South Tyneside Libraries

The Bedford leaving the Pilot Jetty Boathouse for the first time in 31 years to be displayed at Exeter Maritime Museum, October 1968.

10 Boathouses

In 1789 the Tyne entrance was a tidal sandy foreshore with none of the quays or landings that were later to characterise the South Shields and North Shields riverside. The high ground of the Lawe escarpment dominated the southern shore of the river, with the river mouth and Herd Sands immediately below.

Herd Sands, South Shields

The *Original's* boathouse, built in September 1789 at a cost of £58 10s 7d, also provided shelter and accommodation for shipwrecked mariners and served as a depot for ship's materials salvaged from wrecks, reflecting the pilots' commercial aspirations regarding salvage awards.

The location of this boathouse is hard to pinpoint with any degree of accuracy. No detailed maps or charts exist that specifically show where this house was located and historical text is somewhat inconclusive. Greathead, in his submissions to Parliament, stated that the lifeboat was launched into calm waters. This is thought to be a reference to launching over a short stretch of foreshore into the Tyne, rather than transporting the lifeboat across the tidal Herd Sand and launching directly into breaking surf. Greathead's carriage design, with 1ft. diameter wheels, proved impractical, with the carriage sinking into the sand.

E. Mackenzie and M. Ross's *An Historical, Topographical, and Descriptive View of the County Palatine of Durham* Volume 1, published in 1834, states that the *Original's* lifeboat house was situated on the sands, a little beyond the end of Pilot Street, and near to the Lawe House. Pilot Street, now part of River Drive, provided access to the Herd Sand, its seaward end stopping where the South Shields Sailing Club is now located.

George Hodgson, in *The Borough of South Shields*, 1903, stated that at the beginning of the 19th century, the Lawe was occupied only by the old Cross House or Lawe House, apparently originally erected as barracks for the garrison of the battery which existed on the Lawe until after the peace of Waterloo, and by a rope walk and an inn on the site now occupied by the Baltic Tavern. Below, on the edge of the Herd Sand, stood the newly erected Lifeboat House.

A map of South Shields dated 1827 shows two unmarked buildings in locations matching the above descriptions, one building, to the west, with a clearly marked apron extending in front of it, possibly the beginnings of a slipway, facing the river. Whether one of these buildings was the *Original's* boathouse cannot be firmly established in the absence of any descriptive text on this map. However, in the context of

Author's collection

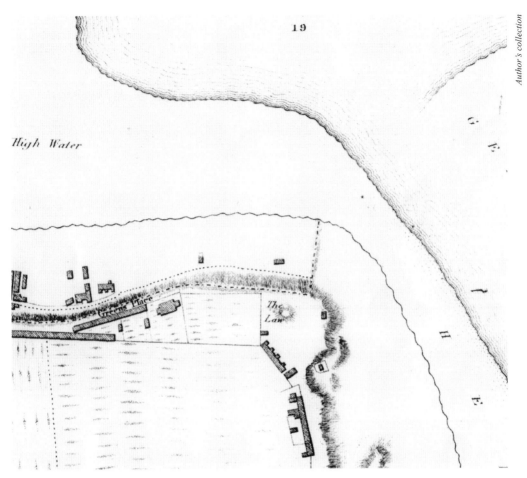

High Water

This 1827 map of the Lawe Top, South Shields, shows the two buildings on the river foreshore, to the north of the Lawe Top and above the high tide mark of the Herd Sands. The Lawe House is the rectangular building projecting beyond the southern end of the smaller terrace of buildings in the centre of the map, and the Coble Landing is located to the extreme left of the map.

the historical text references, it is the likely location of the boathouse. Today it is the site of River Drive and the Harbour View housing estate.

However, this map does not indicate any buildings on what was to become the main South Shields lifeboat station at Coble Landing.

Coble Landing

The first known reference to a lifeboat house at the Coble Landing is shown on a chart of the Tyne entrance, surveyed by Commander Slater and E.K. Calver, RN dated 1838.

Coble Landing, as it name suggests, was a sandy foreshore where local pilots and fishermen launched and stored their cobles. It was approximately 250 metres upstream

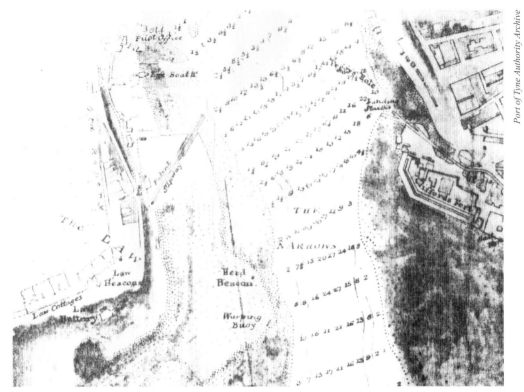

Port of Tyne Authority Archive

The 1838 chart showing, at the top, the single lifeboat house and Pilot's Office at the Coble Landing. The Lawe House is located between the Law Beacons and Law Cottages.

of the Narrows, and the *Original*'s boathouse. The Pilot's Office was also at the landing.

It was the development of shipbuilding at South Shields and the need for land with easy access to the river to launch ships that led to the construction of a boathouse at the Coble Landing.

The *Original*'s boat house was lost sometime during the 1830s following the expansion of adjacent shipbuilding yards, and by 1845, the foreshore to the east of the Coble Landing had been completely developed.

The reorganisation and amalgamation of the North and South Shields Committees soon led to a period of investment in new boats, equipment and shore facilities. In 1841, a double lifeboat house and slipways were constructed at the Coble Landing, on the site of the 1838 house, to accommodate a second boat for the South Shields station, the *Providence*. Whether this was an extension to the 1838 house or a completely new building is not known.

In the 1880s the Trustees had wished to construct a new brick boathouse at their preferred location immediately to the north of the southern wave trap, where the South

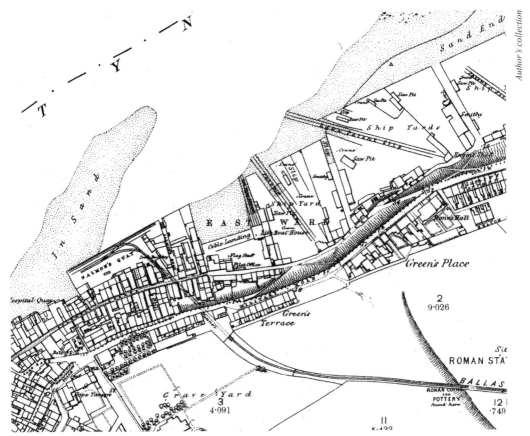

Author's collection

*The Coble Landing double boathouse and slipways, on the first OS map, 1851, with the ship-
yards to the east, and the sandy landing place for pilots which led to the site's name.*

Shields Sailing Club stands today.

However, on 10 August 1885, the pier engineer P.J. Messent, who also held the post
of Honorary Secretary at the Tynemouth RNLI Station, told the Tyne Improvement
Commissioners that as the wave trap was a temporary construction, it would be inap-
propriate to construct a permanent brick building. A temporary structure, of a design to
be approved by the Tyne Improvement Commissioners, that could be removed whenever required would be less objectionable.

This recommendation clearly precluded a permanent solution that would have significantly improved the operational effectiveness of the South Shields lifeboats.

The Trustees of the Lifeboat Institution could not accept this restriction, and in
August 1886, George Lyall, Institution Secretary, wrote to the Commissioners seeking
consent for a new boathouse and slipway at the Coble Landing. Messent responded
less than a month later recommending that the Commissioners give their approval.

In November 1886, a new brick boathouse and slipway was constructed next to the

South Tyneside Libraries

The Bedford Boathouse, 1937.

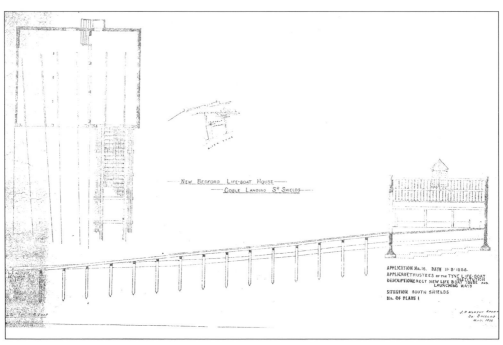

Port of Tyne Authority Archive

J.H. Morton's architectural drawings of the Bedford Boathouse, also indicating the 1841 double boathouse.

South Tyneside Libraries

The redevelopment of the Coble landing, with new quay works under construction and the vacant boathouses waiting to be demolished in 1937.

South Tyneside Libraries

The Lawe Top from North Shields showing the shipyards on the edge of the Herd Sands. The Original's boathouse is thought to have been located on the foreshore to the right of the picture. The building on the skyline, with three chimney stacks to the right of the aft mast, is the Lawe House.

double boathouse that accommodated the *Willie Wouldhave* and *Tom Perry*. This new boathouse, known as the Bedford Boathouse was for the last Tyne Lifeboat Institution boat to be built, the *Bedford*.

The Coble Landing boathouses ceased as an operational station when the *Tom Perry* was sold out of service and the motorised *Bedford* moved to the Pilot Jetty boathouse in April 1936. The boathouses were demolished in 1937 as part of a comprehensive riverside slum clearance scheme undertaken by South Shields Borough Council. A factory now occupies the site of the former boathouses and slipways.

South Beach, South Shields

The first reference to a boathouse at the South Beach was on a chart, dated 1859, indicating the harbour works proposed by the pier engineer, John Ure. This was sited to the south of the South Pier. No records exist as to its precise date of construction.

There are likely to have two reasons for a station being established on the South Beach. First, in the light of the 1849 disaster, a boathouse in this location would have provided a more direct response to a wreck on the Herd Sands, as the boats would not have to cross the Herd Sands and Tynemouth Bar. Secondly, a boathouse may have been provided as a direct response to the construction of the South Pier, to save the

©Crown Copyright

The site of the first South Beach Boathouse, 1871. The tidal gully and sand bar which led to the relocation of the boathouse is clearly shown, as is the Volunteer Life Brigade Watch House.

boats having to be rowed down river and around the pier ends to reach the southern extent of the Herd Sands. Although the construction of the piers did not finally begin until 1854, survey work on its alignment had been in progress since 1849. Whatever the reasons for establishing a South Beach station, it is likely that this was sometime during the early to mid 1850s, as the boathouse is not shown on the 1851 first edition Ordnance Survey map.

The construction of the South Pier began to restrict tidal currents along the Herd Sands to such an extent that the northerly flow on an ebb tide was diverted southwards by the pier and back down the beach. By 1871 the tides had scoured a large gully directly in front of the lifeboat house slip, but with a sand bank formed by the existing beach blocking access to the open sea, which made launching and beaching problematic.

The boathouse was relocated to a more accessible site to the seaward side, and east of the Volunteer Life Brigade Watch House. It opened in around 1875-76. The new boathouse blocked the views to south and east from the Watch House. To maintain their watch capability, the Brigade constructed a tower, as seen today, which was completed in December 1875, and which gave a panoramic view of the harbour, its approaches, and the Herd Sands.

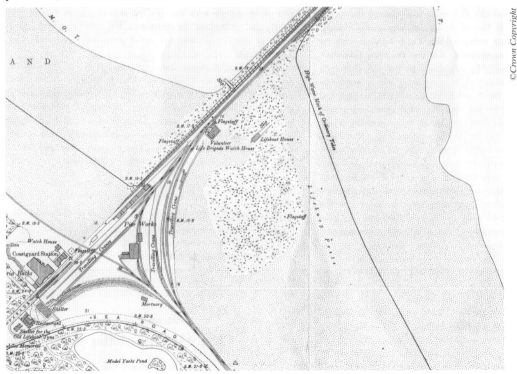

©Crown Copyright

The site of the second South Beach Boathouse and slipway, 1895, now located to the east of the Volunteer Life Brigade Watch House.

In July 1899, the operation of this boathouse was significantly affected because the launchway was blocked by sand and stones. The Tyne Improvement Commission was requested to clear away the obstructions, estimated at between 200 and 300 tons of material. The local Lifeboat Institution offered to pay for this work.

South Tyneside Libraries

The second South Beach Boathouse.

In September 1899, the Trustees decided not to replace the boathouse owing to the high cost of £982. No information exists to indicate why the Trustees were considering the construction of a new boathouse.

The minute book for 1928 records the discovery of a fire at the boathouse in July of that year. It was put out with only slight damage to the building. During World War II, the boathouse was requisitioned by the War Office and used as storage for a searchlight and anti-aircraft battery. The Volunteer Life Brigade was given 24 hours' notice by the War Office to vacate their Watch House, which was used to accommodate the Royal Artillery soldiers who manned the nearby batteries at Trow Rocks and Frenchman's Bay.

The South Beach boathouse was destroyed by fire in the winter of 1947 and with it the *Willie Wouldhave*. The fire was started by a number of small boys playing underneath the boathouse – the house was constructed on piles and elevated above the sands. There were difficulties in fighting the fire, with the nearest water hydrant 300 yards away, and the water partially freezing in the fire hoses laid out over the snowdrifts. All that remained were the large metal wheels of the launching carriage. Following the fire, the Secretary of the Tyne Lifeboat Society, J. Thomson, stated that it was unlikely that the boat and its house would be replaced.

The South Beach area has changed radically since the lifeboat houses and Volunteer Life Brigade Watch House were first built. The development of this area with the Pier Head yard and then, in the 1930s, the construction of a promenade (a job creation scheme during the days of the Depression) and the beginnings of the amusement park, changed the appearance of the area. This culminated with the creation of the sand

Newcastle Libraries

Newcastle Libraries

Two views of the South Beach Boathouse and Volunteer Life Brigade Watch House in the early 1900s. Note the rebuilding of the North Pier following storm damage in 1896.

dunes to the seaward of the amusement park by the tipping of spoil from the excavation of the Brigham and Cowans dock, South Shields, in the late 1940s.

The raising of the land levels as a result of these developments, together with the construction of the South Pier has resulted in the high water mark being pushed eastwards from its 1870s position by approximately 400 metres.

The location of the first South Beach boathouse was within the present-day amusement park on a site to the east of the Dunes Ten Pin Bowling Alley, now occupied by a single storey brown metal-clad building. There are no signs today that indicate the location of the later South Beach boathouse.

Manhaven, South Shields

RNLI Finance Committee Minutes dated 31 July 1854 indicate that the South Shields Lifeboat Committee was considering placing a lifeboat at Manhaven, a small cove to the north of Marsden Bay, and some two miles south of the Tyne entrance.

This small, exposed and unprotected landing place was used by both pilots and fishermen. Landing and getting off were extremely difficult and hazardous with any degree of swell. The space on which to place a boat was restricted, especially at high water and when a gale from the east and heavy breaking surf was running. No records indicate whether a lifeboat was based at Manhaven, and it is likely that because of these operational difficulties the RNLI abandoned their plans

The same RNLI minutes indicate that the Port of Tyne Lifeboat Fund had contributed towards a new lifeboat to be stationed at Prior's Haven, Tynemouth.

Pilot Jetty, South Shields

During the 1880s and 1890s, the Coble Landing boathouse slips were frequently damaged by ships docking at the adjacent Rennoldson's Shipyard, downstream of the boathouse.

Further problems were caused by the boathouse slips suffering from silting brought about, according to the Trustees, when the wind was from the east and by the recent construction of a breakwater and groyne at the nearby Readhead's shipyard. The annual cost of £30 to clear the sand was a considerable charge on lifeboat funds, and the Tyne Improvement Commissioners were requested to instruct the pier engineer, Messent, to survey the locality with the intention of resolving this matter.

Messent responded in December 1882, stating that the problem would resolve itself following the construction of timber groynes downstream and with the further extension of the piers. He also suggested that an immediate remedy would probably be found by raising the slipways, as had been done on the north side at the Low Light boathouse. The Commissioners, however, instructed Messent to present a further report on the state of the launching ways, together with an estimate of the cost of improving their condition.

George Lyall, Secretary of the Tyne Lifeboat Institution wrote to the Commissioners in March 1883, informing them that the situation had deteriorated with the further accumulation of sand and stones on the launching ways. The lifeboat had been damaged on two occasions when launching, despite £17 4s having been spent since the beginning of the year to clear the ways. In 1886 a request to the Commissioners to construct a new boathouse at the southern wavetrap as a solution to these operational difficulties was dismissed by Messent.

Newcastle Libraries

The Southern wave trap, c.1890. The proposed boathouse and slipway would have been located at the top of the beach to the left of the Groyne breakwater. The site is today occupied by South Shields Sailing Club. The wagons contain limestone from Trow Quarry used in the construction of the North Pier.

In March 1891, further damage was caused to the Coble Landing slips when a ship was towed into Rennoldson's yard. In September 1894, the local Institution complained that mooring chains from the same shipyard were lying across the launching ways. Approaches to the yard management to resolve this matter were ignored, and the Secretary, James Robinson, wrote to the Commissioners seeking their help. They tasked the harbour master to investigate and remove the obstruction, which was done in the following month.

Problems at the boathouse continued when, in November 1901, the steamer *Trouper* broke adrift from its moorings and caused considerable damage to the slipways. By December 1901, the boats were unable to launch at certain states of the tide. To address this problem, the Tyne Lifeboat Institution approached the Tyne Improvement Commissioners resurrecting their proposal to construct a new boathouse and slipway at the southern wave trap.

The river engineer could not support the proposal because a boathouse would interfere with the use of the wave trap for the purposes of beaching sunken vessels, which may be raised (as in the case of the SS *Dorothy*) or for the purpose of landing salvaged wreckage, as in the cases of the SS *Maltby* and SS *Knud*.

In October 1905, the Trustees submitted a scheme to the Tyne Improvement

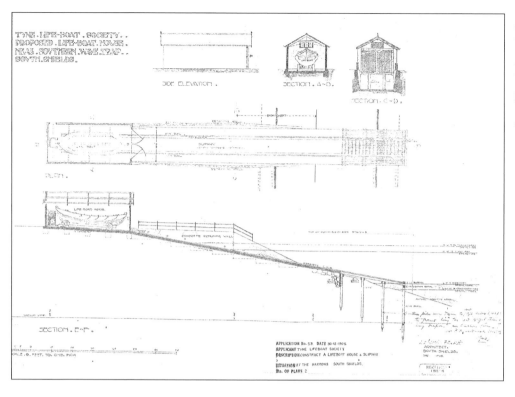

Port of Tyne Authority Archive

J.H. Morton's plans of the Pilot Jetty Boathouse.

Commission, designed by the local architect J.H. Morton, proposing a new location between the Pilot Jetty and Commissioners Wharf, at the Narrows, despite their concerns about the possible steep gradient of any slipway in this location. The proposed lifeboat house would be the same size as that proposed at the Southern Wave Trap. The river engineer recommended that the Commissioners approve this scheme.

Graham Farr Collection (RNLI)

The Pilot Jetty Boathouse.

Graham Farr Collection (RNLI)

The Pilot Jetty Boathouse.

The final approval from the Tyne Improvement Commissioners was received on 10 February 1906, and on the 28th of the same month a tender of £185 16s was accepted for the works.

The land was a gift to the Tyne Lifeboat Society from the River Tyne Commissioners, the house was constructed by R.W. Iversen, contractor, of South Shields. The launching ways and concrete works were carried out by J.H. Hall, also of South Shields.

The *Tom Perry* was transferred to the new boathouse, which opened on 19 July 1906. It was constructed of corrugated iron, painted dark green, and the interior lined with varnished timber panelling. The slipway was formed in concrete and a gap was cut through the rock embankment to beyond the low water mark.

This site was ideal as it was nearly one third of a mile nearer to the harbour entrance than the Coble Landing boathouses. Directly opposite, at North Shields, was moored the new Tynemouth motor lifeboat *J. McConnell-Hussey,* which had arrived on station on May 3, 1905.

In October 1907, the unoccupied double boathouse at the Coble Landing was leased to the Tyne Pilotage Commission as a store, at an annual rent of £5. The *Bedford* remained in operational use in its own house at the Coble Landing.

Graham Farr Collection (RNLI)

The Pilot Jetty Boathouse and Slipway.

The *Tom Perry* was stationed in this boathouse until 1936 when she was sold out of service. The *Bedford* had a petrol engine installed in 1935 and was transferred from her boathouse at the Coble Landing to the Pilot Jetty house a year later. All of the Coble Landing boathouses were demolished in February 1937.

The Pilot Jetty boathouse and slipway, near to the site of the *Original's* boathouse, was demolished in 1990, with the redevelopment of the former Velva Liquids Oil Depot into the Harbour View housing estate. All that remains of the lifeboat station at this location are the slipway abutment walls within the stone quayside, and the supporting timber piles of the slipway which can be seen at low water.

North Shields

The first lifeboat house at North Shields, a timber lean-to shed, was constructed against and on the seaward side of the Low Light, the boat launching over skids directly into the river. This boathouse was in an exposed location, on the Sand End, and is shown on a map dated 1827, of North Shields and the river entrance, commissioned by the Duke of Northumberland.

As at South Shields, station improvements were undertaken during 1840 and 1841, with an extension to the 'timber ways' and a new carriage for the *Northumberland*. In 1855, due to its exposed position on the sands, the boathouse was destroyed in a gale, and subsequently rebuilt.

The 1857 first edition Ordnance Survey map shows a larger boathouse and exten-

North Tyneside Council

The earliest known image of the North Shields lifeboat house, c.1810. The boathouse lies just behind the freestanding scullermen's shed, next to the Low Light.

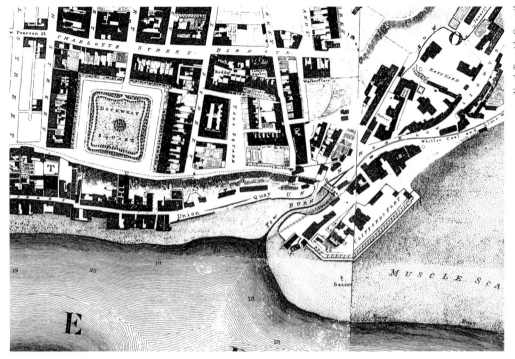

North Tyneside Council

The 1827 map showing the site of the first North Shields Lifeboat House 'X' adjacent to the Low Lighthouse.

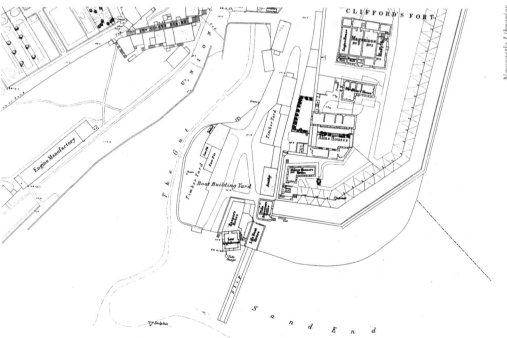

Newcastle Libraries

The Lowlight Boathouse, North Shields c.1857, from the first edition Ordnance Survey map.

Author's collection.

The North Shields Lifeboat House, on the seaward side of the Low Light, with a lifeboat on the slipway, around 1880.

Chris Lambert

The 1884 boathouse in 1999, prior to its demolition.

sive slipway facing due south into the river, the high tide mark midway along the length of the slipway.

Major changes occurred at the station during in April 1884, with the Tyne Improvement Commission giving their consent, following a recommendation made by the Pier Engineer, P.J. Messent, to replace the earlier wooden lifeboat house at the Low Lighthouse with a bigger boathouse to accommodate the new and larger lifeboat, *James Young*, recently built for the station. This consent was subject to the building being removed at any time in the future upon the Commissioner's request and the payment of a nominal annual ground rent of 2s 6d.

In November 1884, the idea of extending the Fish Quay was first put forward, but it was not until October 1885, that the Commissioners received a formal application from Tynemouth Corporation for these works and, at the northern wavetrap, the con-

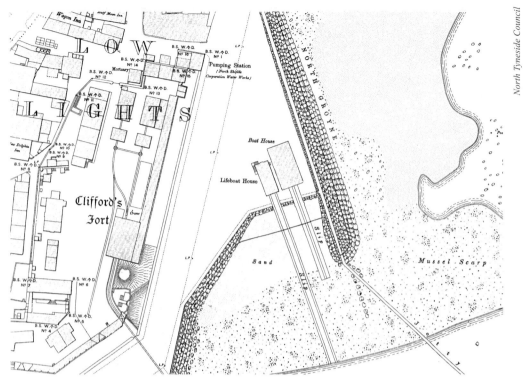

North Tyneside Council

The East Fish Quay Boathouses of the Tyne Lifeboat Institution, with the longer slipway, and to the east, the RNLI boathouse.

Graham Farr Collection (RNLI)

The North Shields Boathouses of the Tyne Lifeboat Society and RNLI.

North Tyneside Council

North Tyneside Council

Two views of the RNLI and Tyne Lifeboat Society Boathouses, North Shields, the lower photo dated 1936. The site of the first boathouse can be seen adjacent to the Lowlight. The RNLI motor lifeboat J. McConnell Hussey was moored immediately upstream of the Lloyds Hailing Station jetty, where the line of fishing cobles are moored. The present Tynemouth RNLI station is located on the site of the jetty that projects into the river from the Fish Quay.

struction of a replacement lifeboat house and a new War Department boat house, with each boathouse having its own separate slipway. These quay works, were approved in November 1885, and upon completion resulted in the severance of the Low Light boathouse from the river.

The 1884 boathouse was converted into a post office and telegraph office, and latterly a café. This building was demolished in 1999, and the site can still be seen today adjacent to the Low Lighthouse.

The replacement boathouse for the *James Young* was completed in 1886. It had a first-floor watch tower. Being located to the east of the Fish Quay and Clifford's Fort, it was protected from the harbour and incoming swells by the Lloyd's Hailing Station jetty. However, this new station suffered similar problems to the Coble Landing boathouse through silting on the launching ways.

On 27 March 1888, the Tynemouth Council Town Clerk wrote to the Tyne Improvement Commissioners concerning a recent half-hour delay in the launching of the *James Young* as a result of sand and stone deposits on the slip. The Pier Engineer, P.J. Messent, replied in May 1888 that an examination of the launching ways showed no signs of silting, and that he was of the opinion that the delay in launching was caused by the boat's carriage coming off the slipway, or the slipway not being long enough at an extraordinary low, low water. He concluded that if the delay had been caused by the state of the tide, an extension of the slipway would resolve the matter.

Immediately adjacent on the seaward side of the Tyne Lifeboat Institution boathouse, was the War Department boathouse, which the RNLI acquired in 1921 to house the 40-foot self-righting motor lifeboat *Henry Vernon.* This boat, and its predecessors, had previously been kept at moorings immediately upstream of the Lloyd's Hailing Station jetty.

In October 1939, the new 41-foot Watson lifeboat *John Pyemont* was allocated to the Tynemouth station. On the night of 10 April 1941, both the Tyne Lifeboat Society and RNLI boathouses, together with the *James Young* and *John Pyemont,* were destroyed in an air raid from two direct hits. Both slipways into the river remained intact.

This led to the Tyne Lifeboat Society's North Shields station being permanently closed, and the RNLI station being temporarily closed until October 1941, when the former Tynemouth lifeboat *Henry Frederick Swan,* now in the reserve fleet was sent to the station. Initially kept on moorings, the boat was subsequently kept in the open on the launching trolley, using the existing slipway.

At the end of the war, the site was cleared and a new boathouse and slipway, together with a watch house, were completed in 1947, the watch house standing on the same site as the two bombed boathouses. The boathouse and slipway were demolished in 1999. The watch house was demolished in December 2005 to enable a flood defence wall to be constructed the following year.

Prior's Haven, Tynemouth

After the tragic loss of life at the mouth of the Tyne during the great gale on 4 January 1854, and following the Cullercoats lifeboat crew's claims that the proposed Tyne Piers would make it difficult to get into Prior's Haven, also known as Tynemouth Haven, in March 1855 the Tyne Lifeboat Institution placed a lifeboat, the *Prior*, at this location.

RNLI Management Committee minutes indicate that in November and December 1854, Robert Plummer of the Port of Tyne Lifeboat Fund had informed the RNLI that a lifeboat was to be stationed at Tynemouth, and a new slipway and gangway would be required to accommodate the boat, which would use the 1832 boathouse occupied by the Coastguard. The Finance Sub-Committee of the National Institution agreed to give £50 to the Port of Tyne Lifeboat Fund Trustees as a contribution towards this new lifeboat.

An article in the January 1855 edition of RNLI's *The Lifeboat* reported that a new lifeboat had been built, and stationed at Tynemouth Haven, by the Shields Life-Boat Association. The boat, constructed on the same design as the Shields lifeboats, was 28ft. long, and pulled ten oars. She was built by Anderson of North Shields. There had originally been three lifeboats, two stationed on the south and one on the north side of

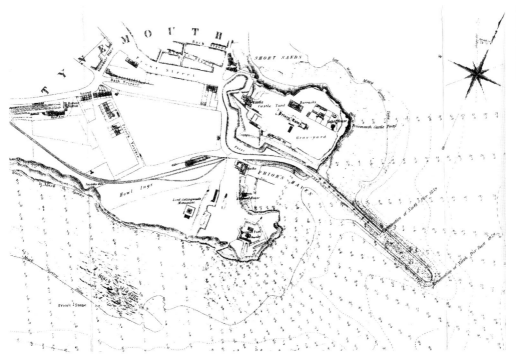

©Crown Copyright

A chart, dated 1859, showing the location of the first boathouse at Prior's Haven, Tynemouth, predating the boathouse built by the RNLI in 1862.

Newcastle Libraries

Prior's Haven Lifeboat House, c.1850s.

the river. Following the gale on 4 January 1854, when many vessels were wrecked on the north side of the Tyne before the Shields lifeboats could reach them, the Shields Lifeboat Committee decided to build another boat.

Following a letter to the RNLI from Mr James Pointon, expressing concern at the number of shipwrecks in and around Prior's Haven, the RNLI Committee of Management, at their meeting on 7 March 1862, decided to reopen the lifeboat station at Tynemouth.

The Tyne Lifeboat Society objected, albeit unsuccessfully, and following the reestablishment of the Tynemouth RNLI station in the summer of 1862 the *Prior* was withdrawn and re-allocated to the South Beach boathouse at South Shields.

A new boathouse and rocket house were built on the same site as the earlier boathouse. They were designed by P.J. Messent, who was to hold the post of Honorary Secretary of the Tynemouth RNLI station between 1865 and 1897. This boathouse survives today, and is used by the Tynemouth Rowing Club.

11 Matters ashore

Operational organisation

A Committee of Trustees ran the Tyne Lifeboat Institution with an elected President, Vice-President, Secretary and Treasurer. The society operated from offices at 11 Greens Place, on the Lawe Top in South Shields, overlooking the Coble Landing boathouses. This terrace was demolished in the 1970s.

Operational responsibility for each of the stations, and the floating fire engine, were in the hands of the superintendent coxswains, who were experienced pilots. Each coxswain was paid £5 at the end of each year.

The Institution also had their own call-out procedure, separate to, and operated independently from that of the Coastguard, whose headquarters were below the Lawe House, on the beach facing the Herd Sands.

A retired pilot, paid £5 a year, was based in the Pilot's Lookout, Trinity Towers, on the Lawe Top. This was yards from the Lawe House and commanded panoramic views

South Tyneside Libraries

The Pilot's Lookout, Trinity Towers, on the Lawe Top, South Shields.

HMS Castor.

of the river entrance, the Black Middens and Herd Sands. This lookout, built in 1810 by Trinity House, was within a third of a mile of the Coble Landing and Pilot Jetty boathouses, and next to the terraced housing of the Lawe Top where the majority of the pilots and lifeboat crew lived. The pilots could watch ships approaching the river and immediately call out the lifeboats if they spotted any vessel in difficulty.

The coastguards at the Spanish Battery, Tynemouth, had their own system of firing two cannon shots to indicate a wreck on the north side of the harbour and three for a wreck on the south side. HMS *Castor*, the Royal Navy guard ship moored at Peggy's Hole, North Shields, would repeat this signal for those out of earshot of the Spanish Battery guns.

When the two local societies amalgamated to form the Tyne Lifeboat Institution in 1841, lifeboatmen were paid 10s 6d for each service. 1892 accounts show that this same sum was still being paid, with 5s to shorehelpers. In March 1909 the payment was increased to 15s 6d for night service calls, day calls remaining at 10s 6d. If lives were saved each crew member received an extra 2s 6d.

The equipment carried in the boats was very basic, but effective, and not substantially different from that first used in 1789. Equipment comprised anchors, grappling hooks, ropes, axes, bailing buckets (for those boats that were not fitted with relieving tubes) cork and canvas fenders and spare oars. Boats carried a unique design of rescue float or slip buoys in the form of a small dumb bell, with cork buoyancy cubes attached at each end of a wooden rod. The whole assembly was attached to a coil of rope and thrown to the shipwrecked seamen who would hold it against their chest while being hauled aboard the lifeboat.

Another innovation was the use of gloves for the rowing crew, which worked on the principle of today's wetsuit. They were dipped in water so the layer of water between the hand and glove was warmed by body heat and kept the oarsmen's hands relatively warm.

Lifejackets were available for crews but these were rarely worn because they were cumbersome and hindered rowing, but also because crews had supreme confidence in their boats.

Lifelines were provided outside the boats, at the waterline and underneath the gunwales. In addition, lines were rigged inside the boats, along the thwarts and inside the gunwale for the protection of the crew.

None of the boats used rowlocks, but a rope grommet that attached the oars to the thole pins running along the gunwale kept the oars securely in place. Later boats were built with rowing board footrests, which ended the earlier design requirement that

Author's collection

The canvas fenders and rescue floats on the Bedford, Eyemouth, 2004.

these boats should be double-enders.

Following the local competition of the 1840s, boats were fitted with water ballast tanks and relieving tubes. A single pump handle, located in the centre of the boat, operated the water ballast system.

Until 1849, boats operated individually, but following the disaster, the boats often worked in pairs, one acting as back up. Institution rules required boats to be in the water, fully manned, within five minutes of the order to launch.

Robert Anderson, Secretary of the local Institution, in submissions to the 1851 Northumberland Committee stated that there were many ways of approaching a wreck:

... they never go to windward of a wreck, and drop an anchor and veer down to her; they carry grappling irons, with the finest white ropes attached to them, to hook on to channels or shrouds, or any place they can get hold of, when the crew (as it often happens) cannot throw them a rope; and they approach mostly to leeward, and rarely go alongside, generally receiving the men into the end of the boat, which renders it necessary to keep the end as clear and roomy as possible.

The Tyne Lifeboat Institution was able to call on the services of the local tug fleet to tow the lifeboats to the wreck site, especially if there was a strong flood tide and gale from the east.

Service records at the RNLI station at Tynemouth outline that the local institution boats were only first on the scene because of this assistance. Certainly, in 1898, the RNLI District Inspector approached local tug owners to seek a formalised arrangement for tugs to tow the RNLI boats when on service. The owners did not agree to a permanent arrangement, but would assist when required.

The independent Tyne lifeboats also helped in the fundraising efforts of the RNLI. On Saturday 5 September 1903, a lifeboat regatta was held at Tynemouth (Prior's) Haven, attended by eleven RNLI boats, the *Charles Dibdin* (Tynemouth No. 1 Prior's Haven), *Forester* (Tynemouth No.2, Black Middens), *George Woofindin* (Sunderland, North Dock), *John and Amy* (Sunderland, Hendon Beach), *Richard and Nelly Hodges* (Sunderland South Outlet), *Robert and Susan* (Newbiggin), *Co-Operator No. 1* (Cullercoats), *Dash* (Blyth), *William and Charles* (Whitburn), *Skynner* (Seaham) and *John Anthony* (Cambois). These boats were towed to the regatta by steam tugs, and were joined by the Tyne Lifeboat Society's *Willie Wouldhave* from the South Beach, South Shields boathouse and *James Young* from North Shields.

It was estimated that over 70,000 people attended the event, with special train and tram services being laid on. They were treated to a programme of demonstrations: a rescue display involving the launching of the Tynemouth No.1 boat into the Haven, and Tynemouth Volunteer Life Brigade carrying out a breeches buoy drill.

Author's collection

RNLI Lifeboat Regatta, Tynemouth Haven, 1903.

RNLI Archive

The Lifeboat Regatta at Tynemouth Haven 1903 showing the Willie Wouldhave and the
Tynemouth No. 1 Lifeboat Charles Dibdin approaching the low tide slipway. The James Young
can also be seen in the company of the RNLI boats.

A procession of lifeboats rowed across to the South Pier, and assembled to participate in a lifeboat handicap race comprising of a number heats and a final; the course ran from the seaward end of the South Pier and across the harbour. The final was won by Tynemouth No. 2 boat, Coxswain T. Smith, with Cambois, Coxswain Anthony Nixon, second and Blyth, Coxswain J.W. Bustell, third.

A similar regatta had been held at Cullercoats in July 1898, on Lifeboat Saturday, attended by seven RNLI boats and the *Bedford* and *James Young* from the Tyne Lifeboat Institution.

On 16 December 1916, during the First War, the Lifeboat Secretary received a letter from the South Shields Recruiting Officer regarding the age and make-up of the lifeboat crews. The Society responded that the only permanent members were the five coxswains, all over military age. The crews were made up from foyboatmen, pilots and pilots' assistants.

Author's collection

A crew list for the North Shields lifeboat James Young for the service to the steamship Waterloo, 16 December 1891. The crew lists for the first services of the Tynemouth motor lifeboat also include the names of J. Brownlee, J. Turnbull and the Bruntons.

Salvage boats

In addition to the Tyne Lifeboats and RNLI boats there were two other boats, mainly used as salvage boats, but manned by pilots and foyboatmen, which occasionally carried out lifesaving services.

By 1843, the Tyne Lifeboat Institution had prohibited the use of their lifeboats in salvage work, a sideline that gave a lucrative boost to the income of pilots and fishermen. This led to a number pilots purchasing the first *Northumberland*, when she was sold out of service in 1844. Renamed the *Noble Institution*, she was used as a salvage boat and based at North Shields. She also undertook a number of rescues. When the Tyne Lifeboat Institution boats were unable to launch she was sometimes used as a lifeboat manned by a crew of pilots. The Tyne Lifeboat Trustees approved payment of the crew on these occasions.

On the 3 December 1871, the *Noble Institution* launched, together with two lifeboats from North Shields and the Tynemouth Lifeboat to the wreck of the Dutch schooner *Fresia*, which, when leaving the river, grounded on the South Pier stones. She soon became a total loss. Three of her crew of six were rescued by the South Shields Volunteer Life Brigade but the rest all drowned.

On 19 November 1875, in a north-easterly storm, the barque *Barbra Avano* went ashore on the Herd Sand. The 13 crew and a pilot were rescued by the *Noble Institution*.

On February 8, 1883, the *Noble Institution* was launched to the brig *Ann* of Guernsey and rescued the crew of four. The *Noble Institution* was launched because the *Willie Wouldhave* was damaged.

In 1884, three pilots purchased the second *Northumberland* lifeboat, for £10 without oars, when it was taken out of service. They used it for salvage work.

Another salvage boat was the *William Wake*, named after the harbour master and built for the ballast keelmen by Mr Stewart at the Low Lights in North Shields in January 1859. She was 22ft. long and rowed 14 oars and was crewed by local foyboatmen. However, she proved to be a failure as a lifeboat being too heavy and beamy, and was used as a salvage boat, removing cargo and equipment from wrecks, and refloating ships ashore on the Herd Sand or Black Middens.

On 8-9 February 1861, the *William Wake* and the *Northumberland* lifeboat were launched on service. In March 1861, the coxswains and crews of both boats were presented with testimonials in appreciation of their services.On the 11 February 1865, the *William Wake*, manned by 21 pilots went to the aid of the schooner *Providence*.

The *William Wake* attended the naming ceremony of the RNLI's *Constance* on Friday 13 November 1862. The last known coxswain of this boat was Skipper Appleby.

The James Mather ship's lifeboat

The pioneering spirit of Shields folk was not confined to shore-based rescue. They were also involved in the welfare of mariners who got into difficulties in the open sea. One such person was James Mather, born in South Shields in 1799, the son of a local shipowner.

In March 1824, Mather, in an article published in the *Newcastle Magazine*, maintained that distressed seamen should not be reliant upon the services of others, but should have the opportunity of being able to save their own lives, especially in those locations where there was no shore-based lifeboat, or where the foundering ship was too far to be reached by lifeboat.

Henry Greathead had tried to sell the idea of a ship's lifeboat to be carried on Royal Navy vessels. His idea was based on the design principles of the *Original* but much smaller in size. The cost of this boat proved too prohibitive to be viable.

In December 1824, Mather, then a philosophy student at Edinburgh University, wrote to the President of the Royal National Institution for the Preservation of Life from Shipwreck, Lord Liverpool, with his ideas and a sketch design for a ship's lifeboat. He did not receive a reply so on 3 March 1826 he commissioned a South Shields boatbuilder to build his ship's lifeboat.

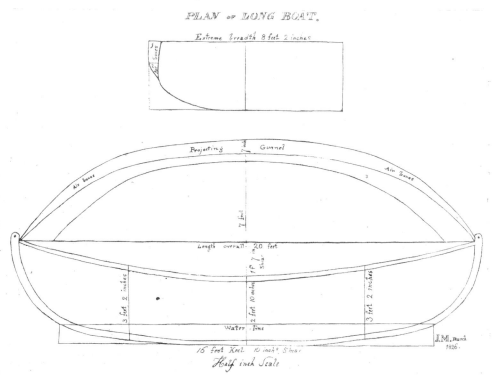

Reproduced from a copy in the British Library

James Mather's pamphlet sketch of his ship's lifeboat design.

She was 20ft. in length and 8ft. 2in. in width. She had an internal breadth of 7ft., with a continuous line of air boxes 1ft. 4in. in depth projecting 8in. running around the gunwales. Like the *Original*, Mather's boat had a pronounced sheerline, a curved keel in order to make the boat highly manoeuvrable, and was steered by a sweep oar.

The completed boat was taken out into Shields Harbour on trials on 26 May, in a strong north-easterly wind with heavy seas breaking on Tynemouth Bar. Skippered by a local pilot, Mather and local fishermen rowed towards the Bar where they encountered 6ft. breaking seas, and not having shipped any water, continued on into Tynemouth Haven. Having rested, the crew successfully tested the stability of the boat by laying broadside onto the seas. The pilot then took the boat into the surf on the Herd Sand, where again the boat proved satisfactory. The crew declared that they would entrust their lives to the protection of such a boat, even in the worst of weathers.

By 22 July 1826, Mather had designed and installed both a launching frame and the boat on one of his father's brigs, the *Mary*. The rectangular oak frame was attached to the ship's deck. The boat was placed on removable chocks on an iron cross piece that pivoted on the frame, and lashed to the frame itself. This enabled the boat to be swivelled and launched to leeward. The *Mary's* crew of four launched the boat within a minute.

Despite advice from friends, Mather refused to take out a patent on his design of the boat and launching frame, claiming that his boat was designed for saving lives and not for his own financial gain. The boat cost £10 more than a ship's longboat.

In 1826 Mather published 'A Description and Recommendation of a Lifeboat and Launching Frame to be carried by Ships, Illustrated by Plans in a Letter to The Right Honourable The Earl of Liverpool*', outlining the design and subsequent trials of the boat and launching frame. He hoped that legislation would be passed making it compulsory for ships to carry their own lifeboat. It is not known whether Mather received a reply from the newly established Committee of the RNIPLS.

However, in July 1827, the *Mary* was wrecked in a gale on rocks at Lessoe in Sweden. The crew took to the boat and, 30 hours later, sailed into a nearby port. The ship's lifeboat must have either returned to South Shields or others of its design were built, as *The Times* of 23 April, 1859 stated that when the brig *Schiedam* came ashore on the Herd Sand in rough seas, at 9 o'clock in the evening, the *James Mather* lifeboat and two local lifeboats launched to assist her.

The *James Mather's* crew returned three hours later but the *Schiedam's* crew decided to remain onboard their vessel. *The Times* stated that the crew of the *James Mather* received no remuneration for their efforts, though each man from one of the lifeboats (which arrived late on the scene) received half a guinea from the Lifeboat Fund of the Tyne.

The *James Mather,* crewed by seamen, launched to the brig, *Speculator*
of Wisbech, which went ashore on
the rocks at the entrance of the river.
Six of the *James Mather's* crew
boarded the brig and helped to refloat
her and bring her into port.

It is interesting that this report
states the boat had been crewed by
seamen, and not pilots. This is the
only known record of the *James
Mather* lifeboat, now 32 years old,
carrying out a lifesaving service.
While the actions of the crew were
admirable, it begs the question
whether their sole motive was to secure a salvage award from the vessel's owners.

Mather's boat was also trialled in
Copenhagen by the Danish Admiralty
but there are no records indicating
whether the prototype ship's lifeboat
was used by the Danish Navy.

PLAN OF LAUNCHING FRAME.

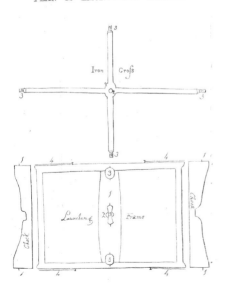

Author's collection

A

DESCRIPTION AND RECOMMENDATION

OF A

LIFE-BOAT AND LAUNCHING-FRAME

TO BE CARRIED BY SHIPS,

ILLUSTRATED BY PLANS,

IN

A LETTER

TO

THE RIGHT HON. THE EARL OF LIVERPOOL, K. G., &c.

BY JAMES MATHER.

" The storm-lash'd surges furious rise,
And wave uproll'd on wave assails the skies——
With ever floating bulwarks they surround
The ship, half-swallow'd in the black profound.
By secret ambushes, their force to prove,
Through many a winding channel first they rove,
Till gathering fury, like the fever'd blood,
Through her dark veins they roll a rapid flood.
No season this for counsel or delay,
Too soon th' eventful moments pass away !"
FALCONER'S SHIPWRECK.

LONDON:

PUBLISHED BY J. W. NORIE AND CO.

No. 157, LEADENHALL-STREET ;

And sold by all the Booksellers in the principal Sea-ports throughout the Kingdom.

The Lifeboat Memorial

The idea for a Lifeboat Memorial was first suggested at a public meeting held on 3 May 1887 to consider the best way of celebrating Queen Victoria's Jubilee. The meeting agreed that the most suitable location for a permanent memorial, possibly a bronze statue or drinking fountain, would be next to the newly completed Marine Park. The type of memorial would be decided by the amount of subscriptions raised.

An Executive Committee was formed, and by 20 May 1887, £304 had been donated. An article appeared in the *Newcastle Courant* three days later, suggesting a drinking fountain and a bronze statue of either Queen Victoria or Willie Wouldhave should be erected on the broad thoroughfare between the North and South Marine Parks.

A meeting of subscribers on 28 May agreed to erect a memorial to Wouldhave.

A competition for designs for a memorial costing no more than £500 was agreed at the Committee meeting on 2 June. Adverts were placed in the Newcastle and Shields newspapers, the *Scotsman* and *Leeds Mercury*, offering a first prize of ten guineas and second prize of five guineas. By 10 June, 12 applications had already been received, but the Committee decided to extend the deadline from 15 July to 1 August.

The Committee also agreed that because opinions differed as to who actually was the inventor of the lifeboat, the monument should be called the 'Wouldhave and Greathead Memorial of the lifeboat'.

The winner of the competition was J.H. Morton, an architect of South Shields. Messrs. Stout and Dockwray, also architects of South Shields, came second. Morton had previously designed the 1886 Bedford boathouse at the Coble Landing, and would go onto to design the 1905 Pilot Jetty boathouse.

The winning entry, 45ft. high, consisted of a drinking fountain with a surrounding basin 21.5 ft. in diameter, dog troughs, various representations of Wouldhave and Greathead, suitable inscriptions and a clock.

Newcastle Libraries

The Lifeboat Memorial c.1900.

Author's collection

The Lifeboat Memorial and Tyne in 2010.

The winning tender of £490 was from R.B. Farbridge of South Shields. Work began on 20 May 1889 and the memorial was completed in October.

In May 1894, the *Tyne* was moved from the Coble Landing to a new shelter on the seaward side of the Lifeboat Memorial. The boat and shelter were moved to the current location during the mid 1930s, and were substantially rebuilt following bomb damage in 1941.

The Tyne Wrecked Mariners' Home

Before the days of an organised rescue service, many shipwrecked seamen, some with injuries, were left to fend for themselves having lost all their possessions and money. With the establishment of a lifeboat service on the Tyne, many of the rescued crews were cared for by the local pilot community, either in their homes, or put up in local boarding houses and public houses. The wives of the lifeboatmen and pilots invariably tended to the needs of survivors, but this required a financial outlay that the community could ill afford.

In December 1839, following the wreck of three ships at the mouth of the river, local inhabitants became concerned at the plight of the rescued mariners.

In response, the Tyne Wrecked Mariners' Home was established in February 1840. The Duke of Northumberland donated £50 and was appointed patron. Trinity House donated 25 guineas and further donations were received from local notable families. 1,500 seamen enrolled in the first year, with an annual subscription of one shilling. The first home was established in South Shields, soon followed by one in North Shields. By 1842, 3,300 seamen had enrolled.

The then Secretary of the Tyne Lifeboat Institution, Robert Anderson, was a Committee member, as was James Mather. The President of the Tyne Shipwrecked Mariners' Home was Doctor Thomas Masterman Winterbottom who, in August 1837, had founded the South Shields Marine School, a seamanship school for boys.

In January 1841, the home struck the Tyne Shipwrecked Mariners Medal. On one side was the inscription 'Tyne Wrecked Mariners' Home 1841', and on the reverse an engraving of the lifeboat, in a stormy sea, about to rescue the crew of a ship wrecked under Tynemouth Priory.

According to reports in the *Port of Tyne Pilot* newspaper, members should produce of this medal if shipwrecked and in need of help. The Home encouraged other coastal communities to set up reciprocal arrangements. Agents of the Tyne Wrecked Mariners' Home acted also as agents for the Fishermen's and Mariners' Benevolent Fund, although approaches from this organisation to take over the Tyne Wrecked Mariners' Homes in the early years of its existence were initially rebuffed.

The work of those helping wrecked sailors was recognised by the Shipwrecked Mariners' Society in 1854, following the Great Gale, when two widowed sisters, a Mrs Young and Mrs Jackson, gave comfort to shipwrecked crews, as crew after crew were landed. The sisters had very little sleep for a week. The Shipwrecked Mariners Society sent a donation of £4 to the two widows for their 'energetic, untiring and most praiseworthy exertions in ministering to the necessities of the shipwrecked crews when brought on shore'. Each of the four masters received a silver medal and £26 was divided amongst the crews of the lifeboats.

Author's collection

The Tyne Sailors Home, North Shields.

In May 1848, the Committee of the Newcastle upon Tyne Sailors' Home decided to raise funds to build a Sailors' Home with sleeping berths and coffee room to accommodate sailors who were between jobs. This campaign faltered, and it was not until November 1852 that the Mayor of Tynemouth resurrected the idea for a home for those 'saved from the sea but shipwrecked on the shore'.

By 1853, the Port of Shields was the third largest in the United Kingdom, with 879 sailing ships registered, totalling 238,498 tons. 16,000 vessels used the river each year, and it was estimated that up to 30,000 sailors could be in port at any one time, the majority needing a temporary or permanent place to live.

Algernon, the 4th Duke of Northumberland, took up this idea pledging that if £2,000 could be raised through public subscription, he would donate the balance of the cost of a Sailors' Home. The Tyne Sailors Home at the New Quay in North Shields cost £8000 and was opened by the Duke on 21 October 1854. It could accommodate 60 seamen, with the potential for a further 90. It also housed the offices of the Marine Board, the Shipping Master and had a savings bank. This building has now been converted into apartments.

The South Shields Borough Coat of Arms

Following a campaign that had its origins in the 1830s, South Shields became a Municipal Borough in September 1850. The machinery and legalities required to operate the local authority were established soon after in early 1851.

The coat of arms that was adopted by the Council was designed by a local landscape artist, Robinson Elliott. Its centre piece was the lifeboat and pilot crew, representing 'Humanity', a South Shields sailor representing 'Courage' and a figure representing 'Commerce', with these words in a scroll surrounding the circular centre piece.

To recognise South Shields as the birthplace of the lifeboat, the words 'Always Ready', the lifeboatman's motto, was adopted as the Borough Motto.

Author's collection

The Borough Coat of Arms, South Shields Town Hall.

12 The building of the Tyne piers

From the 12th century up to 1850, the River Tyne was controlled by the Corporation of Newcastle. The way the Corporation carried out its duties met with considerable criticism because the large income derived from port dues was not spent on maintaining and improving the river as a navigable channel. The Corporation took the view that, as conservators of the river, they only had to maintain its condition and prevent it from getting worse.

Entering the harbour, even in ideal conditions, was not straightforward, with ships having to cross the Tynemouth Bar while maintaining a steady course in the tidal channel to avoid grounding on the Herd Sands and Black Middens rocks, before entering the river through the Narrows. To gain the safety of the harbour in rough seas and high winds would have taxed the skills of the most experienced master mariners and their crews.

The lack of action to improve the safety and navigability of the river and harbour approaches was having an impact upon trade and frustrating local shipowners. There was a need for larger harbour and docks facilities that could accommodate the rapidly developing steamships and stave off competition from other ports. Newcastle Corporation was disinclined to do anything to improve the river as it would mean a diversion of revenue from their own town improvements. They maintained that engineering works would be of no benefit against to the forces of nature.

In 1840, the shipowners of South Shields campaigned to remove the responsibility for the river from Newcastle Corporation and put it in the hands of a Commission. The Corporation, alarmed at the prospect of loss of control and revenue, appointed W.A. Brooks as river engineer to recommend river improvements. Two years later, Brooks proposed the narrowing of the river through the creation of groynes and quays that, in increasing the river flow would scour and remove sand banks and shoals, and deepen the navigable channel.

To further consolidate their control, the Corporation promoted a Parliamentary Bill that became law in 1845. The Newcastle Port Act, created a body of 21 Commissioners, with the Mayor of Newcastle as Chairman. Newcastle Corporation still had a majority interest on the Commissioners Board and the Shields shipowners and merchants were still dissatisfied with Newcastle's lack of management of the river. In 1848, they found that the City of Newcastle was seeking to extend and strengthen their river powers through the promotion of a further Bill through Parliament.

This led to the quiet resurrection of the campaign movement, and Committees were formed in both North and South Shields to promote an independent and elected trust to manage the river. The Tyne Conservancy Bill was drafted for the 1849 Parliamentary session.

In February 1849, an Admiralty Inquiry into the Bill was opened at North Shields, chaired by Captain John Washington R.N. who was later to become a member of the 1851 National Lifeboat Competition Committee and RNLI Committee of Management.

The evidence of the Corporation's own river engineer revealed that no river survey had been carried out nor soundings recorded for 42 years. In the same period, the Corporation had received £957,973 in shipping dues, but had spent only £40,000 in river improvements.

In May 1849, the Admiralty found in favour of the proposed Bill and ordered a new river survey to be undertaken. Despite Parliamentary opposition from the Members for Newcastle, the Bill passed through its second reading, both in the House of Commons and House of Lords. Two months later, with Newcastle MPs continuing their campaign of opposition, the Bill came before a Select Committee. However, the Bill could not complete its Committee stages and it dropped off the Parliamentary programme.

The promotion of the Bill cost £8,000, a considerable amount of money for the time, all raised by subscription. To raise further funds for the reintroduction of the Bill, North and South Shields Councils approved an increase in the local rate for a period of three months. With this additional funding, the Bill was reintroduced in the following Parliamentary session. At the same time, the Corporation of Newcastle, promoted the Tyne Navigation Bill.

The Tyne Navigation Bill proposed a Commission of 17 members, with Newcastle Corporation having the controlling majority interest and the Mayor of Newcastle as Chairman. The Tyne Conservancy Bill, promoted by North and South Shields, proposed that the tidal waterway of the Tyne be placed under the responsibility of an elected Commission, consisting of 15 members, three from Newcastle, one from Gateshead, three each from North Shields and South Shields, and five appointed by the Admiralty.

Both Bills passed through their Commons second readings in February 1850 and were referred to a Select Committee, which took 25 days to consider them in detail. The Committee found in favour of an elected Commission of four Life Commissioners, six to represent Newcastle, three each for North and South Shields, and two for Gateshead.

The Bill received Royal Assent in July 1850 as the Tyne Improvement Act.

The Commission held its first meeting in November 1850, and instructed J.M. Rendel, a river and pier engineer, together their own river engineer, W.A. Brooks, to report separately on improvements to the river and, more especially, only 13 months after the 1849 lifeboat disaster, on the construction of piers at the harbour mouth. The reports were published in October 1851.

Both engineers agreed that the river channel and bar had to be deepened, as had been recommended in 1842. They proposed partial dredging but did not advocate the comprehensive use of steam dredgers.

Brooks and Rendel also proposed similar schemes to construct north and south piers, a dredged river channel and smaller piers either side of the Narrows. In 1845, Brooks had recommended the construction of the two piers to Newcastle Corporation but no action was taken until 1849, when test borings were made on the Herd Sand. It was these boring rods that had caused much controversy at the inquest following the 1849 lifeboat disaster.

The Commissioners decided to opt for elements of both Rendel's and Brook's schemes and proceeded to promote a Parliamentary Bill to raise the necessary finance and obtain the powers to undertake the improvement works.

Although the Bill received Royal Assent in May 1852, the Admiralty would not approve the Tyne Improvement Commission's proposals. The Commission then requested the Admiralty to nominate an engineer to undertake the complete design of the piers. This was agreed on the condition that the appointee would have complete control of the project, the designs should be accepted by the Commissioners, and the Admiralty would have the final consent.

The engineer appointed was James Walker, then President of the Institute of Civil Engineers, and an eminent engineer in breakwater construction. In August 1853, Walker held a number of meetings hearing evidence at Tynemouth, from experienced pilots and local seamen, and at Newcastle and London. His report, in November that same year, found that the previous schemes of Rendel and Brooks were unsatisfactory, but considered that the removal of the Bar was essential for improving the safety of ships entering and leaving the harbour.

Walker proposed the removal of Tynemouth Bar, and the construction of two piers, the North Pier, at 2,100ft. in length, starting under Tynemouth Castle at Prior's Haven, and the South Pier crossing the Herd Sands, with a length of 4,200ft.. Both piers would terminate at a depth of water of 15ft. above low water spring tides, with an entrance width of 1,100ft.

In deciding upon the siting and direction of the piers, Walker had been influenced by the principle considerations of creating a sheltered harbour: the retention of a sandy beach within the harbour for vessels to beach on if in difficulties; to give laden outward-bound ships shelter from the worst winds until they cleared the pier heads and got into deeper water; and to enable tug-boats to get further out to assist ships in entering or leaving the harbour.

Walker's design was approved by the Admiralty in May 1854, and on 15 June 1854

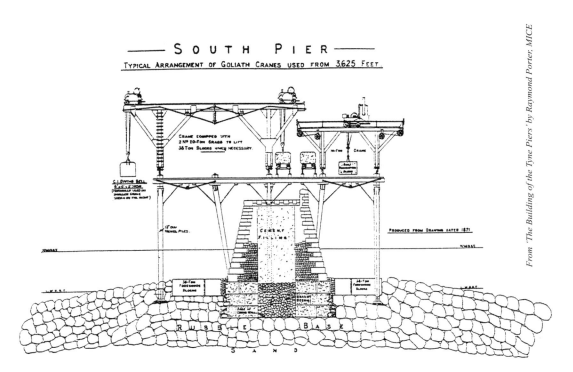

From 'The Building of the Tyne Piers' by Raymond Porter, MICE

The arrangement of staging and cranes during the construction of the South Pier, 1872.

the ceremonial laying of the foundation stones took place for each pier.

It was not until October 1855 that works commenced on the North Pier, and March 1856 on the South Pier. There had been delays in the preparation of working drawings due to a dispute between Brooks, the Commissioners' river engineer, and Walker. The dispute was settled when the Commissioners appointed Walker to undertake all draw-ings and to recruit a resident engineer, Philip J. Messent, one of Walker's assistants from London. Though only 25 years old, Messent had been in charge of the harbour works at Great Yarmouth and Dover, and had been responsible for the preliminary sur-veys and design drawings for the two piers.

The Cullercoats lifeboat crew pointed out that the proposed Tyne Piers would make it difficult to get into Prior's Haven. While the Tyne Lifeboat Institution had stationed a lifeboat there in March 1855, soon after construction works commenced, it was not until 1862 that the RNLI re-opened the Tynemouth Station. A new boathouse and rocket house were built on the same site as the earlier boathouse. They were designed by Messent, who was appointed Honorary Secretary of the Tynemouth RNLI station in 1865, holding this post until his death in 1897. His son Frank took over as Honorary Secretary until 1900.

In April 1854, the Commissioners purchased 36 acres of land at Trow Rocks, South Shields, one mile to the south of the South Pier, to quarry magnesium limestone for the piers. A railway was constructed from the quarry to the South Pier head works, and continued on to the Commissioners Staithes at the Narrows, from where the stone was transported in bottom-opening barges to be deposited on both pier sites. The staithes were next to the site of what was to later become the Pilot Jetty lifeboat house.

The construction of the South Pier changed the direction of the tidal currents along the sands and created a sand bar and gully in front of the first South Beach lifeboat house. This hindered the launch and recovery of the lifeboat so, in 1875, the South Beach boathouse was relocated to a site next to the Volunteer Life Brigade Watch House. Four feet of the Brigade Watch House had also to be removed to enable the pier crane to be taken down the pier.

On 24 October 1885, the steamer *Fir Dene* got into difficulties entering the harbour, nearly stranding on the end of the South Pier. Members of the South Shields Volunteer Life Brigade were on bad weather watch in the Watch House, and a large crowd had gathered on the South Pier to observe events. This large crowd in a relatively confined space obstructed the Brigade. Two boys were swept away by a heavy sea that broke over the pier; one was drowned and the other rescued. As a result of this tragedy, and following a request from the Brigade, the Tyne Commissioners erected storm gates on the pier in 1886. They prevented the public from gaining access to the pier during heavy weather and when the Brigade were undertaking rescues from the pier.

As works progressed it became clear that the planned depth at the pier ends, would not accommodate the increasing size of steamships. Furthermore, the Royal Commission on Harbours of Refuge had recommended, in March 1859, that the piers be extended to a depth of 36ft. at low water.

In 1861, it was decided to double the depth, but as the extent of the piers was now well advanced, in order to preserve the 1,100ft. width between pier ends, the piers had to be turned outwards before making a final sweep inwards at the entrance. This extended the North Pier by 800ft. to 2,900ft., and the South Pier by 1,200ft. to 5,400ft..

The piers were built by constructing staging that allowed for the stone rubble base to be deposited and constructed before the masonry walling was lowered into place by cranes. As the outer and cross walls were built up, the core was filled by quarry debris and concrete. The outer walls, when brought above the low water mark, were immediately protected from the scouring effect of the tides by tipping large rubble stones along the outside. Similar protection was given to the ends of the piers when underwater work was suspended during the winter months.

Walker died in October 1862 and was replaced by J.F. Ure, the Commissioner's Chief Engineer.

Work on the piers was also greatly disrupted by winter gales. A northerly gale on 20 and 21 December 1862 carried away 72ft. of the completed South Pier, and in December 1864, 90ft. of the upper works to the North Pier were destroyed. A severe gale in December 1867 destroyed 480ft. of the North Pier and 300ft. of the South Pier. The pier design was modified to provide deeper foundations.

In March 1887, Ure and Messent proposed a wider pier entrance of 1,300ft. to accommodate the greater tidal flows in the river as a result of river dredging works. In November 1893, just before the roundhead was completed, the large Titan crane on the North Pier was washed away in a gale, and in October 1894, the crane on the South Pier was washed away in similar fashion.

It was not until November 1895 that the lighthouses on both piers were lit. The South Pier light was 39ft. high and today has a range of 13 miles. In February 1896, it was found that the foundations of the North Pier had been undermined and weakened through storm damage. To extend the period of underwater working outside the summer months, the iron vessel SS *Roxanna*, 220ft. in length, was loaded with concrete, and sunk parallel to the seaward part of the damaged section of pier. The ends of the vessel were sealed off to the pier side creating a coffer dam, which afforded protection to the divers and reduced the scouring action of the sea in filling up newly excavated foundations.

However, during successive gales in December 1896 and January 1897, the uncompleted repair works on the North Pier were breached at a point 2,306ft. from shore. By

Newcastle Libraries

The original alignment of the North Pier prior to the 1896 storm damage, with Tynemouth Lighthouse on the cliff top.

Newcastle Libraries

South Tyneside Libraries

The North Pier following storm damage in 1896.

June 1898, 300ft. of the pier had been carried away. At the time of this breach Philip Messent was in failing health, and there is little doubt that this setback affected his chances of recovery. He died in April 1897 at the age of 66.

The Tyne Improvement Commission agreed a revised design for the North Pier to be rebuilt in a straight line from a point 2,200ft. from the shore, for a length of 750ft. These works were completed in 1906. A larger and higher lighthouse, 55ft. in height, its flashing white light visible for 26 miles, was completed on the end of the new pier in 1908, with the original, smaller lighthouse being demolished. The foundations of the pier destroyed in the storm were retained as a protective breakwater, and can still be seen today at low water.

While the piers were under construction, significant improvements were also being made to the river channel, and having dismissed W.A. Brooks, the Commissioners appointed J.F. Ure, as river engineer. Ure, unlike Brooks, was an advocate of dredging, and in 1860 prepared a comprehensive scheme for deepening the tidal river from the east of Tynemouth Bar to a point 19 miles upstream, to depths between 12 and 15ft. at low water spring tides, and the removal of the Insand and Middle Ground shoals between North and South Shields and the removal of the Herd Sand enclosed by the piers.

In 1862, three steam dredgers were built, the largest in the world at that time, and these commenced work a year later. Within ten years, Tynemouth Bar had been removed, together with over half of the Herd Sand within the newly created harbour. The Narrows had also been widened with the removal of the Herd Sand Beacon, and the South Shields Groyne constructed in this location. By this time, over half of the length of the North Pier, and three-quarters of the South Pier had been constructed.

The completion of the piers and removal of the Herd Sand and Tynemouth Bar removed the hazards that had first led the Gentlemen of the Lawe House to consider the provision of a lifeboat at the mouth of the Tyne, although during the construction of the piers there were still many reminders of the force of the sea with ships running aground on the partly completed structures that led to the call-out of local lifeboats and Volunteer Life Brigades.

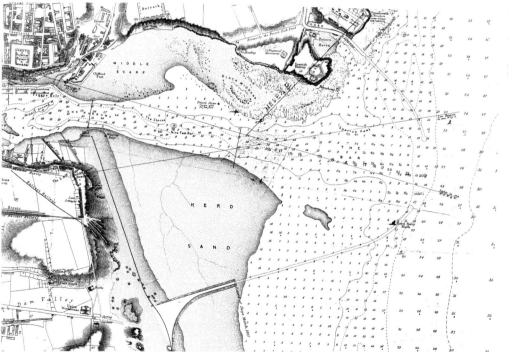

©Crown Copyright

The progress of the piers by 1859, indicating their original proposed alignment. River dredging works had still to commence, and the riverside quays, prevalent along today's river frontage had not been built.

©Crown Copyright

By 1862, works on both piers were well underway. The South Groyne at The Narrows was complete and the Herd Sand was being removed.

©Crown Copyright

By 1872, pier construction had been slowed by construction works having entered into deeper waters. The river channel at The Narrows had been widened and deepened. The first South Beach boathouse is also shown.

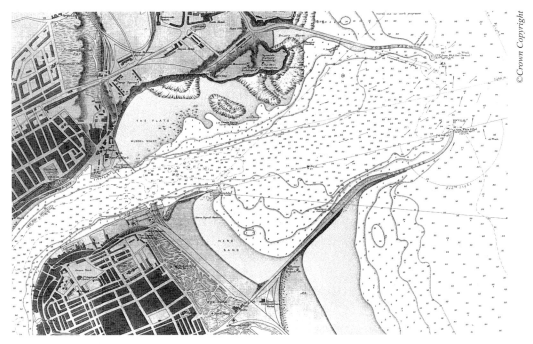

©Crown Copyright

By 1900 the pier works, northern and southern wavetraps, quayside works at North Shields Fish Quay and South Shields riverside had been completed.

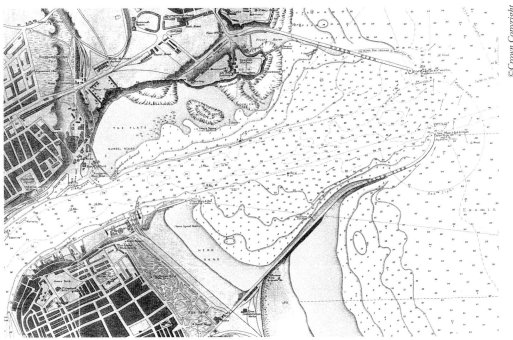

©Crown Copyright

By 1909, works were complete. The North Pier had been reconstructed following storm damage. The new Pilot Jetty boathouse at the southern wavetrap and the second South Beach boathouse are also shown.

South Tyneside Libraries

Victorian Pilots with their distinctive top hats.

13 The Shields pilots

Pilotage on the river is recorded as far back as Henry VIII and was the preserve of Trinity House. It later developed, still under the control of Trinity House, into the provision of River Pilots and Bar Pilots.

The Bar Pilots conducted ships in and out of the harbour and over the Bar, but they were not allowed to take any vessels upstream past Whitehill Point, this being the preserve of the River Pilots. There was originally no formal training of pilots. They were trained by more experienced pilots until the Newcastle Port Act of 1801, which empowered Trinity House to issue licences to those who gave proof of satisfactory skill, knowledge and experience.

By December 1862 there were around 170 pilots as well as apprentices, some of whom were boys of no more than 12 years of age. They took five to six years to qualify. If he passed an examination, a newly qualified pilot would be recommended to the Master and Brethren at Trinity House, should a vacancy become available. After a two-year probationary period they were granted a full pilot's licence.

The pilots were under the control of the Captain of Pilots and had to obey very exacting rules. Strict discipline was enforced, with any breaches of the rules being punished by fines, suspensions, or revocation of the pilot's licence. Bar Pilots were fined if they took ships up to Newcastle, as were River Pilots who took ships out of the harbour and over the Bar.

The Shields Pilots were based at the Coble Landing at South Shields, a sheltered shelving beach from which the pilots could launch their cobles into the river. At one time between 60 and 70 cobles were based at the landing.

A coble, usually about 26ft. in length, with oars and a lug sail, was manned by the pilot and his apprentice. In order to find work the cobles waited out to sea for ships making for the Tyne. This was known as 'seeking'. To seek work, cobles sailed as far south as Flamborough Head and Yarmouth Roads if a ship was known to be heading for the Tyne, and as far north as Holy Island. In one seven-year period, 12 pilots and five apprentices, together with a greater number of cobles, were lost at sea.

The competition to put a pilot aboard a ship was fierce, with many cobles racing each other to be the first. Once on board, the coble was towed stern first. The flatter bottom of the stern being was able to plane over the sea, while the flared bow acted as a skeg keeping the coble on a straight course behind the ship.

To sail such small boats in all conditions and over great distances would have demanded the highest degree of seamanship, local knowledge and endurance – skills eminently suited for the perils of manning the lifeboat in and around the Black Middens,

South Tyneside Libraries

Pilot Coble 72 Jubilee.

Herd Sand and Tynemouth Bar. Trinity House inserted in the pilots' licences a condition that they should man the lifeboat whenever required. This condition was never enforced; indeed the problem was trying to keep the pilots out of the lifeboat when its services were called upon.

The pilots, through the offices of Trinity House, also secured the provision of basic navigation marks in the river channel between the Herd Sand and Black Middens. In March 1786, a beacon was placed on the edge of the Herd Sands, and in 1787, a buoy was placed on the Mussel Scarp sands. In September 1789, a further beacon was placed on the Herd Sand, and a ring placed on the Prior's Stone for ships to make fast to. The Prior's Stone was the only tide gauge the pilots had, as when covered, the pilots knew that there was then sufficient water on the bar for a fully laden ship to enter or leave the river.

In 1799, local shipowners successfully lobbied Trinity House to erect two leading beacons on the south side of the river entrance, adjacent to the Lawe House, and lay buoys either side of the river channel. The original timber pole beacons were replaced by brick beacons in 1832. Both these structures are still in existence today at the Lawe Top, South Shields, and next to the site of the now demolished Lawe House.

James Purvis, centre, with sons George, left, and Jim, right, at the Lawe Beacons, South Shields, in the 1920s. James and George were both coxswains of the Shields lifeboats.

Right: the RNLI Silver Medal awarded to Joseph Smith 1851 now at Trinity House, Newcastle.

In 1810, Trinity Towers was built on the Lawe Top as a watch house for the pilots and lookout for the lifeboats. The location commanded the best view over the Tyne entrance. This building became a radar training school for seamanship students at the local Marine School before being demolished in 1971.

While the pilots embraced the new technologies of the time, such a progressive approach was not applied by the Tyne Lifeboat Institution to the future design and development of the local lifeboat service in adapting operations to changing conditions.

As the Tyne was one of the first ports to build and use steamships, the pilots could see the benefits and power of this new technology. In the 1850s two steam tugs were obtained to tow cobles out to sea in poor weather, although when they reached a ship, boarding could still be a dangerous operation. In heavy seas, when the small tug punt could not be used, the pilot was hauled through the sea on the end of a rope.

The Shields Bar pilots were hardy independent men, described by William Blackburn, the Pilots' Society Secretary during the latter part of the 18th century, as 'a strange set of unruly fellows', but with good hearts under their rough exteriors. They lived in a very close-knit community and tended to marry young, inter-marrying into other pilot families. The profession passed from father to son, with this family exclusivity of profession reinforced by Trinity House who only issued new Pilot Licences to the relatives of pilots.

The pilot community resided in the eastern part of South Shields in the narrow streets along the river bank such as Pilot Street, Shadwell Street, Wapping Street and Heron Place and latterly on the Lawe Top, overlooking the river entrance and within walking distance of the Pilot Watch House, Coble Landing and Pilot Jetty lifeboat houses.

The majority of the main pilot families of Ayre, Burn, Bone, Harrison, Milburn, Phillips, Purvis, Stephenson, Thurlbeck, Tinmouth, Whale, Wright and Young all lived in this small area of South Shields.

It is from these same family names that the majority of the lifeboat crews were drawn. The use of nicknames was common in this community. They reflected personality and attributes of the individual but were also handed down from father to son.

There was 'Horse's Heed' Purvis, 'Over the Shoe Tops' Purvis, 'Panama Jack' Phillips and 'The Woolwich Mystery' Phillips. Woolwich Mystery was so named as he had invented and then sold an ointment of the same name reputed to cure all ills. One of the pilots was nicknamed 'Target' as he always moored his coble to the buoy used for target practice by the artillerymen stationed at the Spanish Battery at Tynemouth.

The pilots of the Victorian era wore a distinctive uniform of khaki trousers, blue monkey jacket and tall hat, as illustrated in the photographs of Coxswain Andrew Harrison on the lifeboat *Tyne* in 1858, and the group of Victorian pilots.

Many of the pilots who manned the lifeboats were also members of the South Shields Volunteer Life Brigade and manned the breeches buoy apparatus.

On 26 June 1851, the National Lifeboat Institution awarded silver medals to the Tyne pilots, Jacob Harrison, John Burn snr, Joseph Smith and John Milburn, for the 'intrepid and successful exertions of the Pilots of the Tyne during the past nine years in saving lives from shipwreck.' The medals were awarded to these pilots who had gone off in the lifeboat 48, 25, 22 and 16 times respectively.

The Tyne Lifeboat Institution did not, at any time during its existence, introduce or award any medals for meritorious service.

On the 20 June 1913, the Tyne pilots hosted the National Pilots' Conference on the river. As part of the conference and celebrations there was a parade of lifeboats with the *Tom Perry*, *Bedford* and *Willie Wouldhave*, under the commands of Coxswains John Whale, Richard Harrison and Thomas Wilson, proceeding up river from the harbour.

Despite their idiosyncrasies and the fierce independence of the pilot community, their seamanship was second to none. To go out in an open surf lifeboat, unprotected from the elements, in the clothing of the day, and in the conditions then experienced at the mouth of the Tyne, illustrates the courage, character, strength, and humanity of this brave band of men.

South Tyneside Libraries

The National Pilots' Conference, May 1913, with, in the centre, the Bedford, Tom Perry to her left and the Willie Wouldhave to her right. The Tyne Pilot cutter Protector can be seen to the left of the photo. This boat sank at the mouth of the river on 31 December 1916 with the loss of 19 lives.

14 The Volunteer Life Brigades

The Volunteer Life Brigades, like the origins of the *Original*, were established as a direct consequence of a double shipwreck that occurred on the Black Middens on the night of Thursday 24 November 1864.

During a south easterly gale, just before low water and with heavy rain and following seas, the schooner *Friendship* and steamer *Stanley* came ashore. The service report in the *Lifeboat Journal* for 1 January, 1865 stated that the storm had produced the heaviest seas in living memory, and the recent removal of the Bar resulted in bigger breaking seas coming ashore.

The tragic events of that day began at around 4pm when the tug *Escort*, which had gone to the assistance of a vessel entering the river, herself ran aground on the Herd Sands. Her crew of four was saved by the South Shields lifeboat *Tyne* that had launched with a crew of 16 pilots, Andrew Harrison in command.

The *Friendship*, of Colchester, laden with coal, was the first to run aground on the Middens, at around 4.30pm, the strong ebb tide still running. The Tynemouth RNLI lifeboat *Constance*, with a crew of 13, launched and, while the coastguard were preparing the rocket apparatus, a message came through that the crew had been rescued by one of the Shields lifeboats. The rocket apparatus was returned to its store, and the *Constance* returned to its boathouse at Prior's Haven. However, the crew had not been rescued and remained onboard the stricken schooner.

Meanwhile, the *Stanley*, a screw steamer built in 1848, bound from Aberdeen to London with a deck cargo of 50 cattle and sheep, 30 passengers and 30 crew, made for the Tyne for refuge. Upon arrival off the river, the captain, Thomas Howling, fired rockets for a pilot at the same time as a steam tug was leaving the river, and a barque in the tow of a tug was entering the harbour. The rocket signals were ignored.

Despite the harbour lights not being lit, the captain decided to make an attempt to enter the river, as the mate, John Main had entered the river on numerous occasions and knew that at low water there would be 17 feet of water over the bar. The *Stanley* drew 13 feet. Running at around five knots, the ship crossed the bar at around 5.15pm and fired two more rockets for a pilot. At this moment the steamer was hit in quick succession by three heavy seas on the starboard quarter that caused her to broach. Before the ship could recover she struck the Black Middens at around 5.30pm, shortly after the rocket apparatus had been returned to store. The captain signalled for assistance a few minutes before 6pm.

Upon hearing that the crew of the *Friendship* had not been rescued and the *Stanley* had now run aground nearby, the *Constance* launched again and the coastguard began

North Tyneside Council

The wreck of the Stanley.

to set up the rocket apparatus, this time opposite the *Stanley*. A line was successfully fired onto the ship, but was attached so low down on the forecastle, contrary to the master's orders, that after three lives were saved by breeches buoy; it got snagged on the rocks and could not be used.

The crew of the *Stanley* had cleared the decks of all cattle, throwing them overboard. Some managed to swim ashore. A lifeboat containing four sailors and four female passengers was lowered. Unfortunately, a davit gave way and the boat was swamped. Three of the seamen were pulled back onboard but the passengers and the fourth crewman drowned. The crew refused to launch any further lifeboats, most of which had been washed away. Meanwhile, after the unsuccessful attempt with the rocket apparatus, the chief officer of the coastguard at Tynemouth decided to take the apparatus down to North Shields and put it on a steam tug so a line could be fired from the seaward side of the wreck. No tugs would put off – several had been damaged by the storm. The apparatus was brought back to Tynemouth.

By this time, the flood tide had began to run, and the *Constance* had battled through the heavy seas and reached a point to the east of the wreck. The coxswain, with bow to the incoming breakers, backed towards and soon reached the port bow of the *Stanley*. Two of steamer's crew hailed the lifeboat and informed the coxswain that they had ropes ready on their starboard bow. As the lifeboat manoeuvred around the bowsprit, at about 11pm, a heavy sea broke over the bow of the *Stanley* and engulfed the

Constance, washing all but two oars out of the boat. The next sea lifted the lifeboat, now perpendicular, into the fore rigging of the *Friendship,* with the end box of the boat completely buried; the steering oar hit the bottom and broke into three pieces. Four of the crew were washed out of the boat.

On seeing the events unfolding on the Black Middens, the North and South Shields lifeboats both launched. The South Shields lifeboat *Providence,* with a crew of 26, was immediately disabled in the heavy seas with most of her oars smashed and several of the crew stunned. The North Shields lifeboat *Northumberland,* with a crew of 21 pilots, could not reach the wreck due to rowing against the flood tide, wind and surging breaking seas.

The *Constance* managed to get clear of the Black Middens and encountered the Shields lifeboats and the salvage boat *William Wake.* Coxswain James Gilbert asked for oars, but none could be spared. The *William Wake* took the *Constance* in tow to North Shields.

The *Lifeboat Journal* report commented that the Shields boatmen did not think it possible that a lifeboat could have come out of the haven in the prevailing conditions. The Shields lifeboats went out, but were unable to approach the wrecks. The crew of the steamer were themselves astonished to see the *Constance* lifeboat approaching them from the sea in such a storm.

Of the four lifeboatmen from the *Constance,* James Grant was crushed between the two boats, but was hauled onboard the schooner, still alive, but critically injured. Edmund Robson, Joseph Bell and James Blackburn all managed to jump onboard, and were secured into the rigging by the crew. When the schooner finally broke up, at around 10pm, all six of the crew and the two lifeboatmen, Grant and Robson were drowned. Bell and Blackburn, both wearing their cork lifejackets, were washed ashore and saved.

At 9pm, the brig *Ardwell* ran ashore onto the Black Middens. Her crew of four was rescued by the South Shields lifeboat *Tyne* and her crew of 19 pilots.

Meanwhile, the deckhouse and bridge on the *Stanley,* on which a number of the crew and passengers had taken refuge, was washed away with all those on it by a series of heavy seas. At 11pm, the steamer broke in two, the fore part, with main mast and foremast still standing, now facing east, and the after end, with the mizzen mast still standing, lying where she had struck. Those onboard the stern of the vessel were all drowned. Those on the foredeck were still alive – this part of the ship was held by an anchor which had been swept overboard still attached to its chain.

All the rockets held by the coastguard at Tynemouth had been fired, and messages were sent to nearby Cullercoats requesting their rockets and apparatus, which duly arrived at 5am, accompanied by the coxswain of the Cullercoats lifeboat and local fishermen. With the tide falling, the apparatus was set up near to the wreck. Four rockets were fired over the after end with no response from the wreck. The apparatus was reset, and the final rocket was fired over the foredeck. The survivors attached the hawser to the foremast. Thirty-two passengers and crew were landed. By this time the tide had turned and the heavy seas had totally destroyed the *Friendship*, leaving only a few timbers lying amongst the rocks.

The *Providence,* with a crew of 18 pilots, had also launched at 5am the following day to render further assistance to the *Stanley,* but it was too late as the surviving crew and passengers had been rescued. Later that same day, the brig *Martin* was lost with all hands on the South Pier, and on the 28 November, three days after the wreck of the *Stanley*, the barques *Reaper* and *Amy Robsart* went ashore onto the Black Middens. Their crews were saved by the lifeboats.

The Board of Trade Inquiry into the wreck of the *Stanley* reported on 17 December 1864 that the removal of the Bar and the advantages of the deepening and widening of the river channel were neutralised by the absence of buoys and beacons to mark this new deep water channel. The practice of extinguishing lights at half ebb tide and re-lighting them upon the flood tide also had to be rectified. The Board also commented on the difficulty experienced by the *Stanley* in obtaining a pilot. Steamers that frequently visited the river retained the services of a pilot, and the pilot steamer that was outside the harbour wrongly assumed that the *Stanley* had a pilot awaiting her arrival. This explains why the *Stanley*'s rocket signals requesting a pilot were not returned. In their evidence the pilots stated that their services were often refused by steamships so they had ceased to communicate with these vessels.

The Board of Trade concluded that the master of the *Stanley* was justified in making for the Tyne and entering the river as there was sufficient water over the Bar. The loss of the steamship was caused by the heavy sea conditions, the absence of leading lights and other circumstances beyond the control of the master.

However, at the Coroner's Inquest, which was held after the Board of Trade Inquiry on the 29 November 1864, the jury returned a verdict that the losses of the *Friendship* and *Stanley* were accidental, but blamed the mate and master of the *Stanley* for entering the harbour before the lights were lit. The jury recommended that the lights be kept lit during the night, so long as there was 17 feet of water on the bar.

Among those that had been watching the tragic events unfold from the cliffs at Tynemouth was a young rifleman, John Morrison, who considered fewer lives may have been lost if the coastguard had been able to call upon a trained body of men to help operate the rocket apparatus, rather than relying on spectators. Morrison found support from two prominent local brothers, John Foster Spence and Joseph Spence. At a public meeting on 5 December 1864, The Tynemouth Volunteer Life Brigade was born. John Foster Spence was elected secretary, a post he held until 1901, and Joseph Spence treasurer. John Morrison became the Brigade's first member.

The Board of Trade approved of this new organisation subject to the Brigade working under the direction and control of the coastguard. Several potential members objected to this stipulation and withdrew their applications. The Brigade was fully constituted on January 13 1865, and the first practice drill was held on Saturday 11 February at the coastguard station on the Spanish Battery, with over 50 men turning out.

A Volunteer Life Brigade was established at Cullercoats in March 1865. This Brigade continued until 1925 when it was disbanded by the coastguard on cost grounds.

South Shields was soon to follow. On 16 December 1865, a meeting was held in the Mechanics Institute, South Shields, where it was agreed to establish a Brigade. A deputation led by the Town Clerk, Thomas Salmon, met local pilots to explain the role of the organisation. The pilots were unanimous in their support.

On 15 January 1866, the South Shields Volunteer Life Brigade was formed. One hundred and forty men enrolled on the same evening. Archibold Stevenson and Samuel Malcolm were elected joint honorary secretaries, Stevenson subsequently became treasurer and Malcolm, who later held the post of Vice-President of the Tyne Lifeboat Institution, was made honorary secretary. The services of the Brigade were accepted by the Board of Trade on January 30, 1866.

After 14 months the Tynemouth Brigade had trained to a state of operational readiness. In March 1865, the collier brig *Burton* ran aground on the stone rubble of the under-construction North Pier. Despite getting a line aboard, a series of heavy seas prevented the crew from attaching it to the mainmast, and with the brig rolling in the seas, she eventually rolled over and broke up with only the mate surviving. He was rescued by the lifeboat.

In 1865 it was decided to raise funds for the construction of a watch house on the Spanish Battery, Tynemouth, overlooking the harbour entrance, from which volunteers could mount bad weather storm watches. The watch house, completed in September 1874, was built of wood with a slate roof. It comprised a lookout, office and a room with bunks and baths for seamen saved from wrecks. There was a fully stocked surgery and gas lighting. In the event of a ship coming ashore, the Brigade would be mustered by the firing of two mortar shots.

In October 1865, the brig *Ringwood* was swept onto the Black Middens, with the Tynemouth Brigade and Tyne lifeboats going into action. The first attempt to get a line onboard failed, the *Ringwood* drifted further onto the Black Middens, near to where the *Stanley* had struck. Having re-sited the rocket apparatus nearer to the wreck, the Brigade fired two successful lines, but did not get a response from the crew. The lifeboats *Providence* and *Northumberland* got alongside the wreck, but no contact could be made with the crew. Assuming all had been drowned, the boats returned to their boathouses at North and South Shields. The crew of five had in fact taken to their boat which had capsized in the harbour. Only two crew members managed to get ashore.

In December 1865, three vessels went ashore and the Tynemouth Brigade got lines across to two of them. However, the lifeboat *Tyne* and salvage boat *William Wake* had both launched, managed to get alongside the vessels and rescued all of their crews.

The RNLI, as a direct consequence of the wreck of the *Stanley,* decided to open a second station at Tynemouth, directly opposite the Black Middens, with a 32ft. standard self-righting boat, rowing ten oars. She became operational in December 1865.

The first rescue to be carried out by a Volunteer Life Brigade was at South Shields, on 2 April 1866, when the schooner *Tenterden*, of Sunderland, ran ashore during a north-easterly gale onto the South Pier stones.

The signal gun was fired three times to summon Brigade members, and within ten minutes between 50 and 60 men had assembled. The first rocket fired was unsuccessful, but following the second, the breeches buoy was rigged and within 30 minutes of mustering, the crew of seven, including the Captain's wife and 18-month-old daughter were rescued.

The South Shields lifeboat *Tyne* launched, with a crew of 19, when the flood tide had been running for an hour, and thinking that the ship was aground on the Herd Sand was towed down the river by the tug *Little John* to a point opposite the Black Middens, and then cast off. Before the coxswain could gain command of the boat, a tremendous sea carried the lifeboat 200 yards smashing her against the jetty on the south side of the Narrows, resulting in her being stove in along her port side in several places. The two bowmen were washed overboard before getting ashore. The remainder of the crew got ashore once the boat had grounded. As the tide fell, 32 pilots got the *Tyne* back into the water and returned her upstream to her boathouse at the Coble Landing to be repaired.

South Shields VLB Archive

'Saved' by T. Watson.

This rescue, the first by a volunteer organisation, was immortalised in the painting 'Saved' by T. Watson. In 1946, an old lady visiting the South Shields Watch House was reputed to have looked at the painting and said, 'I was that child.'

The first rescue carried out by the Tynemouth Brigade took place on the evening of Tuesday 8 February 1870, when the *Susannah* ran aground on the rocks under the Spanish Battery. The Brigade fired three rockets over the wreck, the third line going through the rigging. One of the crew, in attempting to secure the line to the foremast, was washed off the wreck which took the foremast with it. It was not until a fifth rocket had been fired that the breeches buoy was successfully rigged and the four crew members brought ashore.

A few hours later, the barque *Helena* ran aground on the Black Middens, and the Brigade again were successful in getting a line onto the ship. However, at the same time, the North Shields lifeboat *Northumberland* got alongside and took off the ship's crew.

In January 1887, Tynemouth's original watch house had to be demolished to make way for coastal defence works undertaken by the War Department.

It was not until December of that same year that a much larger watch house, with a lookout tower, was completed. It is still used today as the Brigade's operational head-quarters.

In October 1866, the Tyne Improvement Commissioners gave permission for a watch house to be erected on the South Pier at South Shields, the cost of £800 being raised by public subscription. In 1875 the building was extended with a lookout tower, and in 1879, a drying room and infirmary were added. A wooden equipment store was built in 1868 and was replaced by the present brick building in 1894. These buildings remain largely unaltered and, as at Tynemouth, the South Shields Watch House is still used today as an operational rescue base.

The Brigades augmented the work of the lifeboats, as they could rescue people that the lifeboats could not reach. On 13 October 1891, the schooner *Peggy* was struggling to enter the river and drifted onto the eastern extremities of the Black Middens. When this was seen from the shore, the rocket apparatus was readied. Soon after the schooner had grounded, a line was successfully fired over the ship, although the crew did not know how and where to secure the line and use the breeches buoy equipment. As this was going on, the South Shields lifeboat *Bedford* and North Shields Lifeboat *James Young* had both launched, but the conditions were such that the boats could not reach the *Peggy,* which had been driven high onto the Middens. The RNLI's Tynemouth No. 2 lifeboat *Forester*, stationed at the nearby boathouse, could not launch due to the lack of water resulting from the falling tide.

With seas constantly breaking over and battering the *Peggy*, and the Brigadesmen fighting to erect and operate their equipment, it took 30 minutes for a line to be fired

Tynemouth No. 2 lifeboat, Forester, around 1870. See also the photograph on page 163.

successfully over the wreck. Four men were brought ashore through the breaking seas. However, the ship's cook had made two unsuccessful attempts to get into the breeches buoy from the schooner's rigging and, having fallen heavily onto the deck, he retired to the rigging, which, exhausted and soaking wet, he was unable to leave.

One of the coastguards, George Hoar, then volunteered to be carried out in the breeches buoy to the *Peggy* to rescue the remaining crewman. Upon reaching the wreck, Hoar could not get onboard because the hawser cable was not taut enough and he signalled to be pulled ashore. The cable was tightened and Hoar went back out to the wreck, where he was able to reach the ship's cook in the rigging. The cook was reluctant to leave so Hoar forced him into the breeches buoy and signalled the shore team to haul them both ashore. The combined weight of the two men made it extremely difficult to keep the hawser taught, and they were dragged through the breaking surf to the shore. By this time, Hoar was completely exhausted and the ship's cook unconscious. Both were taken to the Watch House where the Brigade's Honorary Medical Officer revived the rescued seaman.

George Hoar was awarded the Albert Medal, the Board of Trade's Gold Medal and the Tynemouth Gold Medal for his bravery.

Christmas week 1876 proved to be busy for the South Shields Brigade. On 21 December, five ships ran aground on the southern side of the South Pier during an easterly gale. Between 2am and 7.30 am, the steamships *Claremont, Tyne* and *Fenella* came ashore in front of the Watch House followed in the afternoon by the *Blenheim*

South Shields VLB Archive

Herman Sauber, Claremont and Fenella, and in the foreground the only remaining timbers of the Tyne.

and *New Cornwall.*

The Brigade rescued all 21 crew of the *Claremont*, the crew of the *Fenella* came ashore as the tide fell, but the 19 crew on the *Tyne*, including one who was a member of the Brigade, were drowned. The ship broke into pieces. The *Blenheim* struck the partly-built pier and broke in two. All the crew, except one, were rescued by breeches buoy. The *New Cornwall* capsized with the loss of all five crew.

In the early hours of Christmas Eve, while the south easterly gale was at its height, the German steamship *Herman Sauber,* of Hamburg, struck the rocks on the south side of the pier. The Life Brigade hauled its gear along to the end of the pier and fired four rockets over the wreck.

Unfortunately, the crew did not know how to operate the equipment, so the *Willie Wouldhave* launched on one of her first services from the newly erected South Beach boathouse and battled through the breaking seas to rescue the 19 crew. During this service, lifeboatman Jacob Harrison sustained a broken leg when one of the crew of the *Herman Sauber* landed on him when jumping into the lifeboat.

The *Northumberland* launched at 2.15 am on Christmas Day and rescued the five crew of the Whitby brig *Mary*, which had gone ashore on the Herd Sand.

Because the Brigades were called to many of the same wreck services as the Tyne Lifeboats, a common signalling system was established in 1883 to avoid any unnecessary delays in mustering crews and launching the lifeboats. When a crew had been taken off a vessel by the lifeboat, the coxswain would burn a longlight as a signal to the Life Brigades that their services would not be required.

On 25 July 1883, following an approach to the Board of Trade, Lieutenant C.H. McLellan, Inspector of Life Saving Stations for the United States Life Saving Service visited the South Shields Brigade on a fact finding mission in respect of the use of the rocket apparatus and breeches buoy equipment. He also took up the invitation to inspect the lifeboats of the Tyne Institution both ashore and afloat. The United States Life Saving Service was formed in 1871, and operated stations comprising of rocket apparatus, breeches buoys and surf lifeboats, manned by six full-time surfmen at each station, with a keeper in charge. The motto of the surfmen was 'They had to go out, but they did not have to come in'.

In 1899, McLellan played a leading role in the development of a motor lifeboat in the United States, with the installation of a 12hp, two-cylinder Superior petrol engine into a 34ft. pulling lifeboat. Following rough weather trials, he realised that the pulling lifeboats were not designed to take an engine in the stern of the boat, and recommended that a boat be designed with additional buoyancy to carry an engine. In trials in 1904-05, this 34ft. boat, a modified pulling boat, was not satisfactory, and in 1907, McLellan designed a 36ft. self-righting motor lifeboat. With improved class variants,

Author's collection

this design became the standard US Coastguard lifeboat in use until the early 1960s. In 1915 the US Coastguard was created by the amalgamation of the US Life Saving Service and US Revenue Cutter Service.

During 1866, the Board of Trade circulated the rules of the Tynemouth Brigade nationally, hoping that further Volunteer Life Brigades would be established around the coast to assist the full-time coastguards in breeches buoy rescue. By 1913, 404 companies were in existence. In 1931, the Board of Trade formed the Coast Life Saving Corps which absorbed many of the old Volunteer Life Brigades.

In 1966, the 7,000 strong Corps became the Coastguard Auxiliary Service, which continued to use the breeches buoy until 1988, when it was withdrawn. The Tynemouth Brigade still retains a breeches buoy capability, using modern rope rescue equipment and compressed air rocket guns developed for the offshore oil industry.

Owing to the popularity of the South Shields beaches during the summer months, in January 1968 the South Shields Brigade decided to expand their rescue role with the addition of an inshore rescue boat. They consulted the RNLI as to what type of boat and equipment would be most appropriate. Following a fundraising appeal, which included a generous donation from the Tyne Lifeboat Society, the *Always Ready*, was named (after the motto of the Tyne Lifeboat Society and South Shields Brigade) in a ceremony in the Watch House on 20 April 1968.

This boat, which cost £537, was a 12ft. 4in. long 'Z' type inflatable powered by a

South Shields VLB Archive

The *Always Ready.*

20 hp outboard engine with a speed of up to 20 knots, and fitted with a radio telephone. Brigade members were trained by Captain Don Atkinson of Tynemouth RNLI station; this station had operated a larger inshore rescue boat since April 1965. In its first four weeks of service during the summer the *Always Ready* rescued six people when their sailing dinghies capsized and towed

Author's collection

Tynemouth Volunteer Life Brigade watch house.

several small craft to safety when they were in danger of being wrecked on the South Pier. In its first year ten people were rescued.

In 1971, following a capsize in heavy surf to the south of the South Pier, which irreparably damaged the boat, the Brigade Committee decided to withdraw the *Always Ready* from service, and to concentrate on their traditional search and cliff rescue function. The larger inshore rescue boat, which had a better launch response time was still at Tynemouth lifeboat station,

The South Shields, Tynemouth and Sunderland Volunteer Life Brigades are still in existence today, being registered charities, and financially and administratively independent of the Maritime and Coastguard Agency. As operational 'declared facility' rescue organisations specialising in coastal search and cliff rescue, the Brigades work regularly with the local RNLI lifeboats from Tynemouth, Cullercoats and Sunderland, and the search and rescue helicopters of 'A' Flight, 202 Squadron, based at RAF Boulmer.

The histories of the South Shields and Tynemouth Volunteer Life Brigades and the Tyne Lifeboat Institution are inextricably linked. The founding members of the shore-based rescue organisations were officers and crew of the local lifeboats. James Gilbert, a founding member of the Tynemouth Brigade was the first coxswain of the RNLI's Tynemouth Lifeboat *Constance.* Samuel Malcolm regarded as the 'Father of South Shields Volunteer Life Brigade' served as honorary secretary, honorary treasurer and president over a period of 69 years. He combined the two principal roles for almost 40 years until 1906, when he became the Brigade's first president, serving until his death in 1935, at the age of 92. As vice president, he represented the Tyne Lifeboat Institution in its legal case against the RNLI in 1904.

15 Rescues

Although lifeboats began operating on the Tyne in 1789, it was not until 1808 and then 1841, with the establishment of the Tyne Lifeboat Institution, that more formal records were kept. Of these, only the service logs for the years 1861-1870 and 1882-1910 remain. What narrative remains today of the exploits of the lifeboat crews comes largely from contemporary accounts or newspaper articles.

The public appeal made by the South Shields Lifeboat Committee, in December 1797, for funds to establish a lifeboat station at North Shields made reference to 200 lives having been saved by the *Original*.

In April 1851, Robert Anderson, Secretary of the Tyne Lifeboat Institution, wrote in response to queries made by the Northumberland Competition Committee that *'in the last 11 years since I have kept an account, our boats have been off 84 times, one or other of them, and the number of persons saved, 493.'* In December 1849, following the *Providence* disaster, Anderson recorded that since 1841, the lifeboats had saved 466 people from 62 vessels.

Contemporary publications record the lifeboat *Tyne* saved 1,024 lives between 1833 and 1887, although this figure cannot be verified.

Not surprisingly, most rescues were carried out between October and March, with very little call for the services of the boats during the summer months. The vast majority of rescues occurred within a mile of the boathouses, to ships that had grounded on either the Herd Sands to the south of the river or Black Middens to the north.

On 18 December 1872 the *Shields Gazette* reported a typical incident at the mouth of the river. A north easterly gale had been blowing for a number of days.

NARROW ESCAPE OF A SCHOONER AT THE ENTRANCE OF THE TYNE AT SHIELDS, 1.20PM

At noon today a Danish schooner, the name of which has not at present been ascertained, was seen approaching Shields harbour, and was watched by an immense crowd from both sides of the river. She came on very well until she reached the Herd Buoy when she was struck on the stern by a tremendous sea, which disabled her steering apparatus. The vessel's sails were partly set, and she turned round with her head seawards, but soon wore round again. She now commenced to drift towards the wreck of the Eagle and every moment was expected to strike the sand. However, she was not so unfortunate as this. A number of steamboats were plying about, and at one time the vessel was entirely surrounded by them. The Friends [a local paddle tug] got a rope out from the schooner's stern and suc-

ceeded in towing her out of her dangerous position, until the tug boat Pilot got a rope out forward. The Friends then slipped her rope, and the Pilot commenced towing away, and brought the vessel safely into harbour. The lifeboats Northumberland and Tom Perry were both alongside the schooner several times, but the men seemed determined not to leave their ship. The alarm guns were loaded and ready for firing at any moment, and the Tynemouth and South Shields Volunteer Life Brigades were in attendance should their services have been re-quired. For half-an-hour the most intense excitement prevailed, and as soon as the vessel was seen to be out of danger, a blinding shower of rain came on, and the crowds soon dispersed. Another schooner has since arrived in safety.

The first rescue

The *Original* first launched on service on January 30 1790 when a vessel came ashore on the Herd Sand. The *Newcastle Courant* reported on 6 February 1790:

We hear from Shields that the boat lately built by Greathead for the purpose of preserving the crews of ships coming on the Herd Sand, was first tried on Saturday last, and far exceeds the expectations of those who had the most san-guine hopes of its utility, for going off three times to a vessel there on shore through a very heavy sea, she scarce shipped any water; and rendered the crew the infinite service – we have the satisfaction to add, that the sailors present were entirely ready in offering themselves upon the occasion.

The vessel was refloated two days later on Monday 1 February.

The first rescue by the *Northumberland*

The *Northumberland* was completed during the summer of 1798, and she had to wait until 16 November to perform her first service. At around 9am, the sloop *Edinburgh* ran ashore on the Herd Sand. Both the *Northumberland* and *Original* launched, but as the North Shields boat was slightly ahead of the South Shields boat, the newly agreed convention dictated that the *Northumberland* would attempt to go alongside the sloop. While doing so, the *Original* went to the aid of a brig which was having difficulties in crossing the bar. In the meantime, the *Northumberland* had taken off the six crew of the *Edinburgh*.

The wreck of the *Glatton* and the loss of the *Original*

At 9am on 21 January 1830, during a south-south-easterly gale and heavy seas, the South Shields brig *Glatton* ran onto the Black Middens while attempting to enter the river.

The *Original* launched from South Shields followed by the *Northumberland* from North Shields. The *Original* came alongside the *Glatton*, and six of the crew of eight entered the lifeboat. Before the remaining two crew members could get into the lifeboat, a heavy sea tore the lifeboat from the sloop's side. She was carried by the breaking surf towards the shore, hit a submerged rock and was beached. The crew and the six survivors were able to climb out of the boat and onto the beach at the Mussel Scarp. Upon inspection, the *Original* was found to have broken her back and split in two. The remaining two crewmembers on the *Glatton* were rescued by the coastguard using Manby's rocket apparatus. Meanwhile, the *Northumberland* was standing by another vessel that was having difficulties crossing the bar. In her 40-year life, the *Original* did not lose a single crewmember. The wreck of the *Original* was completely dismantled by souvenir hunters.

Electra

In March 1845, during an easterly gale, the pilots on morning watch at South Shields observed the brig *Electra* flying a distress signal and trying to reach the open sea against the gale, but being driven slowly towards the shore in the direction of Cullercoats. It was just a matter of time before the brig ran aground so the pilots decided to follow the progress of the *Electra* and launch the lifeboat. Rather than row the lifeboat across the bar and up the coast, they planned to take the boat overland and launch from where the *Electra* came ashore.

The North Shields boat *Northumberland* was being repaired so the *Tyne* was rowed across the river to North Shields and placed upon the *Northumberland*'s carriage. The carriage was hitched up to four horses, and pulled into Tynemouth village, then northwards, across fields and ditches through Cullercoats and Whitley Bay. The boat's wooden carriage collapsed as it was not designed for such a long and difficult journey. At times it caught fire through the friction of the axle; the fire also damaged the lifeboat.

The coxswain, Jacob Harrison, conferred with second coxswain Joseph Smith, and decided to continue the journey having come so far. All loose gear was taken out of the *Tyne* and carried by spectators while the crew and horses continued to drag the boat over the fields, a distance of six miles in total. Meanwhile, the *Electra* was dragging her anchors off Hartley, eight miles to the north of the river. On arrival, the *Tyne* was launched – no mean feat, without its carriage to take the boat into a sufficient depth of water. Twice the boat was thrown back by the surf, and on the third attempt four of the crew were washed overboard. While three of the crew held onto the boat, the fourth, grasping an oar, drifted north for a half mile before being rescued by a gentleman who rode his horse into the surf.

With the *Tyne* preparing to launch a fifth time, the *Electra's* anchors failed and she came ashore. Her crew were able to climb along the jib and drop onto the beach.

The *Tyne,* although severely damaged, was towed back to South Shields by the *Providence,* where she was substantially rebuilt.

The gale of January 1854

During the first two weeks of January 1854, a terrific gale from the east-south-east battered the Tyne Harbour. The following account has been taken from the *North and South Shields Gazette* of 6 and 13 January. It illustrates the conditions the lifeboatmen had to endure in a winter's gale in their open surf lifeboats and the help given to the shipwrecked sailors by the local community once they had been brought ashore.

At 5pm on Tuesday 3 January, conditions at the mouth of the Tyne began to deteriorate, with a full storm blowing by 11pm. At that time, a number of pilots in the lookout saw a light on a vessel that had been driven onto Tynemouth rocks. The South Shields lifeboat, with a crew of 19, was immediately launched, and got alongside the brig *Antelope* of North Shields and took off her entire crew. The brig was totally wrecked.

At 7am, the pilot steamer proceeded to sea with the intention of placing pilots on board vessels making for the harbour. The seas were so high that she had to return. Between 8pm and 9.am, the brig *Elizabeth,* of South Shields, was driven onto the Black Middens. The lifeboat launched, but on seeing that the *Elizabeth* was in no immediate danger, the lifeboat went to the barque *Euretta* of Hull, which had struck the *Elizabeth*, carrying away her bowsprit, and rescued her 14 crew.

The next vessel to come ashore was the coal-laden brig *Anns* of North Shields, whose crew was rescued by the Manby's rocket apparatus; the brig was a total wreck. By this time, there were numerous vessels arriving off the mouth of the Tyne seeking the safety and shelter of the harbour. The inhabitants of Tynemouth, North and South Shields had now gathered on the cliffs overlooking the harbour entrance to view the unfolding events.

The clipper schooner *Eliza* of Kirkwall, made her approach to cross the bar, was struck by a heavy sea and went ashore on the Herd Sand. A second sea struck her and threw her onto her beam ends, her ballast shifting to the starboard side. She lay in this position for about 15 minutes, then she came off the sands and was driven over the bar. The crew had taken to the rigging, three in the main and two in the fore rigging. Lifeboats from South and North Shields launched, but after several attempts were unable to save the crew. The *Eliza,* still on her beam ends, came ashore on Tynemouth rocks, the crew still alive and waving for assistance to the crowds onshore as heavy seas broke over the vessel. A Mr Fry from Tynemouth manned his boat, but this was soon overwhelmed in the breakers. The crew reached the shore safely, righted the boat and launched again, but failed to reach the schooner. While other vessels were successful in entering the river, the barque *Sir Robert Peel* was not and came ashore close to the *Eliza*. The crew of the *Sir Robert Peel* was rescued by the rocket apparatus. Soon afterwards two seamen went back out to the barque, fixed a line to an oar and threw it in the direction of the *Eliza*. The oar and line reached the wreck but her crew were too exhausted to haul it in. Not long afterwards the vessel turned bottom up. From what could be seen from the shore, three of the crew appeared to have died before the vessel capsized, one of whom was hanging from the rigging by one of his legs. A bundle containing a pocket book and documents was washed ashore, but none of the crew were found.

The *Sir Robert Peel* had sailed from Valparaiso with, in addition to its cargo of saltpetre, nine pieces of silver ore, each weighing more than 1cwt. The silver was taken off the barque using the rocket apparatus, and was immediately taken to the Spanish Battery under the protection of the River Tyne Police and officers of the Customs House and Inland Revenue. The *Sir Robert Peel*, a copper hulled vessel, became a total wreck. A number of saltpetre bags came ashore on the beach between the rocks and Low Light.

The rocket apparatus also saved the crew of the brig *New Messenger*, of Sunderland, loaded with salt, which had grounded on the Black Middens.

The next vessel to come ashore was the brig *Amphitrite*, of South Shields, soon followed by the brig *Arethusa* of Blyth. Both crews were saved. At 7pm, a coal-laden schooner came ashore next to the *Euretta*. Her crew was saved by the lifeboat.

At 6.30pm the following day, Thursday 5 January, the pilots on watch in the Lawe Top lookout saw two fully laden vessels attempting to cross the breaking seas on the bar. The first was successful but the second, the brig *Hannah* of Whitby, was struck by a series of heavy seas on her stern, which carried away her taffrail and wheel. The mate, Joseph Smith, who was on the wheel at the time, suffered a fractured right arm, and the apprentice, George Fowler, was washed overboard and drowned. The pilots, seeing the *Hannah* being driven towards the Black Middens, launched the two South Shields lifeboats, each with a crew of 18, into the heavy seas and snow showers. The *Providence* made four attempts to reach the brig, but was prevented from doing so owing to the ropes thrown onto the vessel breaking and four oars being lost. The *Tyne*, after three attempts, succeeded in getting alongside and took off the nine crew. They had considerable difficulty in getting the mate into the lifeboat because of his broken arm.

The two lifeboats had been out for some time and a considerable number of people had begun to congregate at the Coble Landing, anxious about the safety of the boats and their crews.

After three hours both boats returned, and the rescued crew was immediately taken to the home of Mrs Jackson at the Coble Inn. The mate was taken upstairs and the local doctor was sent for to set his arm. He was still in the care of Mrs Jackson a full week after his rescue. One of the apprentices, John Barker Laing, was suffering from the cold and fatigue, but after a period of nursing he recovered and was sent home to Whitby.

The master, Benjamin Harrald (who had severely injured his hand), the mate and the crew had lost all their clothes and belongings. The *Hannah* had sailed from Hartlepool, coal-laden and bound for London, the previous Monday. After she was caught in the gale on the Tuesday evening and driven north westwards, the crew had to man the pumps continuously until just before she came ashore on Thursday evening.

On the morning of Friday 7 January, a schooner was observed riding off Souter Point flying a flag of distress. A message soon reached Whitburn, and the rocket apparatus was taken to where the schooner was lying offshore. Although on a lee shore, the vessel seemed to be riding out the storm a mile offshore and in no danger as long as her anchors held. The Whitburn lifeboat was also sent for.

The pilots at South Shields had also been told about the schooner, and were preparing to go to her assistance. However, the pilot steamer *Pilot* was undergoing repairs, and the departure was delayed until 2pm. Considerable difficulty was experienced in crossing the bar due to the heavy seas, but once clear of the breakers the steamer soon reached the anchored schooner. Using the *Pilot*'s own lifeboat, the schooner was boarded, but no one was found. The pilots speculated that the crew had taken to their own boat. This proved to be correct, as at the time the *Pilot* was crossing the bar, the villagers at Marsden, who had been watching the schooner, saw her crew take to their longboat and pull towards shore. Just outside the surf line, the boat was filled by a heavy sea and one of her crew was washed overboard. He was soon recovered but shortly afterwards the longboat was struck by another heavy sea and capsized in the surf. Three of the crew succeeded in climbing onto the upturned hull. A rocket was fired from the shore. The line fell directly across the boat, but none of the crew could hold it. They were all were thrown into the sea and drowned.

Half-an-hour after this event, the *Pilot* reached the schooner the *Minerva* of Wisbech and she was brought safely into the river. The pilots received a salvage award from the Receiver of Wrecks.

At 8am on Sunday 9 January, the wind was blowing strong from the east south east, with a great number of ships off the harbour entrance waiting to enter. The *Pilot* put to sea with 25 pilots. Shortly afterwards, the barque *Aurora* successfully crossed the bar without a pilot, but then was driven southward by the ebb tide onto the Herd Sand. She was soon followed by the Prussian brig *Armida*, which became a total wreck.

The tide had now receded, but on the next tide, at half flood, some vessels were successful in entering the river, however the brigs *Ann* of Lynn, *Jean* of Inverness,

Breakwater and *Conference,* both of Shields and *Jane and Margaret* of Newcastle, the schooners *George,* of Whitby, *James and Ann* of Ipswich and *Cresswell* of Colchester, the barque *Sarah Midge,* and the French vessel *Bon Virgine,* all came to grief at the harbour entrance.

Upon grounding, the crew of the *Jean* got on board the brig *Breakwater* and were trying to launch the longboat, when the mate was washed overboard. He had sunk and risen twice when the lifeboat, which the crew had not noticed in the spray as it was painted white, rowed up and rescued him.

In total 12 vessels came ashore that Sunday night. The South Shields lifeboats *Tyne* and *Providence* launched at 8pm and rescued 87 seamen, finally returning to their boathouse at the Coble Landing some five hours later. With crew changes, 48 pilots manned the lifeboats throughout the night.

Between midnight and 1am on Monday the stock of clothes kept in the lifeboat house for rescued seamen was used up, despite having been replenished a month before in anticipation of the winter round of wreck services. The lifeboat secretary, Robert Anderson, had to order more. Crew after crew was sent to the houses of Mrs Jackson and Mrs Young to be looked after.

Many of the men brought ashore were members of the Shipwrecked Mariner's Society and they were given money and rail tickets to return to their home ports.

On the Monday morning, with so many ships on the sands, the River Tyne Police and officers belonging to the Customs House were deployed to protect the ships from looters. Despite this, some looting occurred and 12 men were arrested.

Between 9pm and 10pm, the brigs *Lively,* of North Shields, *Savannah,* of London, the billy boy *Happy Return* from Goole, the Norwegian vessel *Junius* and the *Ocean* of Goole came ashore on the Herd Sand. The South Shields lifeboat launched, but owing to the amount of ice in the river, the lifeboat could not proceed down river to the stranded vessels. Fortunately, the crews were not in immediate danger, and remained aboard their vessels until low water, when they came ashore.

On Tuesday the wind was still blowing strong from the east north east, with hail and sleet showers. During the early part of the afternoon, several vessels entered the harbour, but the schooner *Boadicea* of Teignmouth, struck the *Sarah Midge*, carrying away her own foremast, and grounded on the Herd Sand. The lifeboat put off, but the crew of the *Boadicea* refused to enter the lifeboat, and waited for the tide to fall before coming ashore.

Several of the vessels that came ashore were auctioned where they lay and bought by local men for salvage. The *New Messenger* was sold for £38, with the boat and oars being sold separately for £2 11s. The brig *Ann* was sold for £8, the brig *Amphitrite* for £22, the *Arethusa* for £24, the *Antelope* for £5 15s and the *Euretta* for £50.

The Great Gale of 1861: The wrecks of the *Fowlis* and *Minerva*

The 'Great Gale' that occurred during Saturday 9 February 1861 proved to be a busy day for the Tyne Lifeboat Institution, and illustrated the necessity of having four lifeboats stationed at the mouth of the river that could deal with multiple wrecks occurring in a short period of time. A north-easterly gale had been blowing for a number of days, which had resulted in atrocious sea conditions on the bar.

The first boat ashore, in the early hours of the morning, was the brig *Minerva* of Whitby, in ballast, which came ashore on the South Pier stones. The *Providence* launched from the Coble Landing and, having been washed back several times eventually got alongside the brig and took off five of the six crew. The sixth crewmember came ashore on a piece of the ship's timber.

At 7.30am, the schooner *Fowlis* of Inverness, laden with staves, was seen running for the river entrance. Struggling in the conditions, she ran onto the Herd Sands and drifted broadside onto the rubble stones used in the construction of South Pier, approximately 200 yards from the end of the completed pier, and close to where the *Minerva* had come ashore.

Four lifeboats launched; the *Providence, Tyne, Northumberland* and *Prior*. The *Tyne* and *Providence* were unable to reach the wreck because it was low tide. The *Providence* was stove in four places after hitting the rubble stone base of the pier three times, and had to return to the Coble Landing for running repairs. The *Prior*, manned by 19 pilots, could not reach the wreck and put back to shore. The crew tried to relaunch, but the boat was firmly stuck on the sands.

The *Providence* put off a second time and the crew threw grapnel lines toward the *Fowlis*, but they missed their holds. The lifeboat was unable to maintain its position in the high seas and was forced ashore.

While the lifeboats were trying to rescue the crew, Lawrence Byrne, the Chief Boatman at Tynemouth Coastguard Station, and his men had brought the rocket apparatus across the river to South Shields and fired five rockets. Each time the line either fouled or broke on the pier stones.

The *Tyne,* with a crew of 22, returned to the beach and took on board a number of coastguards and their rocket apparatus. Anchored well to seaward of the wreck, the first attempt to put a line on the schooner was unsuccessful.

A crew member then jumped from the *Fowlis* and began to swim towards the lifeboat. On seeing this, the *Tyne* immediately made for the seaman, Peter Mackenzie, and hauled him aboard before landing him on the beach.

The lifeboat then returned, and a second attempt to put a line, with a lifebuoy attached, on board proved successful. This was no mean feat as the Boxer rocket was fired from the small confines of a pitching lifeboat as the crew protected themselves from the rocket as it was fired. The first man to be hauled through the surf to the lifeboat was the mate, Farquhar Fraser, followed by the captain, George Fraser.

Three people remained on board; Hugh Fraser, brother of the mate, George Patience, cook, and Alexander Jack, aged 20. By this time, the lifeboat crew and coast-guards had been struggling for three hours, on a rising tide and increasing wind, and were joined by the *Northumberland* and the salvage boat, *William Wake.*

At around 11.30 am, the *Fowlis* was hit by a series of heavy seas and started to break up. All of the remaining crew were thought to have perished. However, Hugh Fraser and Alexander Jack were seen still clinging to the wreck, while George Patience was on a detached part of the schooner. The lifeboats made as close as they could to the wreck and threw lines to the crew, but these efforts were thwarted by the ferocity of the seas breaking across the *Fowlis*. Hugh Fraser and Alexander Jack died. George Patience was on the last remaining part of the wreck, being constantly washed over by the breaking surf. The flood tide had started to drive the wreck further up onto the pier stones where a number of men formed a line and succeeded in throwing a rope to Patience, who was then hauled ashore.

The *South Shields Gazette* reported that concerns about the condition and state of the rocket apparatus had been raised. It was alleged that the ropes were rotten, which had caused them to break during the rescue attempts.

Thirty minutes later the schooner *Caesar* of Whitstable came ashore on the Herd Sand, with the *Tyne* and *Northumberland* each rescuing four of its crew of eight.

At 12.30pm the brig *Indus* of North Shields ran onto the Herd Sands, with the crew being rescued by the *Northumberland.* The brig broke up on the sands and was a total loss. An hour and a half later, the brig *Sarah Anne* of North Shields came ashore on the Herd Sands where the *Tyne* rescued her crew of six.

Surviving rescue logs also state that at 4am on the following Sunday, the *Tyne* launched and rescued the crew of four from the schooner *Treaty* of Goole. The *Treaty*, laden with potatoes, had earlier sailed from the River Tay bound for London. During the gale she lost her mainsail and made for the Tyne but on entering the river she came ashore on the Herd Sand. She was towed off the sands around 3pm. The *Sarah Anne* and *Caesar* remained on the sands, but by the following day, *Sarah Anne* had gone over onto her beam ends and was a total wreck. The *Caesar* was still on the sands.

On Tuesday 12 February, the wrecks and spars of the *Minerva* and *Fowlis* were auctioned on the beach and purchased by Joseph Wilson, a pilot of South Shields. Scotch fir staves, part of the cargo of the *Fowlis* were sold that same afternoon. The weather continued to be cold, with strong winds from the east, and snow showers and heavy seas on the bar.

The South Shields Shipwrecked Fishermen and Mariners' Society forwarded three of the crew of the *Minerva* to Seaham, three of the crew from the *Sarah Ann* to

London, one to Maldon and one to Dundee. On the following Monday, Farquhar Fraser, Peter Mackenzie and George Patience, all of the *Fowlis*, were dispatched to their homes in Inverness. The three men expressed their thanks, through the *Shields Gazette* to Mrs Heron of the Spring Garden Tavern, who looked after them after they were brought ashore, and to the crews of the lifeboats for their efforts in rescuing them. The body of Alexander Jack was interred in St Stephen's Churchyard, South Shields. His remains were followed to the grave by a number of South Shields seamen. The body of Hugh Fraser was never recovered.

While the Tyne Lifeboats were dealing with these incidents, the Whitby Lifeboat, a 30ft., ten oars, 'North-Country' type built by Falkingbridge of Whitby, capsized on its fourth service of the day, at 2pm, drowning all but one of its 16 crew. This boat was never used again and was broken up the following year.

The wrecks of the *Consul, Duff* and *Gleaner*

The week before Christmas 1872, proved to be tragic for the Volunteer Life Brigadesmen of Tynemouth and lifeboatmen of North Shields. A severe east-south-easterly gale with heavy rain had been blowing for a number of days. At high water, both of the partially completed piers were constantly under water from breaking seas.

On Tuesday 17 December, a number of ships had managed to enter the river during daylight hours. It was not until nightfall that the tragic events of the day began to unfold.

At about 8.20pm, the signal guns on HMS *Castor* and at the Spanish Battery were fired twice to indicate a vessel had gone ashore on the north side of the harbour. This was the 165 ton, Portsmouth-registered coal brig *Duff,* which had left Sunderland fully laden the Saturday before. On hitting bad weather she put about and ran for the shelter of the Tyne. Soon after, the vessel drifted off southwards and went ashore on the Herd Sand. The signal guns were fired three times to indicate the vessel was now ashore on the south side. Two of the crew, the cook and a seaman, were lost when attempting to launch the ship's boat.

South Shields Volunteer Life Brigade mustered and ran out their lines, but the wreck was too far away for the rockets to reach. At the same time, the South Shields lifeboats *Tom Perry* and *Tyne* put off together. The *Northumberland* from North Shields took the remainder of the crew off the brig and landed them at the Sailor's Home at North Shields while both the South Shields lifeboats searched for the ship's boat.

At 10pm the barque *Consul* of South Shields tried to enter the river in atrocious conditions but twice hit the rubble of the partially constructed North Pier before colliding with the staging erected at end of the pier. She came to rest 20 yards off the inside of the pier, her bow facing towards Prior's Haven.

The Volunteer Life Brigadesmen from Tynemouth got a throwing line onboard which was made fast to the *Consul's* anchor. Before the breeches buoy could be rigged, three crew came down the line 'hand over hand'. While a fourth member of crew was being brought ashore in the breeches buoy, a heavy sea rolled the *Consul*, and the crewman dropped into the sea between the barque and the pier. Although he was quickly recovered and brought ashore, he was so severely injured that he died. Only three of the ten crew survived.

During the rescue, a terrific sea came over the pier and swept one of the Brigadesmen, Robert Arkley, a customs officer, into the breaking surf. Immediate attempts to rescue him proved unsuccessful and it wasn't until 1am that his body was recovered. Robert Arkley had also been a member of Tynemouth RNLI lifeboat crew for several years.

The *Consul* had left the Tyne on Saturday 14 December, bound for Genoa with a cargo of firebricks and coke. By the following Monday evening she had only reached a point off Whitby. Her lack of headway was due to adverse winds. On Monday evening a strong gale sprang up and the captain decided to run for the Tyne for shelter, reaching the harbour mouth at daybreak. However, the captain decided not to enter the river, thinking that the storm would soon abate and that he could continue the voyage to Italy. Unfortunately, the gale strengthened, and an attempt was made to reach the safety of the harbour. While passing the North Pier, a heavy sea hit the brig's port quarter, forcing her onto the rubble stone base of the pier. Her bowsprit fouled some of the construction staging and carried away the ship's head. Another sea hit the stern and washed over the decks, driving her further into the pier works. The captain, Thomas Thompson, a Shetlander who lived in South Shields, was killed by the collapsing pier timbers falling onto the brig's deck. The mate, George Fryer of South Shields, had taken to the foretopsail for safety, but this was carried away into the sea following the collision. The remainder of the crew was washed overboard and drowned.

At the same time as the *Consul* had left the Tyne, the 175 ton brig *Gleaner* of Blyth had also set sail from Amble, bound for Boulogne and laden with coal. At sea, the weather started to worsen by early the following week, a south-easterly gale had begun to blow and the brig soon became waterlogged. South of Whitby, the captain, William Gair, decided to put back. By the time she had reached the mouth of the Tyne on the morning of Wednesday 18 December, several feet of water lay in her hold, despite the crew continuously manning the pumps for three days.

That morning, five screw steamers had safely negotiated the harbour entrance. At midday, a Danish schooner, her steering disabled by the following seas, was towed into port by local tugs. They had got a line on board her just before she ran onto the Herd Sand. Both the South and North Shields lifeboats launched to her assistance.

On crossing the bar, a tremendous sea hit the *Gleaner*'s stern, disabling her helm. She became unmanageable and out of control. The seas threw the mate, William Jackson, against a deck house, crushing his arms, chest and legs. The foremast man, John Mole, who had been on the ship's wheel, was washed overboard. To prevent Jackson, who had also been at the wheel, from following him, the Captain lashed him to the vessel.

The *Gleaner* struck the shore near the wreck of the steamer *Eagle*, and the alarm guns were fired to launch the lifeboats and summon the Volunteer Life Brigades. However, the tugs *Friends* and *Robert Bruce* got a line on board the *Gleaner,* and towed her away from the *Eagle*. Nearing the Narrows, the heavy seas broke the tow, and the brig ran onto the Herd Sand, a little to the seaward of the *Duff.*

The *Northumberland,* launching with a scratch crew, was the first boat to make headway. On reaching the wreck, a series of breaking seas lifted, dropped and swamped her, driving her shoreward towards the Mussel Scarp sands, to the east of the North Shields Fish Quay. Six of the crew had been washed overboard, and the remaining crew on the *Northumberland* pulled towards them and picked up the coxswain, H. Sadler, and lifeboatmen G. Thompson and G. Potts. Wearing lifejackets, the three other men were swept ashore where spectators waded into the seas to reach them. Unfortunately, crewmen James Wheatley, aged 31, a ballast keelman, married with three children, and James Watson, a pilot, aged 23, both native of North Shields, drowned.

As the *Northumberland* was being beached to the east of the Fish Quay, the *Tom Perry* battled through the heavy seas and took off the *Gleaner*'s six remaining crew, including the seriously injured mate. They were landed at South Shields, where they were put in the care of the landlord of the Globe Inn at the Coble Landing. The mate, attended by a local doctor, died at 4.30pm, leaving a wife and five children. By 5pm, after a further three screw steamers had safely entered the river on the flood tide, heavy seas were breaking over the *Gleaner*, which became a total wreck.

In two days, three rescuers and nine seamen had been lost. A benevolent fund was started for the wife and children of Robert Arkley, with £321 collected in the three days following his death. A fund was also started for the dependents of the two crew of the *Northumberland* lifeboat, to which the RNLI subscribed 100 guineas.

Immediately following this tragedy the South Shields Gazette reported that Richard Lewis, Secretary of the RNLI, had offered to place a 40ft self-righting lifeboat at Shields. This offer was not taken up.

The wrecks of the *Rhineland, Olaf Kyrre* and *Flid*

What proved to be the last launches of the 49-year-old *Tyne* took place during a severe easterly gale in December 1882, when she was stationed at the South Beach boat-house.

Between 4 and 8 December, the lifeboats *Tom Perry, Willie Wouldhave* and *Tyne* launched on six occasions and the Tynemouth RNLI No. 2 boat *Forester* launched twice.

The first call came on the morning of 4 December, when an east-south-easterly gale, bringing with it heavy snow, blew up quickly. It caught out the Cullercoats coble fleet, which had set sail for the local fishing grounds earlier that morning. On returning to Cullercoats the 30 boats found that it was too dangerous to beach in the harbour, and immediately made for the Tyne. The Cullercoats RNLI lifeboat, attempting to launch, was damaged when it came off its carriage.

In anticipation of the boats arriving off the Tyne the signal guns were fired, alerting the two Volunteer Life Brigades, with the three Tyne lifeboats and Tynemouth's No. 2 boat all launching. All of the Cullercoats cobles made it into the river by midday.

An hour later the signal guns fired again, when the German barque *Rhineland*, carrying a cargo of timber, and being towed into port by the paddle tug *Skylark,* came ashore on the Black Middens near to Battery Point. The towline had parted in the heavy seas. The *Tom Perry* and *Willie Wouldhave* launched from South Shields and soon reached the barque. With heavy seas breaking over the wreck, she took off the crew of 12, which included the captain's wife and two small sons.

Tynemouth's No. 2 boat, *Forester*, launched, with some difficulty, from the Black Middens station at 1.20pm. The boat was filled several times by the breaking seas. She reached the wreck 25 minutes later, shortly after the *Tom Perry*, where she took off the remaining two crew members, landing them at South Shields at 2.30pm. The conditions were so bad that the *Forester* lost her rudder, grapnel hooks and lines on this service. Due to the falling tide and heavy sea, she could not be rehoused and was moored at the North Shields Fish Quay, adjacent to the Low Light. Her crew remained with her.

During the day weather conditions deteriorated, and later that evening the Volunteer Life Brigadesmen at South Shields on bad weather watch in the Watch House tower observed a small boat labouring at the harbour entrance and disappearing when a number of seas hit her.

At 11pm, the signal guns were fired. Tynemouth's No. 2 boat *Forester* launched 20 minutes later followed by the *Willie Wouldhave*. Nothing was found, but later the name board *Catherine and Mary* with some wreckage was washed ashore at Prior's Haven. There were no survivors.

While the *Forester* was searching for the *Catherine and Mary,* she found the Danish schooner *Argo* in a dangerous position near to the South Pier. She escorted the schooner into harbour and returned to her temporary moorings at 1.30am.

Newcastle Libraries

The Tynemouth RNLI No. 2 boathouse and station boat Forester launching at low water. See also the photograph on page 145.

The South Shields Life Brigadesmen had also seen the ship's lights, and, alerted by the signal guns, took the breeches buoy equipment to the end of the South Pier. In the time taken to set up the life saving apparatus, the ship had cleared the danger and entered the harbour. On returning, a huge sea swept over the pier and washed one of the South Shields coastguards 40 yards along the pier, before he got a grip of one of the handrails, saving his life.

At 10pm the following day, 5th December, with the gale unabated, the lights of a ship were seen from the South Shields Volunteer Life Brigade Watch House, and soon after a flare went up. The brig, *Olaf Kyrre* of Frederikstad, Norway, had left the Tyne ten days earlier, but had been driven back by the force of the easterly gale. She had missed the river entrance, coming ashore on a sand bank close to the south side of the South Pier. Between the sand bank and the pier, stones had been laid to protect the pier works from south easterly gales. The alarm guns were fired, and the Life Brigadesmen took the rocket apparatus down the pier. The second rocket fired fell over the ship, but with the crew lashed to the rigging, and seas constantly sweeping over her decks, it was too dangerous to secure the line.

When this rescue attempt failed, the call came to launch the lifeboat. However, the superintendent in charge of the South Beach station refused to sanction a launch due to the dangerous sea conditions, and would not open up the boathouse to the gathered pilots. He went home with the boathouse keys.

The Tynemouth No. 2 boat *Forester* launched at 10.20pm from temporary moorings at the Low Lights and discovered the *Olaf Kyrre* behind the South Pier, but was unable to pass beyond the pier ends due to the atrocious sea conditions. She had to return to the Fish Quay, arriving at 11.45pm.

At the South Beach, the pilots believed that they could launch the lifeboat so they broke down the boathouse door with a spar that had been washed ashore. The *Tyne,* with a crew of 15 under the command of coxswain Andrew Purvis, launched in the early hours of 6 December and battled for two hours through the heavy breaking surf to reach the wreck, three-quarters of a mile offshore.

The launchers sheltering in the boathouse, could see the dim masthead light of the *Tyne* as she battled through the breakers to reach the wreck. Once alongside the wreck, grapnel hooks were thrown into the rigging, but before the crew could jump into the lifeboat, a breaking sea swept the *Tyne* away from the wreck and broadside towards the stones protecting the South Pier. Fortunately, a following sea took her over the rocks, and the crew regained control of the boat and began to row away, south-eastwards, from the pier and seaward of the wreck.

Reaching a position to the north east of the wreck, the *Tyne* dropped her anchor and got alongside the *Olaf Kyrre.* The crew members, frozen and exhausted with seas washing over the wreck and frequent snow storms, were lashed to the rigging and unable to help themselves. The bowman of the lifeboat leaped aboard the brig, cut the eight crew free and took them into the lifeboat, which then surfed through the following breaking seas back to the boathouse.

Once the boat had beached in the early hours of the morning, the lifeboatmen had to be carried ashore with their lower bodies and legs completely frozen. Before they were taken to the warmth of their homes, the coxswain, crew and launchers brought the *Tyne* back up the beach and left her outside the boathouse. They intended to put her back into the boathouse when it was light.

The Norwegian crew was taken to the warmth of the Life Brigade Watch House where they were attended to by the Brigade Doctor, provided with dry clothing and refreshments, and put to bed in the surgery.

Meanwhile, the superintendent read about the rescue in the morning edition of the *South Shields Gazette.* He immediately went to the boathouse to see the *Tyne* on the beach and the boathouse doors damaged.

In a fit of rage, berating the crew for stealing the lifeboat, and declaring they would not receive their service payment of 10s 6d, he went up to confront Andrew Purvis at his home on the Lawe Top. On hearing the coxswain's story of the rescue, and realising his error in criticising the actions of the crew, he sanctioned payment. The evening edition of the *Shields Gazette* pilloried the superintendent for his public criticism, but as the crew received an additional half a crown, the issue was soon forgotten.

On 9 December, the *Shields Gazette* published a letter from Hans Andreasen, Captain of the *Olaf Kyrre*.

Allow me on behalf of myself and my crew (eight men all told) through the medium of your valuable paper, to express our most grateful thanks to the gallant crew who manned the lifeboat 'Tyne' and who, at the imminent peril of their own lives, rescued us from a watery grave early on the morning of Wednesday the 6th inst.

The daring and fearless manner in which the 'Tyne's' crew struggled against the raging and relentless elements in making for our unfortunate vessel, was the most heroic, and we feel unable by words to express the praise they have earned and so truly deserve. We have also to tender our heartfelt thanks to all those kind friends who cared for us after we were brought ashore. The hospitality shown to us in the providing of refreshments and warm clothing will ever be held by us in graceful recollection.

In conclusion, I would add that we had given up all hope of rescue on that dreadful Wednesday morning, and were resigned to meet the worst, when thanks to providence, the gallant crew of the 'Tyne' were enabled to achieve in a most glorious manner their difficult and self-imposed task.

I am,

Hans Andreasen

Master of the unfortunate brig 'Olaf Kyrre' of Frederikstad, Norway,

7ᵗʰ December 1882.

Two days later, at 6.40am on 8 December, another Norwegian brig, the *Flid* of Egersund, came ashore 200 yards south of the South Pier, lying broadside to the seas, which were now sweeping over her. The South Shields Volunteer Life Brigade saw the ship coming ashore and signalled for the guns to be fired at Tynemouth.

The Life Brigade set up the rocket apparatus, fired a line over the stern of the *Flid*, and sent out the hawser, whip lines and breeches buoy. The Norwegian crew, not knowing how to rig the equipment, took it off the hawser line. On seeing this, another breeches buoy was attached and one of the full-time coastguards, Humphrey Ashton, volunteered to be hauled out to the wreck. Although immersed in the surf, he reached the wreck safely, and showed the crew how to rig the rescue equipment. Another coastguard, Thomas Ewart, also made the journey out to the *Flid*. Once the equipment was rigged they brought three of the crew ashore, where they were taken to the warmth of the Watch House.

In the meantime, the *Tyne* had launched from the South Beach boathouse, located next to the Life Brigade Watch House, and battled through the breakers to reach the *Flid.* The remaining eight crew and two coastguards were taken off and landed on the beach. This proved to be the last service launch of the *Tyne.* She was replaced by the *Willie Wouldhave,* which had been transferred from the Coble Landing in September 1887. The *Tyne* was placed in reserve at the Coble Landing, until put on permanent display at the Pier Head, South Shields, in May 1894.

Alphonse

On Friday 28January 1910 a severe easterly storm was blowing frequent snow squalls onto the coast and heavy seas were breaking over the recently completed piers. During that day, members of the South Shields Volunteer Life Brigade had been on bad weather watch, and at 8.30pm, the starboard light of a vessel was seen through the snow and sleet, close to shore and south of the South Pier end. The searchlight in the watch tower picked out a vessel in the breakers coming ashore at the south end of the Herd Sand, 200 yards north of Trow Rocks. She was the 398 ton Norwegian three-masted barquentine, *Alphonse*, built at Arendal in 1903, and loaded with silver sand, on passage from Flushing to Grangemouth.

The alarm guns were fired and the Volunteer Life Brigadesmen pulled the life saving cart half a mile down the beach, setting up the rocket apparatus opposite the *Alphonse*. A rocket line was successfully fired across the ship, but the crew made no attempt to haul out the hawser and whip lines required to use the breeches buoy. A second rocket was successfully fired and fell across the ship near to the mizzen mast. Again, no attempt was made to haul the lines onto the ship.

The *Alphonse* was a steel-hulled ship aground on sand and there was no immediate danger of her breaking up as the tide had begun to ebb. However concern was growing at the delay in getting the crew off the ship so *Willie Wouldhave* was brought out of the South Beach boathouse and pulled on her carriage over the sands to a point 100 yards north of the wreck. This was the first time the *Willie Wouldhave* had been launched on a service since January 1892.

Under the command of Coxswain Richard Harrison, the lifeboat launched into the breakers, and came around the stern of the ship and onto her leeward side. Once alongside, ropes were quickly secured and all 29 crew of the *Alphonse* were taken on board. The lifeboat surfed ashore through the breakers. The crew was taken to the Volunteer Life Brigade Watch House where they were given dry clothing and 'restoratives' by the Brigade's honorary doctors.

Tynemouth's motor lifeboat, *J. McConnell Hussey* also launched. Station records indicate that the signal gun was fired at 8.15pm, from the south side of the river, but due to the north easterly gale, it was not heard by the coxswain or motorman. A scratch

South Tyneside Libraries

The Alphonse, wrecked January 1910.

crew manned the boat, without orders, but failed to start the engine. At 9.15pm
Superintendent Burton was informed that the coastguard had left word at his house
that the rocket apparatus had failed and the lifeboat was required. At the same time,
the Lloyds signalman was using the telephone to trying to establish whether the
lifeboat was still required. At 10pm, after a message was received that the rocket line
had been successfully fired, but the crew of the *Alphonse* would not use it, the *J.
McConnell Hussey* put to sea. On approaching the wreck around 30 minutes later, it
was found that the water was too shallow for the boat to get alongside, and that the
ship could only be approached from shore. As there was no danger to life, the lifeboat
returned, arriving back at her moorings at 11.30pm.

The *South Shields Gazette* interviewed Captain Gallaksen who said that they had
been at sea for 16 days on a voyage that should only have taken between one and two
days in favourable winds. Due to the adverse weather they had covered the distance
three times over and had been in sight of the Firth of Forth on three occasions, but had
been driven back by the northerly and westerly winds. The *Alphonse* had been constantly washed over by heavy seas, and had lost her foretopmast and sails. Arriving off
the Tyne the previous night, with the winds from the east and in a blinding snowstorm,
they had lost the shore lights. When the snow had cleared, the ship had come so close

The wreck of the Alphonse.

inshore that there was no room to turn to windward and she fell into the breakers and grounded.

The captain also explained why the crew did not come ashore in the breeches buoy. Despite the captain's excellent English, they could not understand the instructions on the Tally Board. The Volunteer Life Brigade soon provided an enlarged Tally Board with instructions of how to rig the breeches buoy lines in four languages. The idea was adopted nationally. The *Alphonse* was refloated on 12 February.

Bessheim

On 18 November 1916, a south-easterly gale, with heavy rain and sleet, had been raging for a number of days and had caused considerable damage both on land and at sea. The sea conditions at the entrance to the harbour were so bad that both pier lighthouses were, at times, completely obscured by spray and breaking seas.

The Fred Olsen Line mailboat, *Bessheim,* which provided a scheduled service between Newcastle and Oslo, had already delayed her sailing by 24 hours due to the prevailing conditions. However, on Sunday 19 November, the captain decided to set sail with 88 passengers and a crew of 33. The passenger list included two shipwrecked crews who were returning home.

While the passengers were preparing for breakfast, the *Bessheim* dropped her river pilot next to the Groyne light at about 8am and met the full fury of the gale. With the Black Middens to port, the *Bessheim* reached the pier ends, when her propeller shaft broke. At the mercy of the oncoming seas against her starboard bow, she was soon turned round and driven onto the Black Middens, below the Tynemouth Volunteer Life Brigade Watch House.

The Tyne pilots in their watch house on the Lawe Top had watched the drama unfold, and were on their way to the lifeboat houses before the signal guns were fired. Within minutes, the *Tom Perry,* under the command of Coxswain James Marvin*,* had launched from the Pilot Jetty boathouse, soon followed by the *Bedford*, Coxswain John Whale in command, from the Coble Landing boathouse. Tynemouth RNLI's motor lifeboat *Henry Vernon* under Coxswain Robert Smith, launched at 8.30am and the Tynemouth Volunteer Life Brigade mustered and set up the rocket apparatus on shore.

Battling the heavy seas, the two rowing lifeboats slowly made their way towards the *Bessheim* half a mile away. The *Henry Vernon* overtook them and reached the stranded ship at 8.40am. However, with the tide having just turned after low water, there was insufficient water for the *Henry Vernon,* with her draught of 3ft., to get over the Black Middens and alongside the *Bessheim*.

While the motor lifeboat lay off, the *Tom Perry*, with a draught of only 1ft., rowed through a gully between the rocky outcrops known as Sandy Goit and reached the ship's storm ladder which had been rigged on the lee of the mailboat. 16 passengers were lowered into the lifeboat, which transferred them to the *Henry Vernon.*

By this time, the tide had risen sufficiently to allow the larger and more powerful motor lifeboat to get alongside, and the *Henry Vernon*, with the 16 rescued passengers on board, took onboard a further 32 passengers and landed them at North Shields Fish Quay. She returned two more times to the wreck, taking off 34 and 36 passengers and crew with each trip. All passengers and crew were cared for at the Sailor's Home at North Shields, where they were given dry clothing and a hot meal.

Author's collection

s/s Bessheim" Fred Olsen Line, Oslo-Newcastle

The single screw steamer Bessheim.

Tynemouth Volunteer Life Brigade successfully fired a rocket over the wreck and, using the breeches buoy, took off three crew.

In view of the tensions between the local and national lifeboats on the river, the station records of the Tynemouth RNLI Lifeboat Station give an interesting account of the wreck service,

Weather being very heavy, Coxswain R. Smith mustered crew for watch at 7.30am. SS Bessheim of Christiania going out became unmanageable between the piers at the mouth of the Tyne, and drifted on to Black Middens about 8.30am. The guns had just been fired. The lifeboat seeing impending disaster had already started and was on the spot when the Bessheim struck. She went alongside between rocks and ship and brought off 48 persons – all passengers and stewardesses; second trip she brought about 34; and third trip about 36, including all the remaining ship's company. On returning from the first trip, the boat touched the rocks two or three times, but does not appear to be seriously damaged, although it will be advisable for her to be examined at an early date. <u>Note</u>: The lifeboat 'Harry Reynolds' of South Shields, having been towed down by the pilot cutter, brought ashore 16 men after 'Vernon's' second trip. No headway whatever could be made by the other S. Shields lifeboat. The Volunteer Life Brigade landed 3 by rocket apparatus. The boat returned to the Fish Dock at 11.00 am.

It is not known why the station log refers to the South Shields lifeboat as *Harry Reynolds*.

While the passengers and crew of the *Bessheim* were being saved, ten miles up the coast at Blyth, the steamship *Muristan* had gone ashore, her steering gear having failed in the heavy seas. The local pulling and sailing lifeboat could not assist and the Blyth Volunteer Life Brigade had fired a number of rockets over the wreck, but without any success. A message was sent to Tynemouth requesting the assistance of the motor lifeboat. The *Henry Vernon* launched at 7.30am on 20 November. She was unable to leave the harbour and sheltered in the lee of the North Pier until 9am when she left the harbour during a lull in the storm.

At the wreck, only the bridge and chart room could be seen. Seas were constantly sweeping over the wreck, and the debris surrounding it prevented the lifeboat from going any closer. Coxswain Smith decided to return to the Tyne, but soon the boat was swamped and the engine stopped. It could not be restarted, so the sails were set and the *Henry Vernon* made for Blyth, entering the harbour at noon.

With the help of the local naval station, the engine was stripped down overnight and repaired. The coastguard had observed that there were survivors on the wreck, and the lifeboat left the harbour at first light in improving conditions on 21 November and rescued 16 crew. She landed them at Blyth and arrived back at North Shields at 10.30am.

RNLI Archive

Tynemouth's 40ft. self-righting motor lifeboat Henry Vernon, built in 1911, at a cost of £3,664. With a single petrol engine, she had a speed of 7.5 knots. Stationed at Tynemouth between 1911 and 1918, she was replaced by the Henry Frederick Swan, a boat of the same class, and restored by the North East Maritime Trust at their South Shields boatyard 2010.

Both these rescues highlighted the power and endurance of the motor lifeboat over the rowing lifeboats. Coxswain Smith and Second Coxswain Brownlee were awarded the RNLI Silver Medal for the rescue of the crew of the *Muristan*, and each was awarded The RNLI's thanks on vellum for the *Bessheim* service.

Linerton

During the weekend of 8 and 9 November, 1919, an easterly force eight gale with snow showers had been blowing for a number of days and a bad weather watch was being kept at the South Shields Volunteer Life Brigade Watch House. On the morning of Sunday 9, the steamship *Linerton,* on her maiden voyage from the Humber to the Tyne to load a cargo of coal was seen riding out the storm. She had developed engine problems off Flamborough Head and the Tyne tugs *George V* and *Conqueror* sailed

South Shields VLB Archive

Within the photo:
LINERTON, OF NEWCASTLE.
9TH NOV. 1919.
IN FOREGROUND REMAINS OF
" CONSTANCE ELLEN "
12TH NOV. 1901.

The Linerton, and the remains of the Constance Ellen.

South Tyneside Libraries

The Linerton, her back broken on the Herd Sands.

south and towed her to the Tyne where she anchored a mile off the piers.

At about 6pm on Sunday, her two anchor cables parted and she came ashore on the Herd Sand about 200 yards south of the South Pier. From their Watch House, the Volunteer Life Brigadesmen could see the lights of the *Linerton* slowly coming towards them and immediately dragged the rocket apparatus down onto the beach. The *Linerton* struck with her head to the south and, with heavy seas washing over her, rocking her on her keel. She soon broke her back. The first rockets were fired just as she came ashore, but the force of the gale blew them back onshore. Several unsuccessful attempts were made to get a line aboard. The *Willie Wouldhave* was brought onto the beach, and launched with Coxswain John Whale in command. The ferocity of the seas broke a number of port side oars, and the *Willie Wouldhave* was forced back onto the beach, narrowly missing the timbers of the *Constance Ellen*, which had come ashore in 1901.

With the help of pilots and Brigadesmen, the *Willie Wouldhave* got away again and her crew managed to reach the starboard, leeside, of the *Linerton*, where she took off 24 crew. She was constantly filled by the breakers as she surfed back towards the beach. While the rescued crew were taken to the Watch House, the *Willie Wouldhave* re-launched and took off the remaining 21 crew. This was the last service call for the 41-year-old *Willie Wouldhave*. Although the crew of the Tynemouth lifeboat *Henry Frederick Swan* had assembled on bad weather watch at 4pm, their services were not required.

The last launch

The *Bedford*, now motorised, performed the last service launch of a Tyne Lifeboat Society boat on 17 November 1937, during a south easterly gale, with a heavy swell running, when she stood by the small coaster *Torborg 1* and the three-masted schooner *Orion*.

The *Torborg 1*, based in Norway, was in ballast. Having suffered engine failure she had been drifting northwards towards Newbiggin when the North Shields trawler *Copieux* had managed to connect a towline and slowly brought her towards the Tyne. At 12.30pm she anchored one mile off Brown's Point, Cullercoats and the coastguard alerted Tynemouth Lifeboat Station. At 3.45pm she was taken in tow by the tug, *Hendon*. Entering the harbour at low tide, at around 8.40pm, the tow snapped and the *Torborg 1* began drifting towards the North Pier and into Prior's Haven. Immediately dropping her anchors to halt her progress, she became stranded in the shallows off the Haven and her master radioed the coastguard to place a lifeboat on standby.

The *Hendon* could not reconnect the tow, but the paddle tug *Corsair*, with a much shallower draught ran her counter stern into the *Torborg 1* and got a line onboard. On the rising tide she towed her into deep water and safety. The *Hendon* took the towrope, and with the *Corsair* at the after end, towed her to Middle Docks.

The Tynemouth motor lifeboat *Henry Frederick Swan* launched at 9.20pm, reaching the *Torborg 1* ten minutes later. Together with the *Bedford*, with Coxswain John Whale in command, she stood by the vessel until she refloated and was towed up river.

While the *Torborg 1* was entering the harbour, the schooner *Orion,* was being towed into the river by the tug *Plover*. When the tow line parted, she drifted and ran onto a sandbank off the Lloyds Hailing Station, within yards of the North Shields lifeboat station, and directly opposite the Pilot Jetty boathouse.

The tug *Joffre* fired a rocket line onto the schooner, and brought her off the sandbank. The *Bedford* launched to the aid of the *Orion* from the Pilot Jetty boathouse but her services were not required.

The decline in the number of launches

The construction of the piers and the dredging of the harbour mouth had removed the dangers to shipping that had led to the establishment of the first lifeboat and created a safe harbour that enclosed the previous operating area of the old rowing lifeboats in and around the Black Middens, Tynemouth Bar and Herd Sands.

The Volunteer Life Brigades also contributed to the reduction in the number of effective services undertaken by both the local and national lifeboats on the river because they were able to rescue crews by breeches buoy.

Following the completion of the piers during the early 1900s, this trend became more noticeable. There was also a reduction in the number of calls to the Volunteer Life Brigades.

Between the 1860s and 1890s, the local independent lifeboats launched, on average, ten to 12 times each year. These calls were spread equally on either side of the new year. After 1901, the boats were launched on only three or four occasions each year. After 1905 they were in competition with the Tynemouth motor lifeboat.

Before the construction of the piers, vessels entering the river were, if the wind was from the east, at the mercy of the elements. The service records for 1854, the year pier construction commenced, illustrate the type of incidents the boats were responding to:

Jan. 4

A tremendous storm from ESE. Loss of schooner *Eliza*, of Kirkwall, and her nine crew, upon Tynemouth rocks. The following vessels were driven ashore upon the rocks: – The brig *Elizabeth,* laden with salt; the barque *Euretta,* light; the brig *Antelope,* light; the brig *Arethusa,* of Blyth; the brig *Anns* and the brig *New Messenger* (both coal laden); the barque *Sir Robert Peel*, laden with saltpetre and about a ton of silver; the brig *Amphitrite*, coal laden; the brigantine *Nerio* of London, and brigs *Harmony* of Blyth, *Amy* and *Elizabeth* of Shields, all wrecked at the mouth of the Tyne. Crews all saved by the rocket apparatus. Over 30 wrecks on the Herd Sand and Black Middens.

Jan. 5

6.30pm. The brig *Hannah* of Whitby went ashore on the Black Middens. The lifeboats went to the assistance of the crew, but did not get them out until after 10pm, with the loss of one of the crew.

Jan. 7

The Pilot steamer picked up the schooner *Minerva,* of Whitby, riding off Souter abandoned, and towed her in.

Jan. 8

Sunday. Eleven ships were driven onto the Herd Sand between 9pm and 2am, the barque *Aurora* of Sunderland (ballast); brig *Ann*, of Lynn; brig *Jean*, of Inverness; brig *Breakwater* of Shields; brig *Conference* of Shields; schooner *George* of Whitby; brig *Armida* of Stettin; barque *Sarah Midge*; schooner *Cresswell* of Colchester; brig *Jane and Margaret* of Newcastle; schooner *James and Ann,* of Ipswich, French vessel *Bon Virgine.*

The lifeboats, *Northumberland, Tyne* and *Providence* returned to their boathouses by 3am having rescued 87 seamen.

Jan. 9

The brig *Lively* of North Shields, billy boy *Happy Return* of Goole, brig *Savannah* of Lynn, the *Junius,* of Christiansand, and the *Ocean* of Goole, were wrecked on the Herd Sand.

Jan. 10

During the week's gale, 35 vessels were wrecked or stranded at the mouth of the Tyne, 31 at Sunderland and 44 at Hartlepool and the Tees, and there were 110 wrecks on the coast within 30 miles north and south of the Tyne.

Oct. 17

Gale from NE A brig drove upon Whitley Sands. Crew saved.

Nov. 15

The Prussian Schooner *Napoleon III,* the brig *Lively*, of Lynn, laden with wheat, and the brigantine *Mary Robertson*, of South Shields, were driven upon the rocks. Crews saved by the lifeboats and the rocket apparatus. 12 vessels ashore at Sunderland, 9 Shields ships wrecked.

In comparison, service records for 1909, following the completion of the piers, illustrate the decline in the number of incidents.

Jan. 25

8.10pm. In dense fog, the SS *Elleray* and SS *Tees* collided. The Tynemouth motor lifeboat *J. McConnell Hussey,* the South Shields lifeboat *Tom Perry,* and North Shields lifeboat, *James Young* all launched, but their services were not required.

Feb. 5

A sudden NE gale caught out local fishing cobles. With so many of the lifeboat crew at sea in their cobles, Cullercoats lifeboat was unable to launch. The *J. McConnell Hussey,* launched at 6am and escorted one coble over Tynemouth Bar and the remainder back to Cullercoats Harbour.

Mar. 3

The South Shields lifeboat *Tom Perry* launched to a false alarm.

June 3

NE gale and heavy seas prevented two fishing cobles from South Shields, with six persons on board, crossing the bar. The *J. McConnell Hussey* launched at 3pm and towed both boats back to their moorings.

July 3

The *James Young* launched to the fishing boat *Nellie* observed to be in danger.

Aug. 31

9am. In a freshening NE breeze, the *J. McConnell Hussey* launched to a fishing coble, with a crew of two, which had been salmon fishing and had lost its oars and had to anchor, towing the boat into the harbour.

Oct. 25

The *Tom Perry* launched to a Hopper Barge in danger of stranding on the South Pier.

During the years from the turn of the century up to the start of the First World War, the boats launched 24 times, with no launches in 1906. During the war years, the boats launched six times in both 1914 and 1915, four times during 1916, twice in 1917 and three times in 1918.

A letter from the Secretary of the Tyne Lifeboat Society to the Tyne Improvement Commissioners, in February 1916, acknowledged that it was only on very rare occasions that the lifeboats were required to go outside of the piers.

The calls declined further after the war with two calls in 1919. There would appear to have been no service launches during the 1920s, and in the 1930s there were only three services, two of these performed by the motorised *Bedford.* The services of the *Willie Wouldhave,* based in the South Beach boathouse, were only required on three occasions between 1897 and its last call in 1919, although the boat's last two services to the *Alphonse*, in 1910 and the *Linerton*, in 1919, saved 29 and 45 lives respectively.

With the completion of the Tyne Piers in 1909 and the removal of the Herd Sand and bar, the entrance to the Tyne was a much safer proposition. This, together with the decline in the number of sailing ships entering the port and the increasing number of safer steamships led to a reduction in the number of wrecks within the harbour.

On 13 February 1937, the *Bedford* launched under the command of John Whale to a vessel ashore on St Mary's Island, some six miles to the north. When the *Bedford* arrived, the vessel had refloated itself. This incident could have been dealt with by the motor lifeboats at the nearer RNLI stations at Blyth and Cullercoats but they did not launch.

There was also a change in the type of calls with fewer services required within the harbour and more calls to vessels outside the pier entrance. Because of the longer distances involved, these were better dealt with by the Tynemouth motor lifeboat, which had proved its technical superiority and endurance during the rescues of the *Rohilla* and *Muristan*. Even when the Tyne Lifeboat Society boats launched to calls within the harbour, to steamships which had collided or grounded in fog, their services were not required and they invariably stood by waiting for the vessels to refloat.

Author's collection

The South Beach lifeboat Willie Wouldhave, left, and North Shields lifeboat, James Young. The subtle differences in the design of the two boats can be seen in the raked bow on the longer James Young. In the foreground is the Society's 'Mascot' boat, a scaled version of the larger lifeboats, used for display purposes.

16 The Tyne Lifeboats and the RNLI

The Royal National Institution for the Preservation of Life from Shipwreck (RNIPLS) was founded by Sir William Hillary on March 4, 1824, and operated in parallel with many of the 50 or so local independent lifeboat stations and district lifeboat associations that had been established during the preceding 35 years.

Thomas Wilson, the first chairman, began the task of creating a single national lifeboat service, but received a poor response when he wrote to all independent lifeboat associations inviting them to join. The Tyne Lifeboat Institution declined as they had successfully managed their own affairs since 1789 and saw no advantage in relinquishing their independence.

However, emerging as part of this new organisation, the Newcastle District Shipwreck Association was formed in December 1824. It comprised the Tyne Lifeboat Institution, the Crewe Trustees, Newcastle Trinity House and other local lifeboat stations, at Boulmer and Blyth, co-operating under the Presidency of the 3rd Duke of Northumberland, but remaining independent of the RNIPLS.

Following the wreck of the *Original,* in January 1830, a shortage of shipping dues arising from a trade recession delayed the construction of a replacement lifeboat until 1833 when the *Tyne* was built. Because of this delay, the Newcastle Shipwreck Association contacted the RNIPLS on September 10, 1832, requesting that a lifeboat be placed at the mouth of the Tyne. The RNIPLS agreed to send a 26-foot, six oared, 'Palmer' type lifeboat. The Trustees of the Port of Tyne Lifeboat Fund contributed towards the cost of £60. The Committee for the Port of Newcastle Lifeboat Institution was responsible for the management of the boat, which was kept in a new boathouse built at Prior's Haven, Tynemouth. It arrived there on October 22, 1832.

The new lifeboat was taken out on trial in a strong NNE wind and high sea. Her four crew wore Lieut. Kennedy's calico life preserving jackets. Her stability under sail was much greater than anticipated, which inspired confidence. After performing a number of sailing manoeuvres, the sea overwhelmed and capsized the boat so the four crew members climbed onto the upturned hull. The heavy seas washed the crew off the boat but their lifejackets kept them buoyant until they were rescued by four South Shields pilots who launched their large coble from the Haven as soon as they saw the lifeboat capsize. The capsize was also witnessed by pilots from the Lawe Top, South Shields, who crossed the river and launched the North Shields lifeboat, *Northumberland.* The *Northumberland Advertiser* reported on the new lifeboat's first outing and described this small lifeboat as resembling a south sea whale boat, but fitted with canvas air cases, a suggestion made by Mr George Palmer, Chairman of the

Shipowners' Society. The article said that local pilots, accustomed to their own cobles, and familiar with the safety and speed of lifeboats recently built in South Shields for Cromer and Bamburgh Castle, considered this new lifeboat to be so dangerous and frail that they would not want to use her.

The capsized lifeboat was eventually washed on shore without much damage, and was taken back to Prior's Haven. This lifeboat was never named. When she capsized again on service in 1842, she was damaged beyond repair and scrapped and the station was closed.

The various Committees of the Newcastle District Shipwreck Association co-operated until 1845, but after that their loose association fell apart. The RNIPLS took over the running of the majority of the local Committees and their lifeboat stations, with the exception of the Tyne Lifeboat Institution.

A period of national economic collapse led to a shortage of funds and a loss of confidence around the coast regarding the effectiveness of the RNIPLS. This in turn led to a short-lived resurgence of independent lifeboat stations. By 1850, the RNIPLS income was only £355, and its future was very much in doubt. That same year, harbour dues received at the Customs House for the running of the Tyne Lifeboat Institution amounted to £245, with, in the mid-1840s, annual receipts of £300 and £340. The local independent lifeboat institution, being in a stronger financial position than the national institution, saw no advantage in being absorbed into the RNIPLS.

Following the 1849 lifeboat disaster public sympathy led to the national institution receiving a much needed influx of funds. The 4th Duke of Northumberland took the initiative to restructure the national institution into an effective and stronger organisation.

In November 1851, the Duke proposed a national design competition to create a better and safer lifeboat. In 1854, the RNIPLS became the Royal National Lifeboat Institution. The expansion of the national institution accelerated, with the majority of the district associations and independent lifeboat stations being amalgamated and incorporated into the RNLI by the 1870s.

The only independent lifeboat service that did not come under RNLI control was the Tyne Lifeboat Institution. This led to a hardening of attitudes when the RNLI came to deal with matters relating to their station at Tynemouth and the Tyne Lifeboat Institution in future years.

The last major associations were incorporated into the RNLI in 1894, with the Mersey Docks and Harbour Board, the Humber Conservancy Board in 1911, and the Aberdeen Harbour Commissioners' lifeboats in 1925.

On 26 June 1851, the National Lifeboat Institution, following a meeting chaired by the Duke of Northumberland, awarded Silver medals to the Tyne Pilots, Jacob Harrison, John Burn snr, Joseph Smith and John Milburn, for the 'intrepid and successful exertions of the Pilots of the Tyne during the past nine years in saving lives from shipwreck.' The medals, recommended by the Treasurer of the Tyne Shipwreck Association, were awarded to the pilots who had gone off in the lifeboat 48, 25, 22 and 16 times respectively.

Over a two-year period the RNIPLS carried out a series of trials aimed at convincing the Shields pilots of the superior merits of the new standard design self-righting lifeboats, with the aim of incorporating the Tyne Lifeboat Institution into the RNIPLS.

In 1852, four self-righting 'Peake' lifeboats, 27ft. by 7ft., rowing ten oars, and intended for use on the Northumberland coast were sent to South Shields for trials by the local pilots that normally crewed the local institution boats. The pilots unanimously disapproved of these self-righting boats, stating that they were too light, not full enough at the bows, and unable to carry both their crew and those rescued. They preferred the original type that was best suited to working in the surf on the Herd Sand and notorious Tynemouth Bar.

The Tyne Lifeboat Institution resisted a further request to become a part of the RNLI in March 1854, on the grounds that their boats were better suited for the conditions at the river mouth. They had operated a successful service since 1790 and had the financial resources to continue doing so.

On 9 October 1854, the *Newcastle Journal* reported on the trial of the self-righting powers of the new lifeboat for Newbiggin, presented by the Duke of Northumberland, that took place in Shields Harbour. Captain Washington, a member of both the 1851 National Lifeboat Competition Committee and the RNIPLS Committee of Management, supervised the trial from the deck of the naval steam tug *Lightening* at the Low Lights. With the aid of tackle and rope, the lifeboat was hoisted up a short distance, keel upwards, and in this position was suddenly dropped into the river whereupon she righted herself. The trial was repeated five or six times.

In terms of lifeboat design, the RNLI considered that their self-righting lifeboat was far superior to the surf lifeboats of the Tyne Lifeboat Institution. A lecture given by Captain J.R. Ward, Chief Inspector of Lifeboats, on 17 January 1862 at the Royal United Service Institution, London, extolled the virtues of the standard self-righting lifeboat and reviewed existing lifeboat types of that era.

Ward commented that the North-Country (Greathead-style) boats had undoubted advantages: they were stable, could turn more quickly, and could run more safely before a surf than a straight-keeled sharp-bowed vessel. However these features made them slower and caused them to steer wildly.

Rowed by between eight and 12 oars, double banked they had no sails as their great curvature of keel made them unsuitable for sailing. The boatmen preferred to steer them with two long oars at the stern, as they could turn a boat much more quickly to meet a sea than with a rudder, so there were no rudders either. Despite their great stability, several of these boats had capsized with the loss of many lives, and they shipped much more sea than a self-righting lifeboat.

Ward believed that lateral stability in a lifeboat was essential:

Great breadth of beam in proportion to length is a certain mode of securing great stability, but it adds to weight, above the centre of buoyancy, and by increasing the area of the midship section would entail a loss of speed that would require a greater propelling power.

The standard self-righting lifeboat ultimately adopted by the RNLI had been designed to operate in all sea conditions, with a greater range and using a smaller crew. The Tyne surf lifeboats had been designed solely to operate in the specific conditions experienced at the mouth of the river. Crews at Redcar and Cromer also preferred this type of lifeboat. However, it is also understandable why the North-Country type lifeboat proved to be unpopular with crews at other locations around the coast, where, essentially, the boats were being used in the wrong operating conditions.

It is also interesting to note a report in the *Lifeboat Journal* dated January 1863, regarding the re-establishment of Tynemouth Lifeboat Station. It stated:

As the neighbouring life-boats at North and South Shields, provided and supported by a local lifeboat society, are on the old north country, or 'Greathead' plan, an opportunity will no doubt long be afforded for testing the comparative qualities of the two descriptions of boats, as no winter passes by without the occurrence of wrecks on the Herd Sands and the shore contiguous to our great coal port.

Following the re-establishment of Tynemouth lifeboat station, both the Tyne Lifeboat Institution and RNLI boats worked in conjunction on many occasions during wreck services. However, the relationship between the two organisations was not a cordial one. In March 1861, the Tyne Lifeboat Institution had objected, to the re-establishment of this station, albeit unsuccessfully, and an account in the Tyne Lifeboat Institution service records for 1865 makes an astonishing allegation concerning the conduct of the coxswain and crew of the Tynemouth Lifeboat *Constance*.

During the late afternoon of 29 December 1865, a southerly gale was blowing and the brigs *Lewis* and *Union,* together with the barque *Wynyard,* were off the river entrance. The *Wynyard* and *Lewis* were under tow, the *Union* under canvas. The *Lewis* was the first to enter, but the force of the storm parted the tow and she grounded on the northern extent of the Black Middens, the Spar Hawk rocks. Soon afterwards the *Wynyard* grounded on the eastern end of the Spar Hawk, and the *Union* came to grief nearby on the Black Middens. The pilots in their lookout had seen the three ships in difficulties, and the lifeboat *Tyne* launched immediately, soon followed by the salvage boat *William Wake*. The signal guns had also been fired resulting in the Tynemouth lifeboat launching, and Tynemouth Volunteer Life Brigade firing a number of lines across the ships.

The *William Wake* was the first boat to get alongside the *Lewis* and secure lines, but a heavy sea broke the lines and forced her away. The *Tyne* then ran alongside and rescued the 11 crew. The *Tyne* returned ashore with the crew of the *Lewis* but the service record states that the *Constance*, for whatever reason, made no attempts to rescue the crews from the other two ships. The *William Wake* had to rescue the crew from the *Wynyard*. The *Tyne* returned to the harbour and hailed the *Constance* to take off the crew of the *Union*, but the log states that this request was ignored. The *Tyne* then proceeded to rescue the ten crew and landed them at Prior's Haven, in front of the RNLI boathouse.

The Trustees of the Tyne Lifeboat Institution decided to award the crew of the *William Wake* the same payment they gave to their lifeboat crews.

In the teeth of a gale on a dark winter's evening, the *Constance* could have failed to hear the request from the crew of the *Tyne* but the incident was an indication that the two organisations would not cooperate in future years.

The loss of two crew members from the *Northumberland* in December 1872, going to the aid of the *Gleaner*, gave the RNLI another opportunity to seek the incorporation of the Tyne Lifeboat Institution. The *South Shields Gazette* reported that Richard Lewis, Secretary of the RNLI, announced a subscription of 100 guineas to the dependents' fund and offered to place a 40ft. self-righting lifeboat at Shields. While RNLI records confirm the donation, there is no reference to the placement of a boat. The staunch independence of the local institution prevailed, and no subsequent offer, if made, was taken up.

The RNLI's Cromer type lifeboat

Before the adoption of a standard lifeboat design in 1852, lifeboats were of different local designs that suited the conditions of the particular area of coast they served. In addition to the North-Country lifeboats, the Norfolk and Suffolk beachmen had their own sailing lifeboat based upon their beach yawls, and the Mersey Docks and Harbour Board operated a modified Mersey Gig.

The first lifeboat at Cromer was built by Henry Greathead in 1805, and was 25ft. long, 8ft. 6in. wide with ten oars. This boat operated for 25 years before being transferred to Wells-next–the-Sea, where it served until 1850. The second Cromer boat, of a similar design, was a larger 12-oared boat, 31ft. by 9ft. 6in., built in 1830 by Robsons of South Shields, serving the station until 1858.

When the RNLI took over the running of the station in 1858, a standard self-righting boat was sent. However many of the crew considered that a self-righting boat did

Randall-Salter Lantern Collection

The Cromer Lifeboat Benjamin Bond Cabbell, 1884-1902. This boat shows similar lines to the later boats of the Tyne Lifeboat Institution.

not suit the local conditions and, in 1884, petitioned for a longer and more manoeuvrable boat, with a greater curvature of keel that could operate in the surf conditions experienced along the shore and nearby sandbanks of the north Norfolk coastline. The Cromer fishermen requested a boat similar in design to the Greathead boat of 1804.

This boat, the *Benjamin Bond Cabbell*, arrived at Cromer in September 1884, and was 35ft. in length, 10ft. 6in. in width, with an inside depth of 4ft. She was clinker

Paul Russell, Cromer Lifeboat Station

The 1830 Cromer Lifeboat. The similarities between this boat and the Tyne Lifeboat Institution boats are self-evident.

built, rowed 14 oars, double banked and was steered by either a retractable rudder or sweep oars. There was a self-draining system, air cases around the sides of the boat between the thwarts and deck and a water ballast tank. In appearance it was not dissimilar to the later boats of the Tyne Lifeboat Institution, the main difference between the two designs being that the Cromer boat could sail and was fitted with a mast and dipping lugsail rig. This boat served at Cromer until 1901. While popular with the Cromer crews, only three boats of this type were built, all stationed on the north Norfolk coast. The *Baltic* at Wells, 1895-1913, and the *Zaccheus Burroughes* at Blakeney, 1891-1908.

Difficulties at Tynemouth Lifeboat Station

Tynemouth Lifeboat Station had, for a number of years, been experiencing difficulties in launching and recovering the rowing lifeboats stationed at Priors Haven (No. 1 Station) and the Black Middens (No. 2 Station). The No. 1 boat could not launch 90 minutes, and the No. 2 boat, three hours, either side of low water, although the No. 2 boat, when it did launch, could do so between ten and 15 minutes from the signal gun first going off.

In some instances, the boats could not be re-housed and had to be moored at North Shields fish quay. The Tyne Lifeboat Institution's boats had no such problems and were able to launch and reach wrecks far more quickly than the RNLI boats.

Extracts from the Tynemouth Lifeboat Station launching records not only illustrate the operational difficulties but also provide an insight into the relationship between the RNLI and Tyne Lifeboat Institution.

The No. 1 station boat, *Charles Dibdin*, launched on 7 February 1883 to the brig *Hannah*, which had been driven ashore in a south-easterly gale, onto the rubble foundations of the partially built North Pier, a short distance from the No. 1 lifeboat house. Despite the lifeboat launching within 15 minutes of the call, at dead low water, and traversing over 600 yards of soft sand, the local lifeboat *Willie Wouldhave*, which was afloat and towed from North Shields by a steam tug to the broken water, arrived alongside the *Hannah* a few seconds before the *Charles Dibdin*. The *Hannah*'s crew elected to go in the *Willie Wouldhave* rather than the RNLI boat or be taken ashore in the Tynemouth Volunteer Life Brigade breeches buoy. However, a number of the *Charles Dibdin*'s crew went on board the brig, after the crew had left, released the rocket hawser line, and let go the anchors in order that there might be a chance of saving the vessel.

There were occasions when the Tynemouth lifeboat did reach the casualty before the local Institution boats. On 25 May 1891, the steamer *Napier*, entering the harbour during a north easterly gale, ran onto the Black Middens, off Freestone Point, and approximately 200 yards from the No. 2 boathouse. The signal guns on *HMS Castor* fired, and three lifeboats launched, the *Forester* from Tynemouth, the *Bedford* from

South Shields and the *James Young* from North Shields. The *Forester* launched at 12.45pm and was first alongside at 12.55pm. The master of the *Napier* requested that the lifeboat remain alongside until his ship was towed clear of the rocks. Six tugs came to the assistance of the wreck, with a seventh towing both of the Shields lifeboats into the harbour. At 1.20pm, the *Napier* was successfully refloated, with the lifeboats standing by during this operation.

With a north-north-easterly wind and strong seas running, at 4pm on 30 June 1888, the pilots in the lookout saw the steamer *Hector*, of Sunderland, being towed into the river. When one of the towlines broke, the pilots immediately alerted Andrew Harrison, the Lifeboat Superintendent, and the *Tom Perry* was launched from the Coble Landing with a crew of 18, and towed into the harbour by the tug *Ulysses*. As this was happening, the remaining tug could not prevent the steamer from being driven onto the South Pier. The steamer had been holed and was filling rapidly on a rising tide, with seas sweeping over her.

By the time the signal guns were fired, the *Tom Perry* was already alongside the *Hector*, and took off 15 of her crew with the exception of the master and mate, who were rescued by the North Shields lifeboat *James Young*. One of the crew was rescued

Author's collection

The Tynemouth RNLI No. 1 Lifeboat Charles Dibdin launching to the Iron Crown, ashore on the Black Middens, 21 October 1881. Tynemouth Volunteer Life Brigade rescued five crew before the lifeboat got alongside and rescued the remaining 15.

by the South Shields Volunteer Life Brigade. Meanwhile, the Tynemouth No. 1 boat *Charles Dibdin* had launched from Prior's Haven at 4.05pm and arrived at the wreck ten minutes later, shortly after the crew had been taken off by the *Tom Perry*. The *Charles Dibdin* remained on scene until the master and mate had been taken off and returned to her station at 6.20pm.

The ability of the local institution boats to call upon the services of local tugs and to reach wrecks before the national institution boats, led the RNLI District Inspector, in March 1898, to approach local tug companies to seek a similar arrangement. This proved unsuccessful, the tug companies only giving an assurance that they would help when they could. This was entirely understandable, as the advantage the local institution boats had was that tugs could pick up their charges within the relative safety of the river, towing the lifeboat into the harbour before releasing them. With the RNLI boats stations adjacent to the Black Middens and pier entrance, tug skippers would have questioned the safety of towing the lifeboat the relatively short distance to the casualty, across the exposed harbour mouth where sea conditions would be at their worst.

Similar circumstances presented themselves in December 1899 when the No. 2 boat *Forester* launched to the steamer *Maltby* that had run aground on the Black Middens in a south-easterly gale. By the time the *Forester* had battled through broken water, reaching the wreck within 30 minutes of launching, the 24 crew had been rescued by the North Shields lifeboat, *James Young*, which had been kept afloat and towed to the scene by a steam tug.

It was clear that the operational organisation of the Tyne Lifeboat Institution, with a retired pilot in the Lawe Top lookout to call out the lifeboats, crews living near the boathouses and the reliable services of local tugs, resulted in much faster response times, in terms of launching and reaching ships in distress within the harbour, than could be achieved by the RNLI boats. They had to rely on the Coastguard and signal guns whose stations were a much greater distance from the homes of their crews.

Relations between the two organisations deteriorated further between September 1883 and May 1890, when the Honorary Secretary of the Tynemouth Lifeboat Station, Philip J. Messent, sent a number of letters to the Tyne Lifeboat Institution, requesting that a portion of the funds collected at the Customs Houses be handed over to the Tynemouth RNLI station. The requests were refused but Messent, and latterly E.P. Adamson of the RNLI Local Committee, continued to try despite repeated rebuffs.

It was also during this period that Messent, in his role as Pier and River Engineer, had objected to the Tyne Lifeboat Institution proposal to construct a new lifeboat house at the southern wave trap as well as dismissing the silting problems at the Coble Landing and North Shields boathouse slipways.

In May 1890, Messent again wrote to the Tyne Lifeboat Committee, referring to his

Author's collection

The Tynemouth Volunteer Life Brigade Watch House can be seen on the cliff top to the right of the boathouse.

previous correspondence regarding the equitable division of harbour dues and suggesting a meeting to discuss the matter in a friendly spirit.

The Trustees responded that they could not allow any part of their funds to go to the Royal Lifeboat Institution and could not see any advantage in meeting. If the Tyne Lifeboat Institution Trustees accepted Messent's proposal, it would have significantly reduced the financial and operational ability of the Tyne Institution and jeopardised its existence as a lifeboat service.

In October 1903, the RNLI Deputy Chief Inspector, accompanied by the district inspector, engineer and architect, visited Tynemouth to inspect the No. 1 and No. 2 Stations and investigate the operational problems being experienced. The Deputy Chief Inspector pointed out that, except when the state of tide was favourable, the North Shields lifeboats, which could launch at any state of tide and command the services of a tug nearly always cut out the RNLI boats. It was agreed that the Tynemouth Lifeboat Station should be put in a thoroughly efficient state, but to do so would be costly. They decided to close the No. 1 Station, at Prior's Haven and put the No. 2, Black Middens, Station in a position to enable the boat to launch at any state of the tide.

Newcastle Libraries

Tynemouth RNLI No. 1 boathouse showing the high and low water slipways, Prior's Haven.

This would be achieved by constructing a new boathouse and slipway near to the Black Middens, connected to the mainland by a gangway, and placing the No. 2 boat in it, and vacating the 1865 boathouse. On 10 December 1903, the Tynemouth RNLI Committee approached the Tyne Lifeboat Institution to discuss the proposed relocation of the Tynemouth station and the future of local lifeboat provision at the mouth of the Tyne. This offer was declined on 22 December.

The deterioration in relations between the two lifeboat services, and the lack of a local solution, encouraged the RNLI's Management Committee to become involved. By July 1904, the District Inspector reported that the Tynemouth Lifeboat Station Committee considered that they were not being kept informed about negotiations with what they referred to as the Tyne Lifeboat Trust. The Management Committee agreed to invite the Station Honorary Secretary to any subsequent meetings between the two organisations. By August 1904, no progress had been made and the Duke of Northumberland tried to arrange a meeting between the Tyne Lifeboat Institution and Tynemouth Local Committee for some time during the autumn.

No record exists as to whether this meeting took place. However, due to the operational problems being experienced by the RNLI, and the cost of building a new boathouse and slipway at the Black Middens, compounded by the exposed location of the boathouse and likely difficulties in re-housing a boat, it is understandable that the RNLI was exploring more cost-effective options.

Although a matter of speculation, possible options would have been the incorporation of the Tyne Lifeboat Institution into the RNLI, which would have given the RNLI access to the boathouses at North and South Shields, or the option of the RNLI coming to an agreement to run their operations from the Tyne Lifeboat Institution's North Shields boathouse, with the Tyne Lifeboat Institution operating solely from South Shields.

Had the RNLI succeeded in securing control of all of the Tyne Lifeboat Institution's boathouses, lifeboat cover as it exists today on the Tyne may well have been significantly different.

The Board of Trade case

The frequency of the approaches by the local RNLI Committee and their agenda to undermine the financial and operational existence of the local institution greatly concerned the Vice President of the Tyne Lifeboat Society, Samuel Malcolm, a founding member and Honorary Secretary of South Shields Volunteer Life Brigade. He initiated legal steps to protect the Tyne Lifeboat Institution.

At the same time as the RNLI was considering the future of the Tynemouth lifeboat station, the Tyne Lifeboat Institution applied to the Board of Trade, in August 1904, to be registered under the Companies Act 1867, as a Limited Liability Company. The RNLI became aware of this application through an advertisement published in newspapers in South Shields and Newcastle. In September 1904, the Board of Trade sought the views of the RNLI, who said that they would object to the application.

Later that same month, the Board of Trade replied to the RNLI's letter, enclosing correspondence from solicitors acting on behalf of the Tyne Lifeboat Institution. This proposed that the Tyne Lifeboat Institution was prepared to withdraw their application to be registered under the Companies Act in exchange for permission to provide lifeboats for the coast outside the Tyne piers.

The RNLI reacted strongly, seeing this as an attempt by the Tyne Lifeboat Institution to secure the closure of Tynemouth Lifeboat Station and gain control of all lifesaving activities on the Tyne. They contested the application and their legal team listed ten objections and requested that the case be heard before the President of the Board of Trade.

The hearing, held on December 13th 1904, at the Board of Trade offices in Whitehall, was presided over by W. A. Bonar Law MP, Parliamentary Secretary to the Board of Trade. It was attended by the Chairman and Members of the RNLI

Committee of Management and their legal team, and Trustees of the Tyne Lifeboat Institution, led by their vice-president, Samuel Malcolm.

The RNLI's objections related to public perception and recognition; the undermining of the RNLI as the sole national lifeboat society; the dissolution of the RNLI; conflicts in public fundraising and legacies; and financial recompense for crews.

The RNLI's action demonstrates its intent to take over sole lifesaving responsibilities on the Tyne, by denying the Tyne Lifeboat Institution any formal legal status.

Since the re-organisation of the RNLI in 1854, they had taken over 18 independent lifeboat societies comprising 58 lifeboat stations. By 1904, the only exceptions were the lifeboats operated on the Tyne and by the harbour authorities on the Humber and at Aberdeen. The RNLI did not gain control of these stations until 1911 and 1925 respectively.

The objections put forward by the RNLI, in the context of their national role, and their far superior technical expertise and resources, together with the high level of public esteem, seem to be a little contrived when bearing in mind the Tyne Lifeboat Institution's predilection for using an outdated and antiquated lifeboat design, and lack of the finances or ability to adapt to changing operational circumstances. For the RNLI to consider this small independent lifeboat service a threat to their public fundraising efforts and wrongful receipt of legacies which could lead to the undermining of the RNLI's national role and ultimately their existence is somewhat disingenuous.

Following the inquiry, solicitors acting on behalf of the Tyne Lifeboat Institution wrote to the Board of Trade on 28 December 1904, conceding one of the contested points relating to the RNLI's objections to the use of the word 'Institution'.

On January 11, 1905, the Board of Trade ruled in favour of the Tyne Lifeboat Institution and granted the Licence of Incorporation. The Board of Trade did suggest that the name be changed to the Tyne Lifeboat Society.

The RNLI wrote to the Board of Trade the following day, drawing to the Board's attention to the assurances given by the Tyne Lifeboat Institution to Bonar Law that their operations should never extend beyond the Tyne and that general appeals to the public for help should not be made, but that the arrangements in future should be precisely the same as they had been in the past.

In taking this position, the RNLI clearly recognised, unlike the local society, that the completion of the piers and removal of the Herd Sands and bar would make the harbour entrance a much safer haven, reduce the number of ships in difficulties within the harbour and create more demand for services outside the harbour, which were ill-suited to the surf boats of the local society

Furthermore, with the advent of larger steam ships carrying a greater volume of cargo, in comparison to the smaller sailing ships, there would be a reduction in the number of ships using the river and a corresponding reduction in the contributions being given at the Customs Houses to fund the independent lifeboat service.

The Board of Trade, in their response on the 16 January, duly informed the RNLI that the constitution and powers of the Tyne Lifeboat Society were now defined by their Memorandum and Articles of Association. The wording of the Articles of Association as registered on 23 February 1905, were not as explicit as the RNLI sought in restricting the local society's boats from operating only within the confines of the recently completed piers. Section (B) of the Articles of Association outlined the Tyne Society's responsibilities as being to build, equip and maintain lifeboats, transporting carriages, boat houses and slipways at or near the entrance to the River Tyne, and to carry out all other purposes incidental to the objects of saving life from shipwreck, and assisting vessels in distress, and generally to carry into effect the purposes of a Lifeboat Society.

In an article in the *South Shields Gazette*, a year before his death in March 1935, at the age of 93, Samuel Malcolm told the story of the legal battle between the RNLI and Tyne Lifeboat Institution:

> *I have been connected with the Lifeboat Service for more than half a century. The Tyne Lifeboat Society is the oldest in the world. It was founded in 1789. The National Society came on the scene 35 years afterwards. There was a strong desire for the National body to take charge of the lifesaving work on the Tyne that meant swallowing the existing Tyne organisation – funds and all.*

> *From the moment I joined the Lifeboat Committee, I felt that our position was not secure against attack. I likened it to a house built on sand, because we had no legal status. That same idea gradually permeated the Committee, of which I was then vice-chairman, and at last, after a long lapse of time, it was decided to go for incorporation. That was in 1905.*

> *Accordingly we went through the usual process. We advertised in the London Gazette, our intention to apply for a charter. That brought the National Society to their feet in strong defiance and opposition. They made their protest through the Board of Trade, and filled, I think 13 or 14 pages of objections why we should not become an incorporated body. The Board of Trade sent the bundle of objections to us for our reply, and we categorically took up every point they raised and answered, I think, satisfactorily.*

> *The result was an inquiry was ordered at the offices of the Board of Trade. The Committee told me I must go and fight the case there and I went and took our Secretary, Mr J. Robinson and our Solicitor, Mr Chapman. Mr Bonar Law was then the Secretary of the B.O.T. and occupied the chair at the head of the table. On one side were my assistants and I – three all told. On the opposite side were fourteen representatives of the National Body, including Sir Edward Birkbeck,*

Chairman of the National Society, and Mr Charles Dibdin, Secretary, and three solicitors.

We presented our case. We fought down the objections they raised against us and we fought strenuously and came out of the ordeal with flying colours. One of their objections was that we called ourselves an Institution, and as a solatium, we gave them that. I didn't like the word Society, but we decided to adopt it. It was the only thing we did concede to them.

We got the charter and we kept our funds. If we were ever in danger of obliteration that danger was effectively and for all time exterminated when we became an incorporated body. It was a strenuous fight, but it was worth all the worry and trouble and expense it incurred.

We have £10,000 on investment and no one can touch it and we have our independence.

Samuel Malcolm stepped down as President of the Tyne Lifeboat Society in March 1916.

Despite the Tyne Lifeboat Society being successful in securing their legal status, the response of the RNLI was swift, with the first experimental motor lifeboat being reallocated from its station at Newhaven to Tynemouth.

The First RNLI motor lifeboat

The decision of the Board of Trade resulted in the RNLI resolving to reorganise their lifeboat operations at Tynemouth. What followed was ultimately one of the contributory factors that led to the demise of the Tyne Lifeboat Society.

Following the Board of Trade decision to support the now renamed Tyne Lifeboat Society, the RNLI were contemplating closing both Tynemouth stations due to the operational problems they experienced. The Chief Inspector visited the Tynemouth station on January 24, 1905 to inspect the working arrangements of the two boats, and to find out, in the event of the Committee deciding that the RNLI should still operate from the Tyne, whether better arrangements could be made for the operation of a more effective lifeboat service.

The Chief Inspector, seeing the problems of launching and recovering the No. 1 and No. 2 Station boats at dead low water spring tides for himself, supported the view of his deputy and concluded that both stations should either be closed, or radically reorganised. Although the financial cost would be large, as had been established in 1903, the construction of a new boathouse and slipway would have resolved operational difficulties.

However, there was also a problem of manning the lifeboats at their current locations. The Honorary Secretary could no longer depend on getting a crew from Tynemouth, but was obliged to fall back on the Cullercoats fishermen to supplement the crew.

The RNLI Management Committee were of the view that as the Board of Trade had granted the Licence to the Tyne Lifeboat Society they had acquitted the RNLI of all responsibility to operate their boats from Tynemouth. Knowing that the Tyne Lifeboat Society exercised little or no supervision over its antiquated and inefficient boats, whose crews receiving no training, the Committee questioned whether the RNLI could, in these circumstances, be justified in closing Tynemouth lifeboat station.

While the RNLI could have ceased operations on the Tyne altogether, this course of action would have been seen as an abrogation of their own lifesaving responsibilities given their grave concerns over the ability of the Tyne Society to operate an effective rescue service.

The result of the Chief Inspector's inspection was to recommend that the new experimental motor lifeboat, currently stationed at Newhaven, be placed on moorings at North Shields, between the Fish Quay and northern wave trap, and under the supervision of the Royal Engineers Submarine Mining Depot based in Clifford's Fort. This solution involved no great financial outlay and the Chief Inspector considered that the only drawback was the situation of the North Shields Lifeboat House and slipway alongside the Royal Engineers boathouse.

The option of stationing one of the existing rowing lifeboats, or a larger sailing lifeboat, on moorings at North Shields did not appear to have been considered.

On 25 January 1905, the Chief Inspector recommended to the RNLI Committee of Management that the new motor lifeboat would be under the supervision of the Royal Engineers, who would form the nucleus of the crew. A Royal Engineers mechanic would be appointed to look after the boat. In the short term, the station would continue to operate, with the No. 1 (Prior's Haven) boat launching only if the No. 2 (Black Middens) boat could not be launched over the foul ground beyond the slip due to the state of tide.

For agreement to have been reached so quickly indicates that discussions on the stationing and manning of the motor lifeboat must have commenced and been informally agreed while the Board of Trade case was still being heard.

On 7 February the Committee of Management decided to refer this matter and new management arrangements confidentially to the Tynemouth Station Committee, with a recommendation that the experimental motor lifeboat, currently at Newhaven, be sent to Tynemouth in the spring, and the existing stations closed. Ten days later the local station Committee unanimously accepted the Committee of Management's proposal. In November 1904, the experimental motor lifeboat had been sent to Newhaven lifeboat station for operational evaluation by the crew. So impressed were the coxswain and crew, that when they were informed of her transfer to Tynemouth, they immediately requested the RNLI to convert and install an engine into their own self-righting lifeboat, which was completed in 1905.

Following trials during 1904 in the Solent and at Newhaven, the former Folkestone lifeboat, *J. McConnell Hussey,* a converted 38ft. self-righting rowing lifeboat built in 1893, arrived at Tynemouth in May 1905. The boat had been previously brought to London and overhauled, then was transported to Tynemouth by rail. The cost of adapting and fitting the motor was £1097 11s 6d. The boat was accompanied by Mr W. French, a cycle engineer from Newhaven, who had been appointed on £5 per week, for three weeks, to give instruction in the use of the engine.

The new boat was taken out by the Chief Inspector, the engines run for a continuous ten hours, and an average speed of seven knots attained on the measured mile, both with and against the tide. Mr French was present at all times, but had little to teach Lieutenant Herbert Burton of the Royal Engineers, who was acting as Lifeboat Superintendent. Burton, a skilled engineer, experienced yachtsman and member of the Tynemouth RNLI Committee, was a strong advocate of the petrol engine and was keen to prove its worth. He had previously taken the boat out on trials soon after its arrival with crews of Royal Engineers and pilots.

The only permanent officials appointed were a bowman and caretaker (they were actually the same man) at 10s per month, and a mechanic at 15s a month. The Chief Inspector expressed his complete satisfaction in the boat.

Whether there was a reluctance from local lifeboatmen to crew the new boat, which is somewhat surprising bearing in mind the reaction of the Newhaven lifeboat crew to the re-allocation of the motor lifeboat, or the problems of finding a full crew that lived close to the new station had not been resolved, the Royal Engineers, crewed and operated the boat.

As a result, the coxswain, Thomas Smith, second coxswain, Thomas Richardson and bowman, Jacob Brunton, all resigned from the crew in July 1905 in protest. Thomas Smith had been coxswain for seven years and second coxswain for five years. Richardson had been second coxswain for seven years, and Brunton had been bowman for 12 years. Each man was awarded an annual pension by the RNLI.

The introduction of a more powerful motor lifeboat was, no doubt, a considered and calculated move by the RNLI and its Chief Inspector of Lifeboats, not only to undermine the operational effectiveness of the 'antiquated and inefficient' local society, but also to convince the traditionalist RNLI crews nationally, of the superiority of the motor lifeboat over the pulling and sailing lifeboats. Where better to illustrate this than where there was direct competition?

The manpower problems of raising a full crew at Tynemouth would have been exacerbated by relocating the lifeboat station to North Shields. The expedient solution of

RNLI Archive

The J. McConnell Hussey undergoing self-righting trials.

using military personnel as boat crew guaranteed that the motor lifeboat could be sent to the Tyne.

It was not until early 1906 that sufficient local men were recruited to form a crew. However, this was only on the basis that Lieutenant Burton remained as Honorary Superintendent. Robert 'Scraper' Smith, a member of the earlier rowing lifeboat crew and a convert to the internal combustion engine, was appointed coxswain in July 1910.

If any rescue was to prove the technical superiority of the motor lifeboat over the rowing lifeboat, it was the rescue of 50 of the crew of the hospital ship *Rohilla,* at Whitby, by the Tynemouth motor lifeboat *Henry Vernon,* on 1 November 1914. The *Henry Vernon* travelled the 44 miles in complete darkness during an easterly gale. Coxswain Smith and the now promoted Captain Burton were both awarded the Institution's Gold Medal for their part in this rescue.

With the motor lifeboat on station, rivalry between the two lifeboat services was still evident. On 21 May 1905, the *J. McConnell Hussey* launched on service to the SS *Broadmayne,* following a collision with the SS *Vauxhall,* which had sunk in the river entrance. The motor lifeboat arrived on scene and circled the wreck, observing that the ship's boats had been lowered from each of the davits. According to the service report it was surmised that the crew had left in the vessel's own boats. The report concluded that this was the first service of a motor lifeboat on the Tyne and it was interesting to note that though the Tyne lifeboat got away about eight minutes earlier than the motor lifeboat, the latter passed the former when about half way to the wreck.

However, according to the records of the Tyne Lifeboat Society, it was the North Shields lifeboat *James Young* that picked up the 17 crew from their boats, bringing them back up river when they were passed by the motor lifeboat. A newspaper report of the time stated that the *James Young*'s crew were justly proud of their accomplishment.

On 8 January 1908, the *J. McConnell Hussey* launched at 11.10pm to the steamers *Burham* and *Norfolk,* which had both run onto the Black Middens in a south-easterly gale. The 17 crew of the *Norfolk* were rescued by the South Shields lifeboat *Tom Perry* (13) and the North Shields lifeboat *James Young* (four). The Tynemouth RNLI station service log states:

The delay in getting away with the motor boat was due firstly to want of management on the part of the Coxswains in not having a foyboat in readiness for shipping the crew and secondly the very cold condition of the motor starting gear. The panels of the starting gear had to be pushed down by a rod into position on the hatcher wheel – an operation which had to be repeated several times owing to the frozen condition of the oil on the spindles. The Coxswains have only recently taken up their duties and have profited by the delay experienced with a run to accompany the steamer Burham at 1500hrs, which was out of control on the bar and in immediate danger of founding. It was interesting – and consoling to the crew- to observe the superiority of the motor boat when started under equal conditions with the Tyne lifeboat. Both boats were moored at the Fish Quay at North Shields when the alarm was given and the crews made for their respective boats at the same time. The motor boat met the Burham and accompanied her into safety before the Tyne boat got into rough water. This was the equivalent to a beating of about ½ mile in the half hour which elapsed between time of alarm and time of return of boats to moorings.

An unfortunate incident occurred in the harbour, which no doubt strained relations between the two organisations. At 8pm on Wednesday, 26 January 1909, the *James Young, Tom Perry* and *J. McConnell Hussey* all launched following a collision in dense fog between the steamships *Tees* and *Elleray*. When returning to station at 9pm, the Coxswain of the North Shields lifeboat *James Young* reported that they had been run into by the motor lifeboat, the *James Young* sustaining some damage. The Trustees of the local society later wrote to the RNLI seeking a joint meeting between respective surveyors to discuss damage and financial remuneration. A month later, a damages claim for of £2 8s and two oars was made to the RNLI.

On 12 September 1912, at 11.45pm, the steamer *Cape Colonna* was out of control

Lifeboat Saturday, Cullercoats, 23 July, 1898. Six local RNLI lifeboats can be seen in the harbour together with the North Shields lifeboat James Young, and the South Shields lifeboat, Bedford. The Cullercoats lifeboat, Co-operator No. 1, is in its boathouse.

when entering the river during a strong north-easterly breeze and heavy seas. She grounded on the Black Middens, and the *Henry Vernon* motor lifeboat left her moorings, next to the Lloyds Hailing Station and in front of the Tyne Lifeboat Society's North Shields boathouse, at midnight, with the *James Young*, and the South Shields lifeboat, *Bedford*, soon following. The *Henry Vernon* reached the wreck within 15 minutes and took off 12 of the 23 crew. The *Cape Colonna* was refloated a few hours later at high water and beached on the Herd Sands. According to the remaining service records of the local society, the *Bedford* also rescued 12 of the crew. This conflicts with the account in the Tynemouth RNLI station records.

Even by 1916, the strained relationship between the two organisations was public knowledge, and had not improved as events following the *Bessheim* rescue illustrated. In recognition of the rescue of the crew and passengers of the Norwegian mail steamer, a ceremony was held on North Shields Fish Quay for the presentation of medals from the Norwegian Government to the crews of the *Henry Vernon* and *Tom Perry*. The Mayor of Tynemouth, Mr H. Gregg, in his speech, stated that this was the first occasion on which the two lifeboat organisations had been brought closely together, and that the crews and officials of the Royal National Institution and the Tyne Lifeboat Society were, for the first time, on common ground.

The lifeboat houses of the Tyne Lifeboat Institution and RNLI were located at the head of the Northern Wavetrap. In November 1947, the RNLI built a new lifeboat station and watch house on this site. It remained operational until 1998 and the boathouse was demolished in 1999. The watch house was demolished in 2005, and in 2006 flood prevention walls were constructed and the site landscaped. All traces of lifeboat stations on this site have now disappeared.

In October 1999, Tynemouth Lifeboat Station received a £1.75 million Severn Class lifeboat. Funded by the Tynemouth Lifeboat Appeal, the name of the boat was chosen by members of the lifeboat station. In recognition of the first lifeboat stationed at North Shields, the current RNLI station being located midway between the first North Shields lifeboat house and the boathouses at the northern wavetrap, the new lifeboat was named *Spirit of Northumberland*.

Author's collection

Spirit of Northumberland at Tynemouth Lifeboat Station.

17 Tyne Lifeboat Institution finances

Before 1841, when the local South and North Shields Committees amalgamated to become the Tyne Lifeboat Institution, funding to operate the two lifeboats was obtained through donations from the Coal Trade and local ship-owners. In 1808, with a decline in this income, Nicholas Fairles, as the driving force, established a commercial lifeboat service with shipowners subscribing to the lifeboat fund or, if not, being charged if the lifeboats assisted any of their ships.

In 1840, following the *Friendship* incident, the levy, based on ship tonnage, put the finances on a more solid and organised footing, and due to the large number of ships that sailed into the Tyne, there was a rapid period of expansion with the construction of new boats and boathouses.

With, in the late 1890s, a decline in the number of sailing ships, at the expense of larger steamships, income began to decline and with four lifeboats, their boathouses, crew payments and general maintenance to fund, the Trustees of the Institution began to look at other means to raise finance.

The annual average contributions received from the Customs Houses, during the 1840s, averaged at £250, peaking in 1882 at £450, but declining in 1905 to £104 and by 1929, to £98.

To counter this drop in income, the Institution invested surplus cash and reserves into stocks and shares, using the interest on this capital to fund a revenue account. The accounts for 1883 indicate that £883 had been invested in stock, this increasing in 1892 to £2,483. Samuel Malcolm, Vice President of the Institution, in the early 1900s had took it upon himself to ensure that the Institution became financially secure with the aim of investing £10,000.

Capital was invested in National Savings Certificates, War Stock, the Newcastle and Gateshead Gas Company, South Shields Gas Company, South Shields Corporation, the Tyne Improvement Commission, Tynemouth Corporation and the South Shields Building Society. The accounts for 1929 indicate that from an invested capital of £8,111, an annual return of £355 was received.

The decline in income was certainly not lost on Messent in his attempts, during the 1880s and 90s, to assert the Tynemouth RNLI station as the sole sea rescue organisation on the Tyne. Obtaining an equal share of the Customs House income would have ultimately led to the closure of Tyne Lifeboat Institution.

The Tyne Lifeboat Institution never relied on voluntary donations or organised collections in the same way as the RNLI did in terms of fundraising, points made by the RNLI at the 1904 Board of Trade case. This decline in financial income and the failure of investments to provide sufficient income to fund the organisation severely hampered the ability of the local institution to react to the changing operational circumstances that had been created following the completion of the piers.

In August 1925, minutes recorded that the *Willie Wouldhave* hull was still in a sound condition, but required repainting and that in August 1928, the *Tom Perry*, stationed in the Pilot Jetty boathouse, was 'leaking like a sieve and unfit for service.' In 1928, the *Tom Perry* was re-conditioned at a cost of £ 76 15s 6d, with similar re-conditioning works being undertaken on the *James Young*, in 1929, at a cost of £84 5s 4d, and to the *Willie Wouldhave* at £95 13s 4d, in 1930.

The Tyne Lifeboat Society kept faith with their tried and trusted lifeboat design. Even the arrival of the first petrol driven lifeboat on the river did not provoke the Society to change their views on lifeboat design. As late as the 1920s, the Trustees considered that the surfboat design was the best suited for the conditions experienced at the mouth of the Tyne.

When the Society, in 1935, decided to embrace modern technology, their solution was to motorise the 49-year-old old *Bedford,* which was not without local controversy. Supporters of motorisation argued for technological change, citing the fitness and availability of finding a crew. On one occasion, they stated the crew, because they were unfit, could not propel the boat against wind or tide. Whilst the conversion of an existing boat, the approach the RNLI took in 1904, was understandable, the conversion of the *Bedford* in the context of the advances in motor lifeboat design undertaken by the RNLI during the 1920s and 1930s illustrates a somewhat conservative attitude, and an unwillingness to change, no doubt dictated by the lack of sufficient financial resources, more so when the RNLI's smallest single screw motor lifeboats, the 32 feet surf light motor, cost £3,200 in 1935.

18 The Tyne Lifeboat Society today

The Tyne Lifeboat Society, a registered charity, is still in existence today, its prime function the distribution of funds to local maritime based charities on Tyneside. There are three officers, a Chairman, Vice-Chairman, and Company Secretary, together with six Trustees who meet annually to decide and distribute donations to local maritime causes. The finance first invested in Victorian times is used today in maintaining the aims of the Tyne Lifeboat Society, with annual donations totaling £1,000 being distributed to the South Shields and Tynemouth Volunteer Life Brigades, the Red Seal Maritime Emergency Unit based at Tynemouth, Volunteer Beach Lifeguards and local Sea Cadet and Sea Scout Units.

Looking Back

The creation and establishment of the first purpose designed lifeboat and lifeboat service on the Tyne arose after a number of South Shields ship owners and businessmen became concerned about the frequent and constant loss of life and property from shipwrecks at the mouth of the Tyne.

Although the result of the Lawe House competition was inconclusive, it was the subsequent drive of Nicholas Fairles that led to a boat being built by Henry Greathead. Greathead saw an opportunity to promote his boat building business, and in securing Parliamentary approval, through a campaign that was less than objective, and being known as the 'Inventor of the Lifeboat' he achieved financial reward.

What was lost in these campaigns, though he appears to have taken an extremely modest view of his actions, was Fairles's pivotal role, and a comparison between the Greathead and Wouldhave competition submissions illustrates that the *Original's* final form bore little resemblance to the ideas of either of these men.

Furthermore, the role of Fairles in taking the responsibility and initiative, in 1808, of putting the organisation and management of the lifeboat on a formal basis should not be underestimated. This ensured the continued future of the South Shields lifeboat station

The demise of the Tyne Lifeboat Institution was due to a number of factors. The completion of the piers, the removal of the Herd Sand and Tynemouth Bar, and the dredging of the river channel created a safe harbour that removed the treacherous sea conditions that had first led to the need for a lifeboat.

Whilst the Volunteer Life Brigades contributed towards a reduction in the number of effective services of the lifeboats, the Brigades, following the construction of the piers, also experienced a reduction in service calls.

The role of the RNLI cannot be ignored. Attempts to take over the local institution were repeatedly rebuffed and, ironically, it was the Board of Trade case in 1904 (though won by the Tyne Lifeboat Society) that sealed the operational fate of the surf rowing boats, with the first motor lifeboat being sent to Tynemouth.

The RNLI's decision to replace their two rowing lifeboats with a motor lifeboat, resolved a number of issues. It would immediately make the surf lifeboats on the river obsolete and prove the technological superiority of the motor lifeboat over the rowing and sailing lifeboats to the traditionalist lifeboat crews nationally. A faster boat with greater endurance would also enable the RNLI to deal with the majority of service calls outside the newly completed piers, ultimately leading to the redundancy of the services of the Tyne Lifeboat Society. This is indeed what happened.

The local society's belated attempt to adapt a rowing lifeboat, which maintained design principles established 146 years earlier, was no match for the motor lifeboats in service and being developed by the RNLI. Even if finance had been available, and a modern motor lifeboat constructed, it begs the question as to what effective purpose this could have served with the presence of the RNLI's motor lifeboat at North Shields.

Ultimately, it was the failure of the Tyne Lifeboat Society to adapt to these changing circumstances that stopped it being an effective operational lifeboat service. The adherence to outdated boat design principles through their strong parochial and independent attitudes, and the lack of finance to undertake the modernisation of an aging fleet, placed the local society at a severe disadvantage compared with the more technically advanced, and better resourced RNLI, who in placing a motor lifeboat on the Tyne resolved a number of operational and political problems prevalent between the two organisations.

With the technological ascendancy of the RNLI, and the local institution boats now seen as somewhat of an anachronism, HM Coastguard called upon the services of the more powerful and better equipped Tynemouth motor lifeboat to undertake rescues. The Tyne Lifeboat Society, as an operational lifeboat service, quietly faded into history.

However, the bravery and seamanship skills of the pilots who manned these open boats in atrocious sea conditions cannot be underestimated. Although no comprehensive records of the Tyne Lifeboat Institution's work remain, the number of lives saved by the Shields Lifeboats is estimated at over 4,000, a record of which Shieldsmen, on both sides of the river, can be proud.

Appendices

Appendix 1 – Lifeboat Stations

Herd Sands, South Shields

Original, 1790-1830
Tyne, 1833-1838?

Coble Landing, South Shields

Tyne, 1838?–1868*? Held in reserve 1887-1894
Providence, 1842-1872
Tom Perry, 1872-1905
Willie Wouldhave, 1884-1887
Bedford, 1886-1935

Pilot Jetty

Tom Perry, 1905-1935
Bedford, 1935-1968

South Beach, South Shields

*Tyne**, 1859?-1862
Prior, 1862-1876?
Tyne, 1868?-1887
Willie Wouldhave, 1876-1882, 1887-1949

North Shields

Northumberland (1), 1798-1844
Northumberland (2), 1844-1882
Willie Wouldhave, 1882-1884
James Young, 1884-1941

Prior's Haven, Tynemouth

Prior, 1855-1862

* With only three lifeboats being operated from South Shields during the 1850s, it has been assumed that the *Tyne* was stationed at the first South Beach boathouse until the *Prior* was transferred from Prior's Haven, certainly no later than February 1861.

Appendix 2 – Lifeboats

Original

Years on Station: 1790-1830
Donor: Lawe House/Coal Trade Committee
Cost: £75
Builder: Henry Greathead, South Shields
Dimensions: 28ft. 6in. x 9ft. 6in.
Oars: 10
Notes: Wrecked on service 1830

Northumberland

Years on Station: 1798-1844
Donor: Duke of Northumberland
Cost: £159 4s 0d
Builder: Henry Greathead, South Shields
Dimensions: 30ft. 6in. x 10ft.
Oars: 10
Notes: Sold 1845. Renamed *Noble Institution.*

Tyne

Years on Station: 1833-1887
Donor: Thomas Forrest, South Shields London.
Cost: £170
Builder: Edward Oliver, South Shields
Dimensions: 32ft. 6in. x 10ft.
Oars: 12
Notes: Rebuilt 1845. Kept in reserve 1887-1894. On display at South Shields 1894.
Saved 1,024 lives.

Northumberland

Years on Station: 1844-1884
Donor: Duke of Northumberland.
Cost: £200
Builder: Thomas Anderson, North Shields.
Dimensions: 33ft. x 11ft.
Oars: 10
Notes: Sold out of service for £10, 1884, and used as a salvage boat.

Providence

Years on Station: 1845-1872
Donor: Tyne Lifeboat Institution
Cost: £234
Builder: Woodhouse, South Shields.
Dimensions: 34ft. 6in. x 10ft. 10in.
Oars: 14
Notes: Fitted with water ballast. Capsized on service 4/12/1849 with loss of 20 of her 24 crew. Sold out of service 1872 and used as a water boat on the Tyne. Broken up 1899.

Prior

Years on Station: 1855-1876?
Donor: Not known
Cost: Not known
Builder: Dowey, North Shields
Dimensions: 28ft. x10ft?
Oars: 10?

Tom Perry

Years on Station: 1872-1937
Donor: Mrs. T. Perry, South Shields
Cost: £200
Builder: James Jackson, South Shields
Dimensions: 33ft. x 11ft.
Oars: 12
Notes: Re-conditioned 1929. Sold out of service in 1937 as a diving boat.

Willie Wouldhave

Years on Station: 1876-1949
Donor: Tyne Lifeboat Institution
Cost: Not known
Builder: William Jackson, South Shields
Dimensions: Not known
Oars: 10
Notes: Destroyed in boathouse fire, 1949.

James Young

Years on Station: 1884-1941
Donor: Tyne Lifeboat Institution
Cost: £260
Builder: James Jackson, South Shields.
Dimensions: 32ft. x 11ft.
Oars: 12
Notes: Destroyed by enemy action April 1941.

Bedford

Years on Station: 1886-1937
Donor: Legacy of Miss Bedford of Pershore
Cost: £330
Builder: L.B. Lambert, South Shields
Dimensions: 33ft. 2in x 10ft. 8in.
Oars: 12
Notes: Converted to motor 1935. Displayed at Exeter Maritime Museum 1968. On display at ISCA Maritime Museum, Eyemouth, from 2003.

Appendix 3 – Service Records

Following the establishment of the South Shields Lifeboat Station in 1790, and the North Shields Lifeboat Station eight years later, no known records of lifeboat launches were kept by local lifeboat Committees. It was not until 1841, following the amalgamation of the local Committees and the establishment of the Tyne Lifeboat Institution that an organised record-keeping regime was introduced.

However, with the passage of time, only the service books for the years 1861-1870 and 1882-1910 survive. The others were lost or destroyed.

The launches listed in this appendix have been compiled from a number of sources in addition to these records. Information on launches before 1842 has been obtained from accounts in newspapers such as the *Newcastle Courant* and the *Port of Tyne Pilot*. For launches after 1842 information was gleaned from the *South Shields Gazette and Shipping Telegraph*.

The various local Wreck Registers, published by George Hodgson and Horatio A. Adamson (one of the first members of Tynemouth Volunteer Life Brigade); the wreck service registers of the Volunteer Life Brigades and the station records of Tynemouth Lifeboat Station have also contributed towards producing as comprehensive a list as possible of the launches of the Tyne rowing lifeboats, the wreck services carried out by the two Volunteer Life Brigades, and the launches of the RNLI boats at Tynemouth.

These records illustrate the frequency and number of ships that were wrecked at the mouth of the Tyne, and the changes in the type and number of services carried out by the Tyne Lifeboat Institution following the completion of the piers.

In a number of cases, especially during the early years of the Tyne lifeboats, only the details of wrecks can be given although it is highly likely the lifeboats did launch to them. The surviving record books of the Tyne Lifeboat Institution are also sparse on information, giving no narrative of the wreck service, but only details of the date, the casualty, the lifeboats launched and their crews and the number of persons saved.

1720
Sept 18 11 vessels wrecked on the Herd Sand.

1730
May The *Nell*, of Rotterdam, having been captured off Dunstanburgh Castle by HMS *Deal Castle*, wrecked on the Herd Sand and sunk while being brought into the Tyne by a prize crew.

1756
Oct 7 Great gale. The *Welcome Messenger* and *Sarah and Margaret* driven out of Shields Harbour and lost.

1763

Dec 1 HMS *Solebay* and 20 light and laden colliers broke from their moorings in Shields Harbour and driven out to sea. Most recovered.

1767

Jan 3 *Morning Star* of Stockton wrecked on the Herd Sand. One crew member died from exposure.

1771

Nov 16-17 The great flood in the Tyne drove many vessels from Shields Harbour out to sea. Several wrecked on the Herd Sand. A boy belonging one of the wrecks remained on the maintopmast head from Sunday morning to Monday morning before it was possible to rescue him.

1782

Mar 11 Great flood in the Tyne. Fifty colliers driven out to sea from Shields Harbour Many wrecked on the Herd Sand.

1789

Mar 15 The brig A*dventure*, of Newcastle driven ashore on the Herd Sand in a violent gale with the loss of her seven crew. The *Pitt* of London, and the *Myrmidon* also went ashore on the Herd Sand.

Oct 31 Two sloops wrecked on the Herd Sand. Crews shelter in new lifeboat house.

1790

Jan 30 The South Shields lifeboat *Original* rescues crew of brig ashore on the Herd Sand.

Apr 3 The brig *Nancy* went ashore on the Herd Sand.

1791

Jun 14 A Danish sloop wrecked on the Herd Sand and her crew rescued by the *Original*.

1792

Mar 18 The brig *Mary and Margaret* was wrecked on the Herd Sand and her crew rescued by the *Original*.

1794

Jan? The colliers *Orwell, Hazard* and *Barbara* were wrecked on the Herd Sand. *Alexander and Margaret* wrecked on the Black Middens. Five ships driven from their moorings in Shields Harbour and sunk in Jarrow Slake.

Dec 31 A sloop was wrecked on the Herd Sand. Two boys were lost, three other crew were rescued by the *Original.*

1795

Jan 1 The crews of the *Parthemius* of Newcastle and *Peggy* rescued by the *Original.*

1796

? The crew of the Scottish sloop the *Countess of Errol* rescued by the *Original.*

1797

Oct 15 The sloop *The Fruit of the Friends* of Leith went ashore on the Herd Sand. Four women, one man and a child took to the ship's boat and were drowned. The crew and the remaining passengers were rescued by the *Original.*

Nov ? The *Gateshead* inward bound from Gothenburg with deals and iron sank on the bar.

Late Nov The *Planter* of London, the *Beaver* of North Shields and the brig *Mary* of Newcastle were wrecked on the Herd Sand. Their crews were rescued by the *Original.* The Duke of Northumberland witnessed these rescues from Tynemouth Castle and was so impressed that he funded a second lifeboat, to be called *Northumberland,* to be stationed at North Shields.

Dec 7 Two armed convoy escort ships, *Good Design* and *Pomoma,* each armed with 14 24-pounders, were wrecked on the Spanish Battery in a westerly gale. The wind swung to SE and drove the brig *Agenoria* and another brig onto the Herd Sand. These two crews were rescued by the *Original.*

1798

Feb 24 A small brig was sunk by a gale in Prior's Haven. The *Friendship,* the *James* of Yarmouth and the *Goldthorpe* of Newcastle all went ashore on Spanish Battery rocks. Crews all saved.

Nov 16 The sloop *Edinburgh* of Kincardine, inbound from Gothenburg with iron and deals, drove ashore on the Herd Sand in a storm. Her six crew became the first to be saved by the North Shields lifeboat *Northumberland.*

The crew of the brig *Clio* saved by the *Northumberland.*

1799

Feb 17 The *Jane* of Newcastle, the *Margaret and Ann* of Blyth, and *Commerce* of Blyth were wrecked upon the Herd Sand. Crews were rescued by the lifeboats *Northumberland* and *Original.*

Oct The crew of the *Quintillian* of St Petersburg saved by the *Northumberland.*

1800

Jan 2 *Triton* of Newcastle, *Kitty* of South Shields and *Venerable* of Hull, were all driven ashore on the Spanish Battery rocks. Crews were all saved. Two brigs were driven ashore on the Black Middens, their crews were saved by lifeboat.

Jan 5 *Tiber* of London, *Britannia* of North Shields and a Dutch brig were driven ashore on the Black Middens. Crews all saved.

Jan 30 Four Sunderland vessels and the *Renown* wrecked at the mouth of the Tyne. Crews saved by lifeboat.

1802

Jan 1 *Sally* of Sunderland was driven ashore on the Black Middens. Crew saved by lifeboat.

Jan 2 *Active,* of Sunderland, was driven ashore on the Black Middens. Crew saved by lifeboat.

Jan 21 *Thomas and Alice* of Blyth went ashore on the Herd Sand. Crew saved by the *Northumberland.*

Apr 13 The brig *William and Henry* went ashore on the Herd Sand. Crew saved by lifeboat.

1803

Feb 6 The *Christian* and *Juno* of Sunderland, outward bound with coal for Aberdeen, and *Hope* of Leith all driven ashore on the Herd Sand. The crews were saved by lifeboats.

Nov 21 The North Shields brigantine *Bee* was driven ashore on the Spanish Battery rocks. Crew saved by the North Shields lifeboat *Northumberland.*

1804

Feb 18 Several vessels driven onto the Herd Sands. The lifeboats saved their crews.

Feb 23 An Aberdeen brig with more than 20 persons aboard was driven ashore on the Herd Sand. All were rescued by the *Northumberland.*

Sept 29 The brig *Lucy* of Sunderland, outward bound for Jersey with coal, went ashore on the Herd Sand. The crew was rescued by the lifeboat *Northumberland.*

Oct 26 The brig *Argo* of Lynn went onto the Black Middens in putting back after springing a leak. Crew was saved by lifeboat.

1805

Jan 13 *Royal Sovereign* of Sunderland, *Burdon* of Sunderland, *Perseverance* of Sunderland and *Leander* of Yarmouth all driven ashore on the Black Middens. The crew of the *Royal Sovereign* got ashore by means of a line, the others were rescued by the lifeboats *Northumberland* and *Original.*

May 19 The collier *Favourite* of North Shields went ashore on the Herd Sand. Crew rescued by lifeboat.

Dec 23 The brig *Mariner* of Newcastle, inbound from the Baltic, went ashore on the Herd Sand. Crew rescued by the *Northumberland.*

1807
Apr 17 The sloop *Margaret* of Dysart, inbound with stone ballast and yarn, went ashore on the Herd Sand. Crew saved by lifeboat.

Nov 11 The brig *Cornelia* of Newcastle, inbound from Liverpool, driven ashore on the Herd Sand. Crew saved by the *Northumberland.*

1808
Apr 8 Two sloops driven onto the Herd Sand by gale force winds. The crews were rescued by the lifeboat.

Oct ? The *Two Sisters, Free Briton, Success, Sanderson*, and *James,* all driven onto the Herd Sand in a high sea. The lifeboats saved the crews and went to lay kedge anchors. The five vessels were later got off.

1809 Jan 9 A frozen River Tyne followed by a great flood broke up the ice on the river. Five HM frigates, including the *Bucephalus*, torn from their moorings, a Humber keel, the collier brig *Hope* and the *Mary,* of Richmond, driven onto the Black Middens. 30 ships driven onto the Herd Sand. The *Original* launched to assist. The *Northumberland* could not launch as her slipway was covered by block ice.

1810
Mar 7 The American-built *Swift* of Poole, inbound with wine and cork from Oporto, went ashore on the Herd Sand. Crew saved by lifeboat. Pilots later boarded the ship but forgot to secure their boat, which drifted away. The lifeboat was launched again and rescued them just before the ship broke up.

Apr 8 *Royal Oak* of London drove ashore on the Herd Sand. Crew rescued by the lifeboat.

1811
Jan 31 *Cadiz Packet* driven ashore on the Black Middens in a gale, *Telemachus* of Shields driven onto Prior's Haven. Crews saved by the lifeboat.

May 15 *Fountain* of Lynn, outbound with coal, drove ashore on the Herd Sand. Crew saved by the lifeboat.

Aug 9 The 130-year-old *Happy Return* of Whitby, outbound with coal, was driven ashore in a sudden NE gale onto the Herd Sand. Crew saved by the *Northumberland*.

1812

Sept 1 Five outbound colliers, including *Mary*, owned by Sheppard, *Oughton* of London, *Medway* of Sunderland and *Friendship* of Newcastle were driven ashore on the Herd Sand. All crews saved by lifeboat.

Oct 10 The sloop *Sally* of Sunderland was wrecked on the Spanish Battery rocks while putting back into harbour. Crew rescued by the *Northumberland*.

Oct 24 *Isabella* of South Shields was wrecked in a gale on the Herd Sand. Crew saved by lifeboat.

1813

Dec 4 The sloop *Mary Anna* of Gothenburg, laden with tar, went ashore on the Herd Sand. Her five crew were saved by the *Northumberland*.

1814

May 9 *John and Jane* and *Amity*, both outbound with coal, went ashore on the Herd Sand. Crews saved by the lifeboats.

Jun 25 *Fermina* of London, outbound with coal, was wrecked on the Herd Sand. Crew saved by the *Northumberland*.

1815

Jan 25 The brig *Mercury* was wrecked on the Black Middens. Crew saved by the *Original*, which was badly damaged in the rescue.

Oct 27 *Favourite* of North Shields, inbound from America, was wrecked on the Herd Sand in a NE gale. Crew saved by lifeboat.

Dec 7 The sloop *George and Mary* of Wells was driven ashore in heavy seas on the Herd Sand. The master and mate were washed overboard and drowned but one man was saved by the *Original*.

Dec 8 *Good Intent* of Dundee, laden with wheat, was wrecked on the Herd Sand. Crew saved by lifeboat.

1816

Dec 26 The brig *Ann* of Yarmouth, loaded with grain, and *Stockton Packet* went ashore on the Herd Sand. Both crews saved by lifeboat.

1817

Oct 9 The sloop *Wheatsheaf* of Faversham sprang a leak and was beached on the Herd

Sand. Crew saved by the *Northumberland*.

1818

Oct 8 *Jane* of Caithness, outbound with coal from Sunderland, was damaged and ran ashore on the Black Middens in seeking safety in the Tyne. Crew saved by lifeboat.

1819

Dec 27 *Lady Sherbrooke* of Shields, inbound with timber from America, lost her rudder on the bar and went ashore on the Herd Sand in heavy seas. Crew saved by lifeboat.

1820

Jul 17 *Charlotte*, outbound, went ashore on the Herd Sand. Crew saved by lifeboat.

1821

Dec 7 *Charles* of Yarmouth, and *Thomas* of Hull, both inbound, were wrecked on the Black Middens. Crew and passengers all saved by lifeboats.

1823

Jan 25 In a heavy snowstorm, *Favourite* of North Shields, *Mary Ann*, of South Shields and *Jonas* of South Shields went ashore on the Herd Sand. Crews saved by the lifeboats. The collier *Aurora* also went on the Herd Sand but was refloated with the aid of the lifeboat.

Feb 1 The small brig *Traveller* of Whitby and the sloops *Brothers* of Hastings and *Martin* of Sunderland, and the large brigs *Dido* of Sunderland and *Albion* also of Sunderland all went ashore on the Herd Sand. All crews were saved by the lifeboats.

1825

Dec 1 The *Laurel* and the *Felicity* of Lynn, both in ballast, were driven ashore on the Spanish Battery in a SE gale. Their crews were saved by lifeboats. The Dutch galliot *Telegraph* from Bremen and the *Newcastle (*owned locally), were both driven ashore near Prior's Haven. Both crews were rescued by Captain Manby's apparatus.

1827

Jan 16 *Rivals*, of Cardiff, drove ashore on the Herd Sand. Crew saved by lifeboat.

Feb 17 ESE Gale. The collier *Betsy Cairns* of Shields encountered heavy seas on leaving the Tyne and was obliged to put back. In entering the port, she struck the rocks on Battery Point and went to pieces. Crew saved by the *Northumberland*.

Mar 7 *Denton* of Sunderland and outbound for the Baltic, ran ashore on the Herd Sand while running in for shelter. Crew saved by the lifeboat.

1828

Mar 27 *Matthias* of Wisbech, inbound, lost her rudder on the bar and drove ashore on the Spar Hawk at Tynemouth in a SE gale. Crew saved by lifeboat.

1829

Apr 10 *Gleadow* of Hull, inbound with barley, went ashore on the Herd Sand. Crew saved by the lifeboat but the vessel went to pieces.

Apr 28 The sloop *Brothers Increase* of Gardenstown, on passage from Inverness to Sunderland with grain, ran for shelter in the Tyne and went ashore on the Herd Sand. Crew saved by lifeboat.

Dec 4 The *Economy* of South Shields driven ashore on the Black Middens. Crew saved by lifeboat.

1830

Jan 21 At 9am, the sloop *Glatton* was driven onto the Black Middens during an ESE gale and heavy seas. The South Shields Lifeboat *Original* had taken off six of the crew when a huge wave tore her free from the wreck and drove her across the Black Middens, breaking her back on a rock. Two men left on the ship were rescued by Manby's Mortar apparatus. The *Original* was declared unfit for further service and was completely torn to pieces by souvenir hunters where she lay. She had saved about 500 lives in her forty years of service and no member of her crew had ever been lost.

Sept 19 The Hull steamer *Suffolk*, inbound in a SSW gale, was wrecked on the Spanish Battery rocks. The *Northumberland* rescued the crew and passengers.

Dec 1/2 SE gale. The *Good Intent,* collier of Shields, and *Argo* of Sunderland, with a cargo of oats, both inbound, drove ashore on the Herd Sand. Crews saved by the lifeboat. *Peterel* of Scarborough, in ballast, and *Union,* owned by *Utting* of Guernsey and inbound with potatoes and onions, went ashore on the Spanish Battery. Crews saved. *Prince Regent* and the *Masham* of Sunderland were also wrecked on the Spanish Battery. The master and a boy from the latter were drowned.

Dec 7 *Eagle* of Scarborough, on passage from Riga to London with deals, went ashore on the Herd Sand. Crew saved by the *Northumberland*.

1831

Feb 1 SE gale. Eight ships wrecked on the Herd Sand.

Feb 12 *Trident* of London went ashore on the Herd Sand.

Sept 13 *Henry and Harriet* and *Commerce* of Newcastle both wrecked on the Herd Sand.

Oct 22 *Victory* of Sunderland, on her maiden voyage, wrecked on the Black Middens.

Oct 26 *Liberty,* of Yarmouth, inbound, went ashore on the Black Middens. Crew rescued by the *Northumberland.*

Nov 10 Two light vessels, the *Arethusa* and *Hunter*, both of Shields, driven ashore on the Herd Sand. Crews saved by the *Northumberland. Fanny* of London was wrecked on the Black Middens and *Inverness* wrecked on the Spanish Battery rocks.

1833
Midsummer The passenger steamer *Lady of the Lake*, outbound for Stockton, shipped a sea that put out her boiler fires and drove ashore on the Herd Sand. The *Northumberland* and *Tyne* (on her first rescue) were launched. The *Tyne* rescued crew and passengers.

1834
Jan 6 *Derwent Spec* wrecked in Shields Harbour.

Jan 17 The *Ives Danier*, inbound from Hull with earthenware and coal tar, was driven onto the Herd Sand. The lifeboat put 12 pilots on board to assist the seven crewmen to refloat her on the rising tide, but all 19 had to be rescued when the vessel began to break up.

Oct 22 *Hercules* of Scarborough and outbound for there with coal, broke up on hitting the Herd Sand.

Oct 24 *Robert Gordon*, owned by Milne of Aberdeen, went ashore on the Herd Sand. Crew saved by the *Northumberland.*

1835
Feb 8 *Sally* of North Shields wrecked on the Herd Sand.

Dec 19 *Elizabeth* of South Shields wrecked on the Herd Sand.

1836 Jan 9 *Hartlepool Packet* of Sunderland wrecked on South Shields Sands.

1838
Jan 16 *Sprightley* of North Shields wrecked on the Black Middens.

Feb 2 S*hakespeare* of North Shields went onto the Herd Sand. Crew saved by the lifeboat.

Feb 23 The brig *Oak* of Poole struck the Spanish Battery Rocks and began to take in water. A Dennett's rocket was fired by the Coastguard but the ship was saved. Manby's mortar was also on standby.

Mar 2 *Loyal Packet* of Sunderland went ashore on the Herd Sand. Crew rescued by lifeboat. Later refloated.

Nov 23 *Two Brothers* of Newcastle wrecked at Tynemouth.

Nov 28 *Trio* of Malden wrecked on Tynemouth Rocks.

1839

Mar 11 The *Progress* of Shields was wrecked on the Spanish Battery. Four men were landed by the rocket apparatus under the command of Mr Cunningham of the Committee of the Shipwreck Society.

Mar 12 The local vessel *Delaval* went ashore beside the *Progress*. As the rocket lines had been damaged in the *Progress* rescue, the Manby Mortar was used to rescue two of the crew. The captain, cook and ship's boy chose to stay on board. The next night the ship began to break up and another line was sent over her. Men from the shore had to go out onto the ship to rescue the three remaining crew.

Mar 16 *Alpha* of Shields drove ashore on the Herd Sand. Crew saved by lifeboat.

Nov 30 *Enterprise* of Shields wrecked on Tynemouth Rocks. Crew rescued by Dennett's rocket apparatus.

Dec 19 *Friendship* of Blyth, wrecked at the mouth of the Tyne.

1841

Jan 24 *Mariner* of Perth wrecked on the Herd Sand in attempting to re-enter Shields Harbour in a great gale and snowstorm; the steamer *Advance* had two men drowned in attempting to rescue the shipwrecked crew, who were saved by the lifeboat.

Mar 16 *Thistle,* inbound from Montrose with a general cargo, parted from tug and went ashore on the Herd Sand. Assisted by the lifeboat.

Sept 1 *Allendale* wrecked on the Black Middens.

Sept 4 *Brothers* of Yarmouth wrecked on the Herd Sand. Crew saved by lifeboat.

Oct 15 *Good Hope* on passage from Yarmouth to Hamburg with herring, driven ashore on the Herd Sand. The crew was all saved by the North and South Shields lifeboats, apart from the master's wife,who drowned.

Oct 24 *Fox* of Gravesend wrecked on the Herd Sand. Nine crew saved by the *Tyne*. *Triton* of Yarmouth, broke free from her tug, outbound, and ran ashore at Tynemouth. Crew saved by the *Tyne*.

Oct 25 *William Wallace*, of South Shields, ashore on the Herd Sand. Thirteen crew saved by the South Shields Lifeboat, *Tyne*.

Nov 14 Russo-Finnish vessel, *Frederika*, ashore on the Herd Sand. 11 crew saved by the *Northumberland*.

1842

Jan 12 The brig *Percy* of North Shields driven onto the Black Middens. The National Lifeboat, stationed at Tynemouth, launched to her assistance, but capsized. The lifeboat was driven ashore with no loss of life.

Jan 14 *Thomas Holmes* of Newcastle, inbound from Antwerp with bark, drove ashore on the Herd Sand. Crew saved by lifeboat.

Jan 25 12.30am. The *Constantine* driven ashore on the Spanish Battery in a SSE gale. Crew saved by South Shields lifeboat.

Jan 26 During a great storm, the *Eliza* of North Shields, *Argus* of North Shields, and *Ocean* of Scarborough, driven onto Tynemouth Rocks and became total wrecks. The crews, 18 in total, were saved by Captain Manby's apparatus.

Apr 2 *Seaforth* on passage from Sunderland to Inverness, driven onto the Herd Sand. Crew saved by lifeboat. Part of her cargo was lime, which later caught fire and destroyed the ship.

1843

Jan 13 *Isabella* of Sunderland and *Percy* of North Shields wrecked on the Black Middens. Manby's apparatus was used from the cliff top and part of *Percy's* crew was taken off by the *Northumberland*. Captain Hair, with a broken leg, made desperate efforts to reach the shore by working hand over hand along the hawser, but was washed off and drowned with one seaman.

Jan 23 12.30am. Hurricane force winds and heavy snow. The *Constantia* driven onto the rocks under the Spanish Battery. One crew saved by the Coastguard breeches buoy before lines swept away. Remaining crew saved by the *Northumberland*.

Feb 6 The steamer *City of Hamburg, Jessie Anne* of South Shields and the sloop *Hesperus* all driven ashore on the Herd Sand. *Diadem* of Aberdeen wrecked on the Herd Sand.

Feb 8 *Emily* of Copenhagen wrecked on the Black Middens.

Mar 24 *Elizabeth* from Stettin wrecked on the Herd Sand.

Mar 27 *Electra* of South Shields foundered off the Tyne.

Apr 5 SS *Charles Williams* wrecked on the Spanish Battery rocks after being stolen from Shields Harbour.

Sept 25 *Euphemia* of Newcastle driven onto the Herd Sand, took fire and destroyed.

Oct 17 *Eleanor* and *Lark*, both of Yarmouth, wrecked on the South Sands, South Shields.

Oct 24 *Jane Helen* of Newcastle abandoned off the Tyne.

Oct 28 *Active* of Newcastle, wrecked at Marsden. All hands were drowned.

1844
Feb 24 *William* of Shields, wrecked on the Herd Sand. *Endeavour* of Whitstable and *Unicorn* of Yarmouth wrecked on Tynemouth Rocks. The mate of the *Unicorn* was drowned.

1845
Mar ? 7am The brig *Electra* went ashore at Hartley Bates. The *Tyne* hauled six miles overland to the rescue, but crew dropped ashore from the bowsprit.

Aug 16 *Maria*, Dutch vessel, wrecked on the Black Middens.

Nov 29 *Lady Faversham* sank on the Herd Sand. *Sceptre* wrecked on the Spanish Battery rocks.

1846
Nov 20 *Britain* of Newcastle wrecked on Tynemouth Rocks. *Sceptre* of Blyth, wrecked on Tynemouth Rocks; the master was drowned.

Dec 23 *Majestic* of Sunderland, wrecked on the Herd Sand.

1847
Oct 5 *Clythia* of Newcastle wrecked on the Tyne Bar.

Dec 17 *James* of Yarmouth and *Lady Ann* of Wells wrecked at Tynemouth.

1848
Jan 7 *Edward* of Hull wrecked at Tynemouth.

Nov 14 *George* of Sunderland wrecked on the Herd Sand, laden with lime. The ship took fire.

Dec 22 *George* of South Shields wrecked on the Black Middens.

1849
Mar 30 Great gale; 28 wrecks on the Black Middens and Herd Sand, seven at Hartlepool and 31 at Sunderland.

Sept 18 *Louise Auguste* of Aarhus wrecked on the Herd Sand.

Sept 30 Great gale. *Verbena* of Newcastle lost in Frenchman's Bay.

Oct 5 *Vabrino* wrecked on Tyne Bar.

Oct 7 Great gale. The *Emilie* wrecked on Tyne Bar; two of her crew were drowned.

Dec 4 The brig *Betsy* of Littlehampton and the Danish schooner *Aurora* driven onto the Herd Sand. The South Shields Lifeboat *Providence* went to the assistance of the brig, and capsized. Twenty of her crew drowned, and only four were saved. The *Tyne* and *Northumberland* both launched to assist. The *Northumberland* rescued the crew of the Betsy and one of the crew of the *Providence.*

Dec 28 The *Brilliant* passenger steamer foundered off the Tyne. Crew was saved by the *Providence*, with John Milburn, survivor of the disaster on 4 December, coxswain.

1850
Mar 15 The *Edward* of Port Glasgow wrecked on the Black Middens.

Mar 20 The *Eva* of South Shields foundered off the Tyne.

Mar 29 SE gale. During the night, the *Ariadne* and the *Vigilant* of Sunderland went ashore on Tynemouth rocks.

Mar 30 A terrific gale from the SE. The northbound collier fleet, numbering about 500, had been detained in Yarmouth Roads for some weeks, and sailed on the 28th. The gale broke next day, and on 30th, a large fleet of ships arrived in the Tyne, with 30 wrecks on the Herd Sand and Black Middens. The Narrows became blocked. Great damage was done by ships colliding with each other. They were so close that their crews clambered over them from one shore to the other. The *Good Intent* of Yarmouth, the *Theodore* and the *Luna* went ashore in Tynemouth Haven, and the *Mary Anna*, *Union*, *Minuet* and several other ships were driven onto Tynemouth rocks.

Mar 31 During the morning, the *Sally* of Newcastle, drove upon the Black Middens and went to pieces in the afternoon.

Aug 11 The *Favourite* capsized off Souter Point after casting her ballast.

Oct 24 A great gale. The sloop *Jane* of Bath, laden with potatoes, wrecked on the Herd Sands. The South Shields lifeboat saved the crew. The *Urania* wrecked on Shields Bar.

Nov 20 Storm from the NE. A Dutch sloop driven onto the Herd Sand. Crew saved by the South Shields lifeboat.

1851
Nov 6 The Norwegian Schooner *Phoenix* driven ashore on the Herd Sand. Crew saved by the lifeboat.

Nov 23 Between 500 and 600 Tyne-bound colliers, which had been detained in Bridlington Bay and the Humber set sail northward and were caught in a gale. Several were lost. The SS *William and Mary* wrecked on Shields Bar. Engines recovered by dredger in September 1862.

1852

Sept 21 *William and Sarah* of Shields and *Providence* wrecked on the Herd Sand.

Oct 4 *John Wesley* wrecked on Tynemouth Rocks.

Oct 27 A storm from the SE and E by S, seas tremendously high. In the afternoon, the brig *Union* of Wisbech, carrying coal, was driven onto the Herd. Crew saved by the South Shields lifeboat *Providence.* The brig *Unity* of King's Lynn, also carrying coal, went ashore. Crew saved by the *Providence*. 30 minutes later the *Unity* went to pieces. The brigs *Hipolite Maie* of Ricardais, *Union, Lively, Paulitte* and *Marie* were also driven ashore on the Herd. On 28 October these vessels went to pieces. About 8pm, the barque *Marie Elizabeth* of Christiania, laden with a general cargo, drove ashore on the Herd. The lifeboat got the crew and passenger out; but the latter died shortly afterwards from injuries received in getting from the ship into the lifeboat. The cargo of the *Marie Elizabeth*, consisting largely of liquor, was taken by wreckers.

Nov 13 A storm from the ESE. The brig *Dorothy* of South Shields wrecked upon the end of the Herd, and went to pieces. Crew saved by the lifeboat.

Dec 17 Great flood in the Tyne. Fleet of ships moored off Anchor Quay, Shields, broke adrift, 18 vessels badly damaged, two lives lost.

Dec 28 Great gale. *Harmony* and *Margaret* wrecked at Tynemouth. *Flowers of Ugie* wrecked on the Herd Sand.

1853

Jan 13 The *Rosalind* of London capsized and sank in Shields harbour.

Feb 23 Storm from the NE. About 6pm, during a snow storm, the schooner *Sir William Wallace* was lost on the Herd Sand. Her crew (seven men and a boy) and a woman all perished.

Feb 25 The schooners *May Queen* of Peterhead and *Prompt* of Newcastle wrecked on the Herd Sand. The crews were got off by the lifeboats.

Dec 15 The brig *Admiral* of Aberdeen, laden with pit props, was wrecked at Marsden. Crew saved. The brig *Sylph* of South Shields, coming over the bar, was struck by a sea that broke her tiller and she drifted onto the Black Middens. Crew saved by the South Shields lifeboat.

1854

Jan 4 A tremendous storm from ESE. Loss of schooner *Eliza* of Kirkwall and her nine crew on Tynemouth rocks. The brig *Elizabeth,* laden with salt; the barque *Euretta,* light; the brig *Antelope,* light; the brig *Arethusa* of Blyth; the brig *Anns* and the brig *New Messenger* (both coal laden); the barque *Sir Robert Peel*, laden with saltpetre and about a ton of silver; the brig *Amphitrite*, coal laden; the brigantine *Nerio* of London, and brigs *Harmony* of Blyth and *Amy* and *Elizabeth* of Shields, were all wrecked at the mouth of the Tyne. Crews all saved by the rocket apparatus. Over 30 wrecks on the Herd Sand and Black Middens.

Jan 5 6.30pm. The brig *Hannah* of Whitby went ashore on the Black Middens. The lifeboats were launched but did not get the crew out until after 10pm. One of the crew was lost.

Jan 7 The *Pilot* steamer picked up the schooner *Minerva,* of Whitby, riding off Souter abandoned, and towed her in.

Jan 8 11 ships were driven onto the Herd Sand between 9pm and 2am: the barque *Aurora* of Sunderland (ballast); brig *Ann* of Lynn; brig *Jean* of Inverness; brig *Breakwater* of Shields; brig *Conference* of Shields; schooner *George* of Whitby; brig *Armida* of Stettin; barque *Sarah Midge*; schooner *Cresswell*; brig *Jane and Margaret* of Newcastle; schooner *James and Ann* of Ipswich; French vessel *Bon Virgine*. The *Northumberland, Tyne* and *Providence* returned to their boathouses by 3am having rescued 87 seamen.

Jan 9 The brig *Lively* of North Shields, billy boy *Happy Return* of Goole, brig *Savannah* of Lynn, the *Junius* of Christiansand, and the *Ocean* of Goole, were wrecked on the Herd Sand.

Jan 10 During the week's gale, 35 vessels were wrecked or stranded at the mouth of the Tyne, 31 at Sunderland and 44 at Hartlepool and the Tees, and there were 110 wrecks on the coast within 30 miles north and south of the Tyne.

Oct 17 Gale from NE A brig driven onto Whitley Sands. Crew saved.

Nov 15 The Prussian Schooner *Napoleon III,* the brig *Lively* of Lynn, laden with wheat, and the brigantine *Mary Robertson* of South Shields, were driven onto the rocks. Crews saved by the lifeboats and the rocket apparatus. 12 vessels ashore at Sunderland, nine Shields ships wrecked.

1855

Mar 16 During a SSE storm, that raged during the night of 15 and morning of the 16 March, three ships were driven ashore upon the rocks near to the Spanish Battery: the sloop *Thomas and Mary* of Whitby (crew perished); schooner *Hugh Bourne* of Whitby (crew saved); and the brig *Heather* of Shields, the property of George Metcalf and Son (crew saved).

Oct 30 The brigantine *John and Anne* of South Shields lost on the Tyne Bar, *Marco Polo* of Goole on the Herd Sand. Crew saved by the lifeboat. A small vessel went ashore to the north of Souter Point. Crew saved.

Nov 1 The brig *Nautilus* of Seaton Sluice wrecked on the Herd Sand.

Nov 24 The *British Tar* struck on Shields Sands. John Grieves, pilot, washed overboard.

Dec 18 Gale from the S by E. Two vessels stranded on the rocks near the Battery: the *Redwing* of London, and the *Amulet* of Blyth.

Dec 19 Three vessels driven ashore onto the rocks: the *Johns,* the *Comet,* and the *Currah.*

1856

Feb 7 Terrific gale. *Advance* of South Shields sank in the harbour. 243 vessels damaged by breaking adrift in Shields Harbour. Moralee's floating dock sunk. A number of coal wagons blown off Stanhope Drops on to the deck of a vessel, which sank immediately.

July 8 A gale from the NE. The barque *Spring* was driven ashore at Trow Rocks. A dismasted vessel was seen on the Offing, and the *Pilot* steam tug went to her assistance and towed her in.

Aug 16 The *Lively* sunk in Peggy's Hole, North Shields.

1857

Jan 4 A tremendous gale. The *Sarah Ellen* of South Shields driven ashore to the south of the South Pier. She went on her beam ends, but righted herself. Crew saved, with the exception of a young man who was drowned when he fell overboard. The *Active* and French lugger *Alexis Pierre Henri* both driven onto the Herd Sand. The crew of the *George IV* reported having seen nine vessels founder off the Yorkshire coast. 30 Shields vessels lost in this gale.

Jan 5 A small schooner lost her rudder in crossing the Bar and drove upon the rocks. Crew saved by the *Northumberland.*

Feb 21 The *Colony* of Whitby wrecked on the Tyne Bar.

Mar 20 The barque *Spring* drove on the Black Middens. Crew saved by the rocket apparatus. This is the same vessel that went ashore on 8 July 1856.

July 21 The *Elizabeth and Sarah* of North Shields burned out in Shields harbour.

Nov 26 The brig *Brothers,* coal laden, went ashore on the north side of the Tyne. The crew of six saved by the South Shields Lifeboat.

1858

Feb 21 A small vessel drove ashore on the rocks in front of the Battery. One of the crew taken off by the rocket apparatus.

Nov 6 Great gale. The *Lord Hill of Moruco* wrecked on the Herd Sand. The *Gratitude* ashore on the Mussel Scarp.

1859

Mar 14 SE gale. The schooner *George* of North Shields ran onto the foundations of the North Pier. The South Shields lifeboat crew attempted to board her, but could not do so for two hours, during which the crew of the schooner took to the fore rigging. The vessel went over on her beam ends, throwing all the men into the sea. One was saved and four were drowned. The schooner *Elizabeth Palmer* of Boston wrecked on the Spanish Battery rocks.

Mar 19 *David Owen* of Shields burned in Shields harbour.

Apr ? Brig *Schiedam* went ashore on the Herd Sand. The *James Mather* lifeboat and two Tyne Lifeboat Institution boats launched to assist.

Apr 25 Gale from the NE A vessel went ashore upon the rocks. Crew saved by the lifeboat. On 28 April she went to pieces.

1860

Jan 27 Storm from the NE. The barques *Sarah* of Newcastle and *Mediu,* of Blyth, driven ashore on the Herd Sand. Crews saved by lifeboats. The *Gratitude* ashore on the Mussel Scarp.

May 28 Great gale. The *Dublin Lass* and *Fleur de Marie* lost on the Herd Sand. 143 wrecks on the British coast. 100 Tyne seamen lost.

Oct 1 Great gale. Several ships adrift in Shields Harbour.

Nov 22 A severe storm from the East. Sea breaking heavily across the Bar. The brig *Union* of Ipswich was driven ashore on the Herd Sand, a little to the south of the South Pier, and the barque *Arno* of Newcastle, near Frenchman's Bay. 15 crew of the *Arno* saved by the Manby mortar apparatus.

Dec 3 A gale from the SE. The brig *Hugh* of London wrecked on the Black Middens during the night. Crew saved.

Dec 31 *William* of South Shields wrecked on Tynemouth rocks.

1861

Jan 1 A storm from the SE. The brig *Lovely Nelly* of Seaham driven ashore at Whitley

Bay. The Cullercoats lifeboat was taken overland and launched, and saved the crew, with the exception of one man.

Jan 6 *William and Jane* picked up derelict off Tynemouth. No trace of crew.

Jan 15 ESE gale. The schooner *Mariner* of Brixham, loaded with ironstone, was driven onto the Black Middens when crossing the bar. The *Providence*, with a crew of 23, rescued 4 crew and the *Northumberland*, (22 crew) rescued 6. Later that day the *Northumberland* launched to take off nine salvage men working on the wreck.

Feb 9 ESE gale with heavy seas. At 8am, the schooner *Fowlis* of Inverness, laden with staves, wrecked on the stones at the South Pier. She went to pieces. South Beach lifeboat *Prior* (16 crew) and the *Tyne* (22 crew), and *Providence* all launched. The *Providence* was holed in three places, and the *Prior* was unable to reach the wreck. Four of her crew were saved by the rocket apparatus, which was fired from the *Tyne*, and two perished. At 1pm, the brig *Indus* of North Shields and the schooner, *Minerva*, both laden, were driven ashore onto the South Pier stones. At 2pm, the *Sarah Anne* was driven onto the Herd. Six crew saved by the *Tyne* with 14 pilots on board. The crew of the *Indus* was saved by the *Northumberland* (26 crew) and five crew from the *Minerva* were saved by the *Providence* (20 crew). One of the *Minerva*'s crew was washed ashore on a piece of timber. The *Indus* broke up 30 minutes after the crew was landed. The salvage boat *William Wake* also launched to assist the lifeboats.

At 3pm the brig *Caesar* came ashore onto the Herd Sand. Four crew rescued by the South Shields lifeboat (22 crew), and four by the *Northumberland* (23 crew).

Feb 10 The schooner *Treaty* of Goole, carrying potatoes, was driven onto the Herd Sand. Crew of four rescued by the *Tyne* (14 crew).

Feb 15 The *Providence* (23 crew) rescued four from the *Mariner* ashore on the Black Middens. The *Northumberland* (22 crew) rescued six.

Sept 5 10am. NE wind. Four wherries from HMS *Defence*, in difficulties on the Herd Sands. 13 crew rescued by South Shields lifeboat, crewed by 14 Pilots.

Oct 28 3am. ESE strong wind, lights seen in harbour. The South Shields lifeboat *Tyne*, (16 crew) launched and found a screw steamer that required no assistance. The lifeboat returned to her boathouse.

Nov 14 Gale from the NE. The brigs *Albion* of Aberystwyth and *Phrenic* of Aberdeen were driven onto the Herd Sand when crossing the bar. The eight crew of the *Albion* were saved by the *Providence* (24 crew), assisted by the *Tyne* (18 crew). The crew of the *Phrenic* was saved by the *Northumberland,* with the exception of the mate, who fell overboard and drowned.

A Dutch galliot under tow was struck by a sea and the towline broke. She drifted southward and was struck by another sea, which carried away her masts. She drifted until she was driven ashore at Trow Rocks. Four of the crew were saved by rocket apparatus but the mate and a son of the master were washed overboard and drowned.

Nov 15 SS *Albatross* struck the Bar. *Providence* (32 crew) and *Northumberland* (21 crew) both launched and managed to turn the ship's head off the sands. 5s 3d per man awarded to the crews of the *Providence* and *Northumberland.*

Nov 16 10am. A laden schooner, the *Rhodes*, struck on the Bar and was driven onto the Herd. The *Northumberland* (19 crew) rescued the four crew. The South Shields lifeboat put some men on board the *Rhodes* and refloated her.

Dec 14 12.20am. The *Northumberland* rescued five from the *Phrenic* aground on the Herd Sands, ENE wind, 1 crew lost when jumping overboard.

12.30am. The *Providence* (24 crew) rescued eight crew from the *Albion* ashore on the Herd Sands. *Tyne*, 18 crew.

1862
Jan 31 9.30pm. Coastguard signal from Tynemouth for lifeboat. *Northumberland* (14 crew) launched and found SS *Onward* on North Pier foundation stones. Ten crew waded ashore before the lifeboat reached the wreck.

Feb 9 10am. Schooner *Ebenezer* struck the Bar and grounded on the Herd. *Providence* (22 crew) and *Northumberland* (18 crew) both launched in ESE wind with moderate seas. Crew refused to leave.

Feb 20 11pm. Pilots hailed by a passing steamer. A ship aground on the bar, 4ft. seas, 3.5 hours ebb tide. *Tyne* launched (17 crew). Got to Black Middens, nothing found.

Mar 5 9.10am. The brig *Mary Campbell* of North Shields driven onto the Black Middens. The *Providence* (22 crew) saved the seven crew.

The brig *Nautilus* struck the Bar and drifted onto the Black Middens. The *Northumberland* (19 crew) and *Tyne* (19 crew) both launched in SSE gale, strong seas. The crew refused to leave.

Mar 20 Dutch schooner *Catherina Louisa*, got into difficulties when entering the harbour. The *Tyne* launched (16 crew). A tug got a line aboard and towed vessel into river.

Apr 11 9am. E gale and heavy seas. The schooner *Liberal* of Peterhead ran aground on the Herd Sand. The *Providence* launched (19 crew) and saved the crew of five. The *Northumberland* also launched (18 crew).

June 12 6pm The Tyne Improvement Commissioners Lighter *No. 16,* being towed into harbour, struck the Pier Rocks. The *Tyne* launched (16 crew). The Lighter's crew refused to leave.

Aug 5 The *Gallant* of South Shields struck by a squall when discharging ballast off the Tyne, filled through her open ports and sank.

Oct 3 *William Englier* of Shields wrecked on Tynemouth Long Sands.

Oct 10 The steam tug *Integrity* of Shields lost with all hands off Tynemouth.

Nov 23 9.30am. The schooner *Glen Grant* hit Sparrow Hawk rocks. The *Northumberland* (23 crew) launched. The crew refused to leave.

Dec 8 The *Sostrall* wrecked on Tynemouth Rocks.

Dec 20 5pm. The schooner *Isabella* of Montrose ran onto the Herd Sands in heavy seas during a north westerly gale. Her crew of four were rescued by the *Providence* (25 crew). The RNLI lifeboat stationed at Tynemouth, *Constance,* launched for the first time from her boathouse in Tynemouth (Prior's) Haven, but her services were not required.

Dec 26 The brig *Violet* of Shoreham ran onto the Herd Sands. The *Constance* launched, but her services were not required.

1863

Jan 9 11am. NNE gale. The schooner *Maris* of Bergen struck the Bar in heavy seas and drifted onto the Herd Sands. The *Northumberland*, manned by 23 pilots launched. The *Constance* also launched, but her services were not required. The crew of the schooner refused to leave their vessel, which was later refloated and brought into the river.

Jan 29 2am. The brig *Elina* seen in difficulties in high seas from NNE by pilots at the Lawe lookout. Fearing she would drift onto Herd Sands, they launched the *Tyne* (17 crew), which found the brig and towed her clear.

Mar 8 8am. Craft in tow of steamer entering harbour in ENE gale. Tow broke; craft struck by heavy seas and sank. Crew of two lost. *Northumberland* launched (16 crew). The *Tyne* (15 crew) and *Providence* (18 crew) also launched to assist.

Mar 9 7am. Brig *Telegraph* entering harbour went onto the Black Middens. Crew of eight rescued by the *Northumberland* (21 crew). *Tyne* (15 crew) launched to assist.

The Norwegian schooner *Ashea* being towed by steamer, tow broke and drifted onto Herd Sand. The *Northumberland* (22 crew) launched. Crew refused to leave.

Mar 13 Dutch barque *Zeelandia* struck the bar and drifted onto the Herd Sand, in an ENE gale and heavy seas. The *Tyne* (19 crew) launched, but the barque's crew refused to leave. The barque, in tow of steamer, was later refloated. The *Providence* (21 crew), *Northumberland* (18 crew) and *Constance* all launched, but their services not required.

Nov 7 SS *James Dixon,* on leaving harbour, collided with an Italian barque and drove onto the foundations of the South Pier. The *Tyne* (14 crew) and *Northumberland* (19 crew) launched, rescuing six and one respectively. Later that day, lights were seen from the vessel. Expecting the remainder of the crew wanted to be taken off, the *Providence* (16 pilots) *Northumberland* (18 crew) launched. Crew would not leave. Both lifeboats remained alongside for two hours before returning ashore. The *Constance* also launched but her services were not required.

Dec 9 Andrew Purvis, pilot, went to sea in his coble searching for ships and saw a billy boy, the *Mary* of Wisbech striking the wreck of the *James Dixon.* He managed to rescue two men and a boy, brought them ashore and was awarded £1.

Dec 17 Schooner *Tees* struck bar and grounded on the Herd Sand when entering harbour. The *Providence* (21 crew) and *Northumberland* (21 crew) launched in NE wind and heavy seas. A steamer got a rope aboard and towed schooner clear.

Dec 31 Pilots at Lawe lookout saw distress signal, ship ashore on North Pier stones. The *Northumberland* launched (15 crew). Could find nothing.

1864
Feb 8 7am Norwegian barque *San Francisco* struck by heavy seas and driven onto Herd Sands. The *Tyne* (18 pilots) launched and took off her 14 crew.

Feb 10 The barque *Don* struck the Herd sands, while taking the bar at low water in tow of steamer. The *Providence* launched (24 pilots) but a steamer managed to tow the barque off. The *Northumberland* (26 crew) also launched.

Feb 13 Great WSW gale. *Victoria* broke from her moorings in Shields Harbour and drove on to the Herd Sand. Many vessels adrift in the harbour.

Mar 8 11.30am. The schooner *Esther* was driven onto the Herd Sand when entering river during a NNE wind and strong seas. The *Tyne* (18 crew) launched, but the crew would not leave vessel. The *Northumberland* (20 crew) also launched.

Mar 9 3am. The *Argwarn* struck the Herd Sands. The pilots launched the *Tyne* (18 crew) but ship came off the sands as the lifeboat arrived.

Apr 15 The *Paupalos*, in ballast, struck rocks on Spanish Battery in heavy weather. The South Shields lifeboat, *Tyne*, 18 (crew), and North Shields lifeboat, *Northumberland*, (24 crew) launched. The *Paupalous* managed to free herself.

May 23 During a strong ENE wind with high seas running, Hopper Barge *35* was being towed into the river by a Tyne Improvement Commission screw hopper. The tow broke and the barge drifted onto Herd Sands. The *Providence* (18 crew) launched, but the tow was reconnected and the barge towed into the river. The *Northumberland* (18 crew) also launched.

Aug 16 12am. Unknown schooner struck the bar and drifted onto rocks. The *Tyne*, (15 crew) launched, but a steamer got a rope onboard and towed the schooner off.

Oct 23 9.30am. E wind blowing. The brig *Elbe* returning laden with coal through bad weather got out of the channel and drove onto Herd Sand. The *Providence,* (22 crew) and the *Northumberland* (23 crew) launched. The *Northumberland* rescued the crew of nine, and Martin Purvis, a Tyne Pilot.

On the same day, the schooner *John Slater* was driven onto the Black Middens. The *Tyne* (20 crew) and *Northumberland* (22 crew) launched, but could not get alongside due to rocks. The *Constance,* also launched and stood by until the storm had eased and the schooner had refloated. Earlier the crew got ashore in a small boat due to efforts of E. Fry of Tynemouth and four others, who were all rewarded for their services.

Nov 24 A strong ENE gale caused great destruction to shipping and much loss of life. The first casualty was the steam tug *Escort* of Shields, which had gone too far in shore to aid a steamship, and was driven onto the Herd End. The *Tyne*, launched and in getting alongside the tug grounded in shallow water. Having previously got a rope onboard, the steamer succeeded in rescuing the tug's four crew. After two hours aground, the steamship refloated on the rising tide. The *Escort* broke up and became a total loss.

On the same day, the schooner *Friendship* of Colchester, coal laden and returning to the Tyne to shelter from the storm, got out of the channel and drove on the Black Middens rocks. The *Northumberland* (21 crew) and *Providence* (24 crew) both launched, but due to heavy seas it was impossible to help. Meanwhile the *Constance* went to the wreck. Getting too close to the ship she was struck by a heavy sea, driven up against the wreck and stove in. Four of the crew, thinking the lifeboat unsafe, jumped on to the wreck of the *Friendship*, which capsized, killing everyone on board.

The SS *Stanley* of Aberdeen, bound for London with a general cargo, including cattle and passengers, tried to make the Tyne for shelter. It was low water when she took the bar, the harbour lights were not lit, and being out of the channel she was driven ashore close alongside the wreck of the *Friendship* on the Black Middens. The three boats *Providence* (26 crew)*, Tyne* (15 crew) and *Northumberland* (23 crew) again put off and made many unsuccessful rescue attempts. A lot of oars had been broken by the heavy seas so they returned to shore for new oars.

At 9pm, the boats returned to the *Stanley* and observed the brig *Ardwell* returning to the Tyne for shelter, laden with coal, ashore near to the steamer. The *Tyne*, after many attempts, succeeded in getting her four crew aboard. In the meantime the other boats were trying to reach the *Stanley*. It was impossible and after two hours the exhausted crew returned to shore. (Account taken from Tyne Lifeboat Institution Service Log)

Nov 25 8.30am. SSE wind. The brig *Martin Luther* of Sunderland wrecked on the South Pier stones. The *Tyne* (18 crew), *Providence* (19 crew) and the *Northumberland* (19 crew) all launched, but were unable to reach the vessel due to the shallow water and heavy seas breaking on the rocks. They stood by until midday, only 50 yards from the wreck but the brig went to pieces and her crew of eight all perished.

At 11pm, the brig *Robert Scott* hailed the North Shields lifeboat station, requesting the crew to go out to the *Martin Luther*. The *Northumberland* was towed into the harbour by a tug, but found the brig had gone to pieces.

Nov 28 The barques *Reaper* and *Amy Robsart* and were driven onto the Black Middens at 6.30am and 8am respectively. The *Northumberland* (23 crew) launched with the *Tyne* (14 crew), rescuing the ten crew of the *Amy Robsart,* which went to pieces by 14 December. The *Reaper* was towed off the rocks.

Dec 15 10.30am. The schooner *Ann* of Dartmouth was driven onto the Herd Sand. The *Tyne* (14 crew) and *Northumberland* (33 crew), both launched. A passing steamer towed the schooner off the sands.

1865
Jan 16 9.15am. Strong NNE wind. Four feet seas on the bar and harbour lights just put out. The barque *Napoleon* of Antwerp drove onto the Herd Sand. The *Northumberland* (23 crew) launched. The crew refused to leave and the barque re-floated on the next tide.

Feb 3 Russian barque *Warsaw* driven onto the Herd Sand. The *Northumberland* (22 crew), *Tyne* (17 crew) and *Constance* all launched. The crew of the *Warsaw* refused to leave and she was refloated on the next tide without the services of the lifeboats.

10am. The SS *Earl Percy* driven onto the Black Middens and broken in two. The 17 crew, the only passenger on board, an elderly gentleman, and a pilot, rescued by the *Providence* (14 crew) assisted by the *Tyne* and N*orthumberland.*

Feb 11 9.15pm. The schooner *Providence* of Teignmouth was driven onto the Herd Sand and became a total wreck. Due to the state of the tide, the *Northumberland* was delayed in launching. The salvage boat *William Wake* was manned (21 crew) and rescued the five crew. The *Northumberland* eventually launched with a crew of 20.

Mar 11 The brig *Fly* of Seaham returning coal laden to the Tyne to seek shelter in a gale was driven onto the Herd Sand. The *Tyne, Providence* and *Northumberland* all launched. The five crew were rescued by the *Tyne,* just before the *Fly* went to pieces.

Mar 19 9am. In heavy seas, the brig *Border Chieftain* of Hartlepool, under the charge of a pilot, was hit by heavy seas which disabled her steering and drove her onto the south side of the North Pier stones. The seven crew and pilot were saved by the *Constance.* The *Northumberland* (22 crew) also launched.

4.30pm. Wreck of the brigantine *Burton,* of Colchester. The vessel entered the river too far north, close to another vessel to windward, which took the wind from her sails. At the same time she was hit by a series of heavy seas, which drove her onto the North Pier stones. The crew took to the rigging. The Tynemouth Volunteer Life Brigade succeeded in firing a rocket over the wreck, but the crew could not reach it. Within seven minutes of grounding, she went to pieces with the loss of four crew. The *Constance* launched within five minutes of the ship coming ashore and reached the site of the wreck five minutes later, but not before the vessel had broke up. The lifeboat was impeded by wreckage entangling the oars. The crew rescued the mate who was clinging to a spar from the wreck.

The mate and his brother of the schooner *Quickstep* of Exeter and the mate of a Yarmouth brig were washed overboard and drowned.

Apr 5 The *Hedley Vicars* of Seaham sank in Shields Harbour following a collision with SS *Berwick* on the Tyne Bar.

Jun 23 The *Milo* sank in Shields Harbour following a collision with SS *William Hunter.*

Sept 20 The *Johns* sank in Shields Harbour following a collision with SS *John Liddle.* Three lives lost.

Sept 25 The *Betsy* sank in Shields Harbour following a collision.

Oct 10 Gale from the E and S. Wreck of the *Ringwood* on the rocks. Five crew left her in their boat, and three were drowned. The *Tyne* and *Northumberland* both launched. Tynemouth Volunteer Life Brigade got a rocket line onboard the *Ringwood*, but the crew had already left the brig.

At 11am, the brig *Medora* of Shields had her stern stove in when coming across the bar and she foundered. The crew perished. The *Tyne, Providence* and *Northumberland* all launched.

Oct 19 In a severe gale, the tugs *William and Mary* and *Vigilant* broke from moorings and drifted onto the Herd Sand. The *Tyne* launched and found no one on board either vessel. The *William and Mary* later went to pieces on the sands.

Oct 27 The *Iduna* wrecked on Marsden Bay.

Oct 31 5.30am. Schooner *Lively Sheel* of Montrose, in ballast, struck the South Pier stones. The *Tyne* (17 crew) launched, but the schooner's crew reached safety by climbing along the jib boom and dropping onto the pier. Schooner refloated on the next tide.

Nov 16 The *Industry* of Shields lost at Souter Point.

Nov 18 The *George and James* wrecked south of Marsden Rock.

Nov 26 3am. The schooner *Sarah Ann* of Jersey, in ballast, got out of the channel when entering the harbour and let her anchors go near the Black Middens. The *Tyne* (16 crew) launched and stood by for two hours until a steamer towed the schooner into the river on the next tide.

Dec 3 The brig *Harriet* of Plymouth went ashore on the Herd Sand with the tide at half ebb. Her crew of nine was rescued by the *Tyne* (17 crew). The brig went to pieces the next day. The *Providence* also launched, without orders and without Superintendent Coxswain onboard. No reward was made to the crew.

Dec 6 The *Leander* of North Shields sank after colliding with the barque *Saxon* off the Tyne.

Dec 15 1.30am. The schooner *Achien* fired signal rockets when she strayed out of the channel towards the Herd Sand. The *Tyne (*18 crew) launched but the crew of the *Achien* refused to leave their vessel. The *Tyne* stood by until the schooner entered harbour.

Dec 29 4.30pm. Southerly gale. The brigs *Lewis* of South Shields and *Wynyard* of Blyth were being towed into harbour when the tow broke and both vessels were driven onto the Black Middens. The *Tyne* (18 crew) launched, soon followed by the salvage boat *William Wake,* which got alongside the *Levis*, but was washed clear. The *Tyne* ran in and rescued the 11 crew, landing them at Tynemouth Haven.

As the *Tyne* was returning to shore with the crew of the *Lewis,* the brig, *Union* of Shoreham ran onto the rocks. The *Constance* had launched and the crew of the *Tyne* hailed the *Constance* informing them of the wreck of the *Union* but the messages were not heard. The *Tyne* immediately went out and rescued her crew of 10. The *Providence* (18 crew) had also launched to the aid of the *Union.*

The *William Wake* rescued the crew of the *Wynard.* Tynemouth Volunteer Life Brigade fired lines onto the three vessels, but the crews elected to be taken off by the lifeboat and salvage boat.

1866

Jan 13 4am. The barque *Victoria* of Ostend came ashore at Souter Point. At 9am word reached the pilots and the *Tyne* (18 crew) launched and was towed to the wreck. On arrival the steam tugs *Robert Scott, William* and *Pinards*, had rescued the crew of nine using hauling lines. The mate was unaccounted for and the *Tyne* went alongside and rescued him. The *Northumberland* (21 crew) then arrived on scene. Both lifeboats were towed back to the river by the tug *Manner.*

Jan 31 *Nymphia* wrecked in Shields Harbour.

Mar 1 8pm. The *Hygoea* of Kragero, Norway, went ashore on the Herd Sand. The dismasted vessel was pounded by heavy seas. The *Tyne* (18 crew) and *Providence* (19 crew) both launched. The *Tyne* got alongside and rescued seven crew. One man was drowned as he attempted to jump into the lifeboat. South Shields Volunteer Life Brigade mustered for the first time, but their services were not required. The North Shields lifeboat *Northumberland* launched some time later but the Trustees of the Institution refused to pay the crew their reward.

Mar 19 10.30pm. SSE gale, four hours ebb. The schooner *Hesperus* of Newcastle, in ballast, was driven out of the channel towards the Black Middens. The *Tyne* (15 crew) launched, but the crew refused to leave. The schooner was later towed off.

Apr 2 5pm. A tremendous gale. The schooner *Tenterden* of Sunderland was driven ashore on the Herd Sand, south of the South Pier. The crew of seven, including the master's wife and young child, were saved by South Shields Volunteer Life Brigade, the first rescue by the Shields Brigade. The *Tyne* (19 crew) launched and was towed downstream by a tug. After releasing the tow, the lifeboat was swamped by heavy seas, driven against the Groyne and holed in several places. The crew escaped ashore and the lifeboat was later reboarded and returned to its boathouse for repair.

Apr 8 A small boat with two boys on board swept onto the Herd Sand and capsized. The *Tyne* (14 crew) launched, but one boy was rescued by a passing coble and the other drowned.

July 31 Wreck of the barque *Ostrich* of North Shields at Manhaven, Marsden, with the loss of ten crew including the master and his son. Only four of the crew saved.

Nov 10 10pm. S gale. The brig *Quayside* of Whitby, in ballast, was driven onto the Herd Sand. The *Tyne* (18 crew) launched. Crew would not leave their vessel which was later refloated.

Nov 14 The *Constance* launched to the SS *Buda* of Leith, which had fired distress rockets off the river entrance. With the assistance of the lifeboat crew, the vessel was brought safely into the river.

Nov 16 Wreck of the barque *Blossom*, 6.15pm, and the schooner *Sovereign*, 6.30pm, both on the south side of the South Pier. The four crew of the *Blossom* were taken off by South Shields Volunteer Life Brigade, the 11 crew of the *Sovereign* saved themselves. The *Northumberland* (23 crew) launched, but by the time the lifeboat had got around the pier, the crew had been rescued.

Nov 19 6am. NW gale. The barque *Borelia* of Shields, in the tow of a steamer, went onto the Herd Sand after the tow rope had parted. The *Tyne* (19 crew) launched. The steamer got another line onboard and brought the barque into the river.

1867
Jan 5 1am. Signal guns fired twice indicating a ship ashore. The *Tyne* (16 crew) launched, but found nothing.

Jan 6 A severe gale from the SE. Between midnight and 4am, four vessels, following each others' lights, came ashore on the Herd Sand and South Pier, in front of the Volunteer Life Brigade Watch House; the schooner *Merghee* of Whitstable (1am.) the brig *Mary Mac* (2am) and brigantine *Cora* (2am), both of Faversham, and the brig *Lucerne* of Blyth (4am).

South Shields Volunteer Life Brigade landed all 19 crew from the *Merghee*, the six crew of the *Mary Mac*, and eight crew from the *Lucerne*. The crew of the *Cora* saved themselves by crawling along the brig's bowsprit and dropping onto the pier. A boy from the *Mary Mac*, and another from the *Merghee*, were drowned.

The *Tyne* (17 crew), *Providence* (18 crew) and *Northumberland* (18 crew) all launched but could not get alongside due to the rocks.

The brig *Emmanuel Boucher* of Whitby came ashore on the Black Middens. The Tynemouth No. 2 lifeboat *Pomfret and Goole*, launched on her first service from her boathouse overlooking the Black Middens, and saved the six crew of the *Emmanuel Boucher*. The *Tyne* (17 crew), *Providence* (18 crew) and *Northumberland* all launched but their services were not required.

Feb 25 The steam tug *Guide* run down off the Tyne Bar.

Mar 17 SS *Florence* of Sunderland, aground on the Mussel Scarp sands, Black Middens. The *Tyne* (12 crew) gave assistance.

May 17 The *Northumberland* launched to a brig in difficulties and the *Providence* launched to a capsized boat.

Oct 16 7.30pm. Gale from the NNE. The brig *Sea Horse* of Aberdeen, returning to the Tyne coal laden, was driven onto the South Pier stones. Crew rescued by the *Tyne* (22 crew). The *Providence* and *Northumberland* (20 crew) both launched. South Shields

Volunteer Life Brigade on bad weather watch.

Dec 2 Gale from the NNE with a very high sea. The steam tug *Pearl*, returning to the harbour, was struck by a heavy sea, overwhelmed, and foundered with the loss of her crew of four. Great damage was done to the North Pier and 250ft. of the South Pier were destroyed.

1868
Jan 28 *Anne* of Whitstable wrecked at the mouth of the Tyne.

Aug 1 The *Providence* launched to a boat upset in the harbour.

Sept 11 The brig *Nathaniel* and barque *Magna Charta* were making signals to the south of the South Pier. The *Tyne* (18 crew) launched. Later that day the *Providence* (17 crew) launched to the same vessels.

Sept 27 4.30am. Gale from the SE. The schooner *Impulse* of Maldon went ashore on South Pier. The crew of seven, who at first refused to leave, was rescued by South Shields Volunteer Life Brigade.

Oct 4 During a NW gale, the SS *Martlet* of Hull dragged her anchor and drifted onto the Herd Sand, but shortly afterwards got off. Five of the passengers were landed by the *Tyne* (17 crew). The *Pomfret and Goole* launched, but her services were not required. The *Northumberland* (20 crew) launched later the same day.

Oct 23 HMS *Castor* fired her signal guns to indicate a ship ashore. The *Tyne* (18 crew) launched.

Nov 6 9.30am. Gale from the NNW. The galliot *Premier* of Montrose went ashore on the South Pier. Five crew landed by South Shields Volunteer Life Brigade. The *Tyne* and *Providence* launched. The tug *Excelsior* was towing a lighter. The tow line snapped when crossing the bar, the lighter sank and her two crew drowned.

The *Tyne* (18 crew) launched to the schooner *Tom Duff* of Aberdeen aground on the Herd Sands

The *Providence* (24 crew) and *Tyne* (18 crew) launched to the *Inverness-shire*.

Nov 24 2am. Hopper Barge *No.25* ashore on the south side of the South Pier. Two crew landed by South Shields Volunteer Life Brigade. The South Beach lifeboat, *Prior* (16 crew), the *Tyne* (18 crew) and the *Northumberland* (19 crew) all launched.

1869
Jan 18 3.30am. The *Two Brothers* of Holland went ashore on the Herd Sand. The *Tyne* (13 crew) launched, and stood by for two hours until the vessel refloated and entered the river.

Jan 21 11am. The SS *Scotia* ran onto the rocks to the north of the North Pier in dense fog. Tugs were unable to tow her off, and lighters were brought alongside to discharge cargo. Two days later, the vessel began to break up and the crew was taken off by the salvage boat *William Wake*. Tynemouth Volunteer Life Brigade were on standby.

Mar 5 NE Gale. Three pilots, John Heron, John Houlsby and Launcelot Burn were making for the harbour in their pilot coble when the boat was swamped in broken water off the Herd Sand near to the under construction South Pier. The men and boat were saved by the *Tyne* (18 crew). The *Northumberland* (20 crew) assisted.

Mar 23 The *Alert* wrecked on the Tyne Bar.

Mar 29 7.50am. Gale from the NE. Stranding of the schooner *Mary* of Chester on the end of the Herd Sand. Crew refused to leave the ship in the lifeboats that were along-side. *Pomfret and Goole, Tyne* (23 crew) and *Providence* (19 crew) all launched, but their services were not required.

Jun 10 The *Alma* of Aberdeen ashore on rocks. *Tyne* (17 crew) launched.

Jun 15 Terrific gale from the NE. Stranding of the fishing boats *Victo,* of Eyemouth (her crew of five rescued by South Shields Volunteer Life Brigade), and *Ten Brothers* of Weymouth on the Herd Sand. Two of the crew drowned in crossing the Bar, and three were landed by the South Shields Volunteer Life Brigade. At 10pm, the schooner *Annie*, of Rye, came ashore at Manhaven. Seven crew landed by South Shields Volunteer Life Brigade, the schooner later went to pieces. The *Northumberland* (23 crew) and *Tyne* (16 crew) both launched, but their services were not required.

Jun 16 1.30am. Fishing smack aground on South Pier. Three crew landed by South Shields Volunteer Life Brigade. The *Tyne* (16 crew) and *Northumberland* (19 crew) both launched but their services were not required.

Oct 18 8.30pm. The *Mary* of Aberdeen, returning coal laden to the Tyne for shelter, ran onto the Black Middens, The *Tyne* (17 crew) launched, but the crew refused to leave and the vessel was later refloated by tugs.

Oct 19 12pm. The *Friends* of Aberdeen in difficulties at the Tyne entrance. Six crew landed by the *Tyne*. South Shields Volunteer Life Brigade on bad weather watch.

Gale from the NNE. The Prussian brig *Mauritz Reichenheim*, inbound, broke loose from the tug *Reynard* and came ashore at Manhaven. Only one survivor from a crew of ten.

Nov 30 Gale from the NE. Stranding of the schooner *Squirrel* of South Shields, laden with blasting powder, on the Herd Sand. Crew of three saved by the *Tyne* (18 crew). The *Providence* (24 crew) and the *Pomfret and Goole* both launched but their services were not required.

Dec 24 Gale with heavy seas. The *Apollo* of Aberdeen ran onto the Black Middens. The *Tyne* (18 crew) and *Providence* (24 crew) gave assistance.

Dec 26 8pm. Gale from the NE with blinding showers of snow and hail. Loss of the schooner *Viscount Macduff* of Montrose on the Black Middens during a snow storm. The master and one of the crew at the ship's wheel were washed overboard by heavy seas when crossing the Bar. The *Tyne* and *Northumberland* both launched, but could not find the wreck. Tynemouth Volunteer Life Brigade fired lines over the wreck, but without response. The remaining crew of four was saved by the *Pomfret and Goole*.

Dec 27 5.30pm. The brig *Harmony,* riding at anchor in broken water, close to the Spar Hawk rocks, Tynemouth. The *Providence* (25 crew) and *Northumberland* (20 crew) launched to her assistance. The brig was towed into the river by a passing steamer.

Dec 30 During a hurricane force SSE gale, the *Lady Carter* of Liverpool lost her tow when rounding the South Pier Buoy and was in danger of driving onto the advanced base of the North Pier. She dropped two anchors and flew distress signals off the harbour entrance. The *Constance* launched and stood by for six hours until two steamers towed the vessel into the river.

5pm. SSE gale. The brig *Annie* of Shields got too close to the South Pier when entering the harbour and let go her anchors. The *Northumberland* (21 crew) took off nine crew. The *Tyne* arrived on scene and finding no one onboard put a number of pilots on the brig to bring her into the river.

8pm. The *Catherine and Hannah* got too close to the Black Middens and dropped her anchors. The *Providence* (21 crew) and *Tyne* (18 crew) both launched, but the crew refused to leave their ship which was later towed into harbour.

9pm. The *Produce* of Folkestone, in ballast, drove onto the North Pier stones. The *Northumberland* (20 crew) launched, but a passing steamer got a line onboard and towed the vessel into the river.

1870
Jan 31 Wind ESE. Stranding of the three-masted Prussian barque *Astrea* on the North Pier at Tynemouth Haven. The *Tyne* (18 crew) and *Northumberland* (20 crew) both launched. The crew refused to leave and the vessel was towed off the next morning by the tug *Spindrift*.

Feb 8 3.58pm. E gale and heavy seas with sleet and snow showers. Loss of the barque *Helena* of Scarborough on the Spar Hawk. Crew of 16 and one pilot saved by The *Northumberland* (22 crew), with the *Tyne* standing by. Tynemouth Volunteer Life

Brigade fired lines across the wreck, but the crew had been taken off by the lifeboat.

4pm. Loss of the brigantine *Susannah* of Seaham on the Spanish Battery Rocks, master and three of the crew saved by the Tynemouth Volunteer Life Brigade. One of the crew fell overboard with the mast and drowned. This was the first crew saved by the Tynemouth Volunteer Life Brigade. The *Tyne* (17 crew) launched, but her services were not required.

Crew of the *Anne,* ashore on the Black Middens, rescued by the *Providence* (24 crew).

Loss of the schooner *Light of the Harem*, to the north of the North Pier. Crew of five saved by the Tynemouth Volunteer Life Brigade. While a Yarmouth schooner was entering the Tyne, the master was washed overboard and drowned.

Mar 23 7.30am. NE gale. The *Alert* of Wick, in ballast, drove onto the Herd Sand. The *Tyne* (19 crew) and *Northumberland* (19 crew) both launched. The crew refused to leave their vessel, which was later towed off the sands by the tug *William Scott.*

The *Saxon* of Montrose driven onto the Herd Sand. The crew rescued by the *Northumberland* (20 crew). The *Tyne* (18 crew) also launched.

Dec 9 7am. Gale from the SE. South Pier. SS *Eagle*, of London aground on the Herd Sand to the north of the South Pier. South Shields Volunteer Life Brigade fired two rockets over the wreck, but the crew did not understand how to use the line and took to the rigging. Ten crew saved by the *Tyne* (18 crew) and seven crew saved by the *Northumberland (*20 crew).

4.30pm. The schooner *Samuel Barnard* of Boston foundered in heavy seas, 100 yards off the South Pier. Crew of five, including the captain's wife and children, all perished.

Wreck of the Barque *City of Bristol* on Tynemouth Long Sands. Crew of nine rescued by Cullercoats Volunteer Life Brigade. The *Tyne* (18 crew) and *Northumberland* (24 crew) launched but their services were not required.

10.10pm. The schooner *Amalie* of Stavanger driven onto Tynemouth Long Sands. Tynemouth Volunteer Life Brigade fired lines towards the vessel, which was too far offshore to be reached. The crew of six was saved by the *Pomfret and Goole.* The *Tyne* (18 crew) and *Northumberland* (20 crew) both launched, but returned to their boat-houses when it was found that the wreck was north of the North Pier.

Dec 20 7.10pm. Gale from the SE with tremendous seas running. The barque *Union* of Colchester aground on the end of the South Pier. Ten crew landed by South Shields Volunteer Life Brigade. The barque went to pieces during the night. The *Tyne* (18 crew) and *Providence* (24 crew) both launched, but due to the heavy seas, and the danger of capsize, were unable to approach the wreck.

Dec 22 Gale from the SE. The *Margaret and Ann* grounded on the Mussel Scarp, Black Middens. Crew rescued by the *Tyne* (17 crew).

1871

Jan 23 3.50am. South Pier. The brig *Maize* of London stranded on the south side of the South Pier stones. Six crew landed by South Shields Volunteer Life Brigade, using a heaving line. Master taken off by the *Tyne.*

Feb 6 The brig *Gratitude* ashore on Spanish Battery rocks. Later refloated by a tug.

Feb 10 Terrible gale from the SE. Seas between the piers a mass of churning water, with four ships coming ashore within a short period of time and all close to each other.

Wreck of the brigs *Orinoco* of Scarborough and the *Cynthia Ann* of London, on the Black Middens. The crews of six and seven respectively, saved by the *Tyne* and *Northumberland.*

Loss of the brig *Jabez* of Whitby on the Spanish Battery rocks. Four of the crew drowned, and two were washed ashore on planks. Tynemouth Volunteer Life Brigade fired lines aboard, but the brig broke up in a matter of minutes.

Wreck of the brig *British Queen* of London on the rocks near Tynemouth Haven. Crew of seven saved by the *Constance.*

9.30pm. Loss of the schooner *Admiral Codrington* of Colchester ashore on the Spanish Battery rocks. Crew of six saved by the Tynemouth Volunteer Life Brigade.

Wreck of the brig *Valiant* of Newport, which had struck the staging on the end of the North Pier. Crew of seven saved by the *Constance.*

May 6 SS *David Brown* in collision with the SS *Earl Percy*, in dense fog off the Tyne entrance.

Oct 1 Loss of the German barque *Llanelly* on the rubble inside the North Pier. The crew saved themselves by jumping onto the pier.

Oct 2 Gale from the ESE. 10.45pm. The brig *Anne* stranded on the Herd Sand on the north side of the South Pier. South Shields Volunteer Life Brigade set up the life saving apparatus on the pier, but two rockets misfired. Two lifeboats launched, with eight crew saved by the *Tyne.*

Dec 3 10.30am. Wind from the NNE. The German brig *Fresia*, under tow out of the river went aground on the end of the South Pier after the tow broke. The *Tyne* and *Providence*, *Northumberland* and salvage boat *Noble Institution* all launched. Three crew landed by South Shields Volunteer Life Brigade. Vessel broke up within 30 minutes of grounding. Three of the crew drowned.

1872

Apr 21 3.40pm. Gale from the NE with heavy seas, tide on the ebb. The *Amphitrite* of North Shields, built in 1776, came ashore on the Herd Sand on the south side of the South Pier. South Shields Volunteer Life Brigade fired two rockets that fell short of the wreck. Four lifeboats launched but only two managed to get around the South Pier end. Six crew saved by the *Tyne*. The captain, mate and two seamen remained on board while the vessel was left high and dry on the falling tide.

Dec 17 Terrific gale from the SSE. Wreck of the barque *Consul* of South Shields on the end of the North Pier. Loss of her master and six crew. Three of the crew saved by Tynemouth Volunteer Life Brigade. Robert Arkley, a member of the Volunteer Life Brigade, and previously of the Tynemouth Lifeboat, was washed off the pier and drowned.

8.20pm. Wreck of the brig *Duff* of Portsmouth. Having struck the Black Middens she drifted onto the Herd Sand, to the north of the South Pier. Two crew drowned in the ship's boat, the remaining five crew saved by the *Northumberland*. South Shields Volunteer Life Brigade assembled, but the wreck was out of range of the rockets.

9pm. The *Jamais* ashore on the Herd Sand within the harbour. While the South Shields Volunteer Life Brigade were setting up the rocket apparatus, the North Shields lifeboat got alongside and took off the crew with the exception of one crewmember who was washed overboard.

Dec 18 The brig *Gleaner* of Blyth lost one of the men at the wheel and the mate was washed overboard and drowned while coming in to the harbour. The *Northumberland* launched, but as it neared the wreck, six lifeboatmen were washed overboard by heavy seas. Two were drowned and the lifeboat was beached. The five crew of the *Gleaner* were saved by the South Shields lifeboat *Tom Perry*.

1873

Feb 3 11pm. NE gale. Hopper Barge grounded on the north side of the South Pier after losing its tow. Two crew brought ashore with heaving lines by South Shields Volunteer Life Brigade.

1874

July 16 The *Small Advance* wrecked on the Prior's Stone, Tynemouth.

Sept 5 The *William D. Seed* of Fleetwood capsized in Shields Harbour.

Nov 28 10.30pm. SSE gale. The schooner *Lavinia* of Guernsey aground on the Herd Sand, to the south of the Groyne. South Shields Volunteer Life Brigade began to set up the rocket apparatus. The *Tyne* and *Tom Perry* both launched and rescued the crew of nine.

Nov 29 5am. Wreck of the *Scylla* of Whitstable on the Herd Sand to the south of the South Pier. Crew of six saved by the South Shields Volunteer Life Brigade.

3pm. SSE gale. Loss of the sloop *St Albans* of London driven ashore onto rocks behind the North Pier. The master's wife and one crew drowned. The remaining three crew were rescued by Tynemouth Volunteer Life Brigade.

Dec 9 1am.Terrific gale on the coast from the NE. Loss of the barque *Henry Cooke,* of South Shields, driven onto the Herd Sand, on the south side of the South Pier, close to the wreck of the *Scylla*. South Shields Volunteer Life Brigade succeeded in firing lines onboard, but the crew did not know how to use them. The vessel keeled over and immediately went to pieces, and all 17 crew perished.

2.30am. Stranding of the schooner *J.P. Frecker* of Buckhaven on the Herd Sand midway between the South Pier and Trow Rocks. South Shields Volunteer Life Brigade succeeded in firing lines onboard, but the crew did not use them. By 5am, the tide had receded and the crew of seven walked ashore.

Dec 11 SE gale. Stranding of the SS *Breeze* of Hartlepool, on her sea trials, on the rocks below the Spanish Battery, having earlier grounded on the Herd Sand. Two of

South Tyneside Libraries

The Henry Cooke, wrecked 9 December, 1874.

the crew came ashore in the ship's boat. The *Constance* launched but was stove-in after hitting floating wreckage and returned to shore. Tynemouth Volunteer Life Brigade got a line onboard, as the two crew of the SS *Breeze* were being taken off by the *Northumberland*. The *Constance* was damaged beyond repair.

Dec 12 Wreck of the brigantine *Arcadia* of Truro on the Herd Sand, to the south of the South Pier. Two of the crew drowned and the remaining four were rescued by the South Shields Volunteer Life Brigade.

1875

Oct 14 Storm from the E, with a very high sea. Loss of the tug *Robin Hood* of Shields, which capsized on the Bar. The captain was saved by the tug *Toiler,* but her three crew all drowned.

Oct 19 Midday. A tremendous gale from the SE. Wreck of the schooner *Mystery* of Portsmouth on rocks to the south of the North Pier. The crew of five saved by the Tynemouth Volunteer Life Brigade.

Nov 19 5pm. Storm from the NE. The barque *Barba Avano* aground on the Herd Sand. Crew of 13 and a pilot saved by the salvage boat, *Noble Institution*. Tynemouth No. 2 lifeboat *Forester* launched, but her services were not required. Barque later refloated.

Nov 30 9am. SS *Alice* wrecked on the Herd Sand. Passengers taken off by the *Noble Institution*. The vessel was later refloated.

1876

Oct 21 Schooner *Albion* of Whitstable ashore on the Spanish Battery rocks. The new Tynemouth No. 1 lifeboat, *Charles Dibdin*, launched, but her services were not required.

Dec 2 Loss of three Cullercoats fishermen entering Cullercoats Harbour.

Dec 3 Sunday. Gale from the SE with a very high sea. Loss of the SS *Prince* of Middlesbrough and all her 14 crew when making for the Bar.

Loss of the schooner *Seven Sons* of Whitstable on the Black Middens. Crew of seven saved by Tynemouth Volunteer Life Brigade.

Dec 21 4.15am. A fearful SE storm with a tremendous sea. Wreck of the SS *Claremont* of Newcastle ashore on south side of South Pier. Crew of 19, together with the captain's wife and child rescued by South Shields Volunteer Life Brigade. Four members of the Brigade had a narrow escape from being washed off the South Pier. The South Shields, South Beach lifeboat *Willie Wouldhave* launched at 3am, as the first crew were being brought ashore by breeches buoy.

6.30am. SS *Tyne* ashore on south side of the South Pier end. South Shields Volunteer Life Brigade fired lines onto the vessel, whose crew were in the rigging. The waves were running at half mast height and all 17 crew were washed overboard and drowned.

7.30am. SS *Fenella* of London ashore on the south side of South Pier, close to the wreck of the *Tyne*. South Shields Volunteer Life Brigade fired lines onto the vessel, but the crew remained onboard and walked ashore at low water.

11am. Loss of the brig *First of May* of Blyth in Tynemouth Haven. Crew of eight saved by Tynemouth Volunteer Life Brigade.

2.40pm. SS *Blenheim* of Hartlepool ashore on the south side of the South Pier end. Six crew landed by South Shields Volunteer Life Brigade. 14 crew jumped ashore. One fell short and drowned.

3pm. Loss of the schooner *Albion,* of Whitstable on the Black Middens. The Tynemouth lifeboat *Charles Dibdin* was unable to get alongside due to the heavy seas. The crew of seven rescued by Tynemouth Volunteer Life Brigade.

4pm. The schooner, *New Cornwall* of Barnstable foundered with loss of all five crew outside the Piers. South Shields Volunteer Life Brigade on bad weather watch.

Dec 24 1am. SS *Herman Sauber*, aground on the Herd Sand to the south of the South Pier. 19 crew taken off by the *Willie Wouldhave*. South Shields Volunteer Life Brigade on bad weather watch.

Dec 25 Gale from the SE. 2.15am. Stranding of the brig *Mary* of Whitby. Five crew saved by the *Northumberland*.

1877
Mar 8 Tynemouth No. 2 lifeboat *Forester* launched to the barque *Eliza Mary*. No effective service.

Apr 21 The brig *Amphitrite* stranded at midnight on the Herd Sand during a SSE gale. Vessel refloated by tugs. She was stranded five years previously. South Shields Volunteer Life Brigade on bad weather watch.

1878
Feb 11 4am. SS *Mabel* of Montrose stranded 200 yards to the south of the South Pier in dense fog. The four crew came ashore in the ship's boat and were taken to the South Shields Volunteer Life Brigade Watch House. Brigade's members on bad weather watch. The vessel later refloated by tugs.

Sept 15 The *Asia* of South Shields sunk in Shields harbour after a collision with the

Countess of Aberdeen of Aberdeen.

Nov 28 6.30am. Storm from NNE. German barque *Jacob Rothenburg* driven onto the south side of the South Pier. The crew of seven and an English pilot landed by South Shields Volunteer Life Brigade. A Newfoundland dog belonging to the ship drowned.

Nov 29 Stranding of the outward bound SS *Stagshaw* in fog on the Black Middens. The *Forester* and *Northumberland* and the *Tom Perry* all launched, but their services were declined.

1879

Feb 16 Gale from the SE. Stranding of the SS *Mary*, of London, on the Black Middens, laden with copper ore. Tynemouth Volunteer Life Brigade fired a number of lines across the wreck, but got no response. 14 of the crew rescued by the *Northumberland*, and the remaining five crew by the *Tom Perry*. The Tynemouth lifeboat *Forester* could not be launched due to the low tide. The SS *Mary* became a total wreck.

Apr 7 The SS *Ben Ledi* of North Shields wrecked on Souter Point.

May 15 The *Brothers* of Shields lost with all hands off Trow Rocks.

Nov 19 The SS *Emeral* of Whitstable sunk after a collision with the SS *Blue Cross* of Newcastle off the South Pier. The master and two men from the *Emeral* drowned.

1880

Feb 16 6.35pm. Gale from the SE with a heavy sea. The brig *Thomas and Elizabeth* of Sunderland ran aground on the Herd Sand near to the South Pier. Despite the breeches buoy apparatus being set up and rocket lines fired over the wreck by South Shields Volunteer Life Brigade, she broke up immediately, leaving no chance to save the crew.

Oct 22 9pm. *Olymphe Kruper* ashore on the Herd Sand. Eight crew remained onboard. South Shields Volunteer Life Brigade on bad weather watch.

Oct 28 7.50am. Storm from the ESE. The schooner, *Johanna* of Denmark hit the South Pier end and came ashore on the Black Middens. Only one of a crew of four saved by the N*orthumberland*. South Shields Volunteer Life Brigade on bad weather watch.

8.20am. Loss of the steam trawler *Wonga* and her crew of five. She capsized after being hit by heavy seas.

9am. The North Shields steam trawler *Flying Huntsman* capsized after being hit and broached to by a number of heavy seas when crossing the Bar. Eight crew lost.

1.30pm. The schooner *Isis* of Yarmouth ashore on the Herd Sand to the south of the

South Pier. Six crew rescued by South Shields Volunteer Life Brigade.

8pm. The brigantine *Harry Clem* of Faversham ashore on the Herd Sand, a short distance to the south of the *Isis*. Lines fired aboard by South Shields Volunteer Life Brigade, but no response. Two crew lost overboard, four got ashore in their own boat assisted by South Shields Volunteer Life Brigade.

An enormous number of spectators gathered on the beach to the south of the Brigade Watch House to watch the shipwrecks. The high tide suddenly flooded the area and, seeing that they could be cut off, the spectators panicked and stampeded. Two women, two young girls and a boy fell in the shallow waters and drowned.

Wreck of the brig *Astley* of West Hartlepool at Cullercoats. Crew of six saved by Cullercoats Volunteer Life Brigade.

Vessel driven ashore on Whitley Sands, near Briar Dene Burn. Crew saved by Cullercoats Volunteer Life Brigade.

Nov 8 4.45pm *Bertha* aground on South Pier. Six crew remained on board. The pilot drowned.

1881
Jan 19 Gale from the SE with heavy snow showers. Entering the harbour, the brig *Coquette* of Whitby had her main topmast carried away along with one of the crew who drowned. The mate was injured.

Feb 7 6pm. Gale from the SE. While entering the harbour, the three-masted schooner *Faithful* of Ipswich was driven onto the Black Middens. Tynemouth Volunteer Life Brigade got a line onboard, but the seven crew were rescued by the *Tom Perry*.

Feb 14 7.20pm. Gale from the SSE with showers of rain and sleet and high seas. Two vessels drove ashore on the Herd Sand to the south of the South Pier; the brigantine *Ann* of Sunderland and, at 7.30pm, the brigantine *Reaper*, 30 yards to the east of the *Ann*. Lines fired over both vessels by South Shields Volunteer Life Brigade and the crews of six and nine respectively, and a dog, were rescued. Both ships went to pieces next day.

Mar 4 Fearful gale and snowstorm. Loss of the *Cecilia* of Liverpool, and 18 lives, off Souter Point.

Mar 12 11pm. The barque *Fluellen* of London struck the rocks while entering the harbour during a fog. She was got off and towed into the harbour. *Forester* launched, but no effective service was performed.

Oct 14 2.15pm. Storm from the NE. The three-masted schooner *Atlantic* of Laurig, Norway, laden with sleepers and pit props, was entering the harbour under tow. She was driven ashore onto the Herd Sand near to the South Pier when the towline broke. Seven crew and a pilot rescued by South Shields Volunteer Life Brigade. The pilot's coble, which was being towed by the *Atlantic*, was carried away and lost.

A pilot coble returning from sea capsized outside the South Pier. Thomas Young and John Ramsey, both pilots, and Thomas Tindle, apprentice, were drowned. Young was brought ashore alive by South Shields Volunteer Life Brigade and taken to the Brigade Watch House, but the Honorary Surgeon could not revive him.

Oct 19 4pm. Gale from the E. The galliot *Bertha* of Stavanger, was driven onto the Herd Sand. The South Shields lifeboats *Tyne* and *Tom Perry* both launched. Five crew rescued by the *Tom Perry*.

Oct 21 0.15am. The barque *Iron Crown* of Liverpool (995 tons) went ashore on the Black Middens during a severe ESE gale. Five crew rescued by Tynemouth Volunteer Life Brigade and 17 on the first effective service of the Tynemouth No. 1 lifeboat *Charles Dibdin*. The barque went to pieces the following day. South Shields Volunteer Life Brigade on bad weather watch.

Nov 3 Wind from the SE with seas breaking over the Bar. The sloop *Aurora* of Boston wrecked on the Black Middens. Crew of three rescued by *Forester*. Tynemouth Volunteer Life Brigade got lines aboard, but the crew refused to leave by the breeches buoy as they did not understand how to use it. The sloop quickly broke up and became a total wreck.

Shields Daily News

The Iron Crown wrecked on the Black Middens, October 21 1881.

South Tyneside Libraries

The George Clark and Ida.

Nov 26 7pm. Gale from the SW. The brig *George Clark*, in ballast, driven onto the south side of the South Pier. Eight crew landed by South Shields Volunteer Life Brigade.

7.45pm. The ketch, *Ida* of Ipswich, driven ashore onto the South Pier against the *George Clark*. Coastguardsman Frederick Jaggers, stationed at South Shields, volunteered to be taken back out to the *George Clark* in the breeches buoy. He guided the four crew of the *Ida* onto the *George Clark* and took them ashore in the breeches buoy.

Nov 27 Thirteen salvage men onboard the *George Clark* landed in the breeches buoy by South Shields Volunteer Life Brigade, due to increasing heavy seas breaking over the vessel with the onset of the high tide.

South Tyneside Libraries

Coastguard Fred Jaggers

1882

Mar 22 10.15am. NNE gale. The schooner *Mail* of Alloa was being towed into the harbour when the towrope broke and she was driven ashore on the north side of the South Pier. The four crew were rescued by South Shields Volunteer Life Brigade. The *Tyne* launched to assist.

South Tyneside Libraries

The Mail.

7am. The SS *Robert Watson Boyd* lost her helm while leaving the Tyne and came ashore onto the Black Middens. Several tugs tried unsuccessfully to tow the vessel off the rocks due to the deteriorating weather. By 2pm, distress signals were fired, and the *Forester* took off 14 crew and some nautical instruments. The remaining 46 crew were taken off by the *Tom Perry* and *Tyne*.

Apr 15 3.30pm *Glenfinart* in difficulties at Trow Rocks. South Shields Volunteer Life Brigade on bad weather watch. *Charles Dibdin* launched but her services were not required. Vessel got away.

Aug 2 3pm *Isabella* in difficulties at South Pier. South Shields Volunteer Life Brigade on bad weather watch. Vessel got away.

Sept 29 SS *Finlay* wrecked on the Black Middens.

Nov 1 The *Tom Perry* launched to the SS *Preston*.

Dec 4 11.30am. A severe ESE gale. *Emily* in difficulties at South Pier. South Shields Volunteer Life Brigade on bad weather watch. Vessel got away.

The *Tom Perry* launched to escort 20 Cullercoats fishing cobles in difficulties making for the Tyne harbour.

1.30pm. The barque *Rhineland* of Pensacola, laden with timber, was being towed into the harbour by the steam tug *Skylark*. She broke her tow and drove onto the Black Middens. The master, his wife and two children together with 11 crew were rescued by the *Tom Perry*, and two crew were taken off by *Forester.* The *Willie Wouldhave* and *Noble Institution* also launched.

1.30pm. The *Catherine and Mary* of Torquay foundered in heavy breaking seas off the harbour mouth, with the loss of all hands. The *Willie Wouldhave* went to her assistance.

The alarm guns were fired at 11pm, and the *Forester* launched at 11.20pm to the schooner *Argo* of Copenhagen in a dangerous position near the South Pier. The lifeboat piloted the schooner into safer waters inside the harbour.

Dec 5 10pm. The brig, *Olaf Kyrre* of Frederikstad, Norway, was driven ashore to the south of the South Pier end. Eight crew saved by the *Tyne* were landed at 2am. The *Tom Perry* launched but her services were not required. South Shields Volunteer Life Brigade on bad weather watch.

Dec 7 6.40am. The schooner, *Flid* of Egersund, Norway, drove onto the Herd Sand to the south of the South Pier. Three crew landed by South Shields Volunteer Life Brigade. Two Brigadesmen went off to the ship in the breeches buoy to assist the crew. The remaining three crew were saved by the *Tyne*. The schooner went to pieces at 10.30am. This was the last service launch of the *Tyne*.

Dec 8 5.15pm. Unknown vessel in difficulties off Herd Sand. South Shields Volunteer Life Brigade on standby. Vessel got away.

1883
Jan12 SE gale. SS *Libelle* stranded on Tynemouth Long Sands. Tynemouth Volunteer Life Brigade set up rocket apparatus, but the 21 crew and eight passengers rescued by Cullercoats lifeboat *Palmerston*. The *Tom Perry* and *Willie Wouldhave* both launched, but rendered no assistance.

Jan 23 The schooner *Wave* of Maldon ashore on the Black Middens. The *Tom Perry* and *Willie Wouldhave* launched to assist.

Feb 6 9.15pm. Gale from the SE. The Brig *Cactus* of Whitby was wrecked on the Black Midden Rocks. The crew of seven was rescued by the *Tom Perry*. Tynemouth Volunteer Life Brigade fired lines aboard but got no response, despite receiving no signals that the crew had been rescued earlier by the lifeboat.

Feb 7 9.30am. The brigantine *Hannah and Eleanor* went ashore on the rubble foundations of the North Pier. The crew of five rescued by the *Willie Wouldhave,* which had been towed to the wreck by a tug, and had arrived just before the *Charles Dibdin*, which had launched at 9.45am, following a difficult journey across 600 yards of soft sand. The *Tom Perry* also launched. Members of the Tynemouth lifeboat crew and Tynemouth Volunteer Life Brigade boarded the wreck to release rocket lines and lay anchors to try and save the brigantine.

Feb 8 8.25am. The Russian barque *Vega* stranded on the Black Midden rocks, and afterwards drifted to the South Pier, where she grounded. She was later towed out of danger. The *Tom Perry* launched and the Tynemouth Volunteer Life Brigade were on standby.

10am. The Brig *Janet Izat*, an old Tyne collier, went ashore on the Black Middens. The crew of eight was rescued by the *Tom Perry* after a delay of an hour and a half. Tynemouth Volunteer Life Brigade fired lines onboard, but the crew refused to leave the ship. The *Willie Wouldhave* launched and stood by.

6.50pm. The *Ann* of Guernsey struck the ground to the east of the Groyne, South Shields. South Shields Volunteer Life Brigade fired lines and the crew hauled the breeches buoy on board. However everything then went quiet. Later it was learned that three crew had been saved by the *Tom Perry* and three by the *Noble Institution*. The *Willie Wouldhave* fell off her launching trolley, was disabled, and could not launch. Her crew then launched the *Noble Institution*.

Feb 9 11.30pm. The SS *Minnie* of Middlesbrough struck the rocks under the Spanish Battery. Tynemouth Volunteer Life Brigade fired lines onboard, but the crew failed to rig the breeches buoy apparatus. Fourteen crew rescued by the *Willie Wouldhave*, and one by the *Tom Perry*. They were landed at the Tyne Sailors' Home.

Feb 28 SS *Veracity* wrecked at Souter Point. Master drowned.

Mar 9 The *Tom Perry* and *Willie Wouldhave* launched to the SS *Athelstane*.

Mar 18 7.30pm. Storm from the SE. The three-masted schooner *Aleas* of Helsingborg

South Tyneside Libraries

The Ann, of Guernsey, wrecked at South Shields on 8 February, 1883.

went ashore on the Black Middens. Tynemouth Volunteer Life Brigade fired lines on-board, and the crew began to rig the breeches buoy apparatus, when the *Willie Wouldhave* came alongside and took off the crew of eight. The *Tom Perry* launched to assist. The ship went to pieces during the night.

Mar 30 1.30am. Gale from the SW. The steam wherry *Yarr Yen* of Montrose went ashore on the Black Middens. Crew of six rescued by the *Willie Wouldhave*. The *Tom Perry* launched to assist. Tynemouth Volunteer Life Brigade fired a rocket, but the strong wind sent it wide, by which time the lifeboat was alongside.

Apr 17 The *British Enterprise* sunk in Shields harbour after collision with the SS *Warkworth*.

1884

Feb 18 The Tyne Improvement Commissioners' *Hopper No. 28* drove ashore at the back of the North Pier after breaking its towline. The crew of two was rescued by Tynemouth Volunteer Life Brigade. The *Tom Perry* and *Willie Wouldhave* both launched, but rendered no assistance.

Feb 28 4am. The brig *Excel* of Swansea, having hit the South Pier end, grounded on the south side of the South Pier. South Shields Volunteer Life Brigade fired lines on-

South Shields VLB Archive

The wreck of the brig Excel. To the left of the Excel's mainmast stay can be seen the South Beach lifeboat house, and in the background between the Excel and the pier, the Volunteer Life Brigade Watch House.

board, but the eight crew had got away safely in the ship's boat and were picked up by the tug *Expert*. The *Tom Perry* and *Willie Wouldhave* both launched, but rendered no assistance.

Sept 7 Gale from the N and N by E. Loss of Matthew Heslop and William Purvis, two pilots, when their coble capsized off Souter Point.

1885
Oct 19 Signal guns at the Spanish Battery fired to indicate a ship in distress. The *Tom Perry* and *Willie Wouldhave* both launched, but found nothing – false alarm.

Oct 24 Storm from the NE by N. The SS *Firdene* had a narrow escape from stranding on the South Pier end when entering the harbour. Two boys were washed off the South Pier. One was drowned. South Shields Volunteer Life Brigade on bad weather watch.

Nov 25 6.30pm. In a full gale and heavy seas, the rudder of the ketch *Ada* was carried away and anchored in a dangerous position near the South Pier. The *Tom Perry, Willie Wouldhave* and *Forester* all launched and stood by until tugs managed to bring the vessel safely into harbour.

1886
Dec 15 The brig *Agenoria* of Guernsey in danger south of the South Pier. The *Tom Perry* launched to her assistance.

1887
Jan 11 Schooner *Earl of Musgrove* in danger close to Tynemouth rocks. The South Shields lifeboats *Bedford*, on her first service, and *Tom Perry* launched to her assistance.

May 20 The Norwegian schooner *Kaperin* in distress on the north side of the South Pier. The *Tom Perry* and North Shields lifeboat *James Young* launched to her assistance.

Nov 22 Three young men, Wm. J. Sadler, Joseph McGee and Carr Duncan, left the Tyne in a foyboat to attend to their fishing gear. They were caught in a storm from the NE and drowned near the Trow Rocks.

Nov 24 Stranding of the Schooner *Jane Roberts* of Caernarvon on Tynemouth Long Sands during a fog. The crew left in their own boats and were picked up by the steam tug *England* and brought into the Tyne.

1888
Jan 27 The schooner *Balcay* seen riding in a dangerous position near the Herd Sands. The *Bedford* launched to her assistance.

Mar 12 The fishing boat *British Prince* seen in danger near the South Pier. The *Bedford, Tom Perry* and *James Young* launched to her assistance.

Apr 17 The *Diadem* sunk in collision with the SS *Cyprus* in Shields Harbour.

Apr 26 The fishing boat *Maggie Scott* went ashore on the north side of the South Pier. The *Bedford* launched to her assistance.

June 30 3.30pm. SS *Hector* of Sunderland went aground on the north side of the South Pier. One crew landed by South Shields Volunteer Life Brigade, 15 by the *Tom Perry* and three by the *James Young*. *Charles Dibdin* launched, on what proved to be her last service at the station, and arrived shortly after the *Tom Perry*, which had been towed to the wreck by a tug. All lifeboats stood by whilst the vessel was refloated.

Nov 22 The SS *Vauxhall* of London, sunk in Shields Harbour in collision with the SS *Prudhoe Castle*.

1889
Feb 13 SS *Falcon* grounded on the South Pier then cast adrift. Two pilot apprentices, whose coble had been swamped, also rescued by the *Bedford,* with the *James Young* in attendance.

Mar 20 The fishing vessel *Eleanor* in distress at the harbour entrance. *Bedford, Tom Perry* and *James Young* launched to her assistance.

Mar 26 The *Danish Prince* of North Shields lost off Souter Point with all three hands.

Oct 19 SS *Rocklight* in difficulties near the Groyne. The *Bedford* launched to her assistance.

1890
Mar 24 SS *Lillian* of Newcastle ashore on the South Pier. The *Bedford* and *James Young* both launched but their services were not required. The vessel later refloated under her own power.

April 8 3.20pm. NE gale. The iron barque *Abbey Holme* of Liverpool came ashore on the north side of the South Pier when her tow rope parted. Ten crew landed by South Shields Volunteer Life Brigade. The *Bedford, James Young* and *Forester* all launched but all boats returned to shore.

Dec 9 The *Tom Perry* and *James Young* launched to the schooner *Volunteer* in difficulties south of the Groyne.

1891
Mar 15 8.20pm. The schooner *Ploughboy* of Shoreham went aground on South Pier. Five crew landed by South Shields Volunteer Life Brigade. The *James Young* launched

The Abbey Holme.

but her services were not required.

May 25 12.45pm. Strong NE wind. The *Forester*, *Bedford* and *James Young* all launched to the SS *Napier* which had ran aground on the Black Middens. The *Forester* was first on scene, followed by the South Shields lifeboats. They stood by as Tynemouth Volunteer Life Brigade fired lines onboard. The vessel was towed off by tugs on the rising tide.

June 3 6.50pm. SS *Geralda* of Newcastle stranded on Herd Sand was towed off. South Shields Volunteer Life Brigade on bad weather watch. The *Bedford* and *James Young* launched but their services were not required.

Oct 16 The *Tom Perry* and *James Young* launched to the schooner *Peggy,* ashore on the Black Middens. Crew saved by Tynemouth Volunteer Life Brigade. The *Forester* was unable to launch due to the low tide.

Nov 18 The *Bedford* and *James Young* launched to the steam trawler *Advance,* aground on the Black Middens. Services not required.

South Tyneside Libraries

The Huntsman, grounded on the south side of the South Pier, 10 January, 1892.

Dec 18 The *Bedford* and *James Young* launched to the SS *Gracie* of London and SS *Waterloo* of North Shields.

1892

Jan 7 The *Bedford* launched to the outward-bound SS *Crystal*, sunk when in collision with the inward-bound SS *Eider* off the South Pier ends. The crew of the *Crystal* was picked up by the tug *Gauntlet*.

Jan 10 6.30pm. ESE gale, heavy snow. SS *Huntsman* of North Shields grounded on south side of South Pier. 23 crew, one fisherman, the captain's wife and three children were landed by South Shields Volunteer Life Brigade. The *Willie Wouldhave* and *James Young* launched, but their services were not required.

Jan 12 The *James Young* launched to the SS *Orrick*.

Jan 14 The *Lina* run down off Souter Point.

Jan 17 5.30pm. The brig *Wellington* of Whitby went ashore on the south side of the South Pier, next to the *Huntsman*. Captain and one man swept off the wreck and drowned. Remaining four crew climbed on board the *Huntsman* and were afterwards taken off by breeches buoy by South Shields Volunteer Life Brigade. The *Willie Wouldhave*, *Bedford* and *James Young* launched, but their services were not required.

Oct 27 2.30am. SW gale. The schooner *Resolute* of Fowey went ashore on South Pier. The *Bedford* and *James Young* launched. Four crew landed by South Shields Volunteer

Life Brigade. Captain remained onboard till the tide fell.

Nov 17 SE gale. During the early hours of the morning, the barque *Lowestoft*, in the tow of a tug, hit the inside of the North Pier after the tow had parted. Four crew scrambled onto the North Pier. The remaining three crew were rescued by Tynemouth Volunteer Life Brigade.

Nov 20 2.20pm. The storm washed the Mammoth crane off the North Pier.

Dec 17 The *Satellite* run down off the Tyne.

1893
Nov 20 The *Tom Perry* launched to a barque from Lowestoft, aground on Tynemouth rocks.

1894
Jan 1 11.45am. NE gale. The barque *Friederich Ohledrich* of Rostock grounded on the South Pier end, after her tow parted when entering the harbour. 13 crew, the captain's wife and two compass adjustors landed by South Shields Volunteer Life Brigade. The *Tom Perry* and *James Young* launched, but their services were not required.

Oct 20 The barquentine *Fame* went ashore behind the North Pier. Crew of six rescued by Tynemouth Volunteer Life Brigade.

The Fame, wrecked on the north side of the North Pier.

Newcastle Libraries

Newcastle Libraries

The Fame from the North Pier.

South Tyneside Libraries

The Constantine, run on to the rocks south of the South Pier, 20 September, 1895.

1895

Jan 7 12.15pm. *Charles Dibdin* launched to escort fishing cobles from Cullercoats into harbour following a sudden squall.

Sept 20 4.50am. The collier SS *Constantine* of London was entering the harbour and collided with the outward-bound collier SS *Trevithick*. After sustaining damage and sinking, she was deliberately run onto the rocks on the southern side of the South Pier. Five crew were landed by South Shields Volunteer Life Brigade, and three had jumped onboard the SS *Trevithick* at the time of the collision. The remaining seven crew were rescued by the *James Young*, with the *Tom Perry* standing by.

Nov 19 The *James Young* launched to the fishing boat *Margaret Morris*, in difficulties in Tynemouth Haven.

Nov 23 8.30am. Severe NNE gale and heavy seas. The barque *Salween* of Norway was in tow of the tug *Tynedale*. The rope broke three times and the *Salween* drifted and hit the South Pier before coming ashore on south side of the South Pier. Nine crew landed by South Shields Volunteer Life Brigade. The *Tom Perry*, *James Young* and *Forester* all launched, but their services were not required.

South Tyneside Libraries

The Salween.

The wreck of the Rupert, ashore on the Black Middens.

Dec 16 8pm. SE gale. The *James Young, Tom Perry* and *Forester* launched to the SS *Willowdene,* in difficulties near the Black Middens. Tynemouth Volunteer Life Brigade mustered on shore, but the ship was towed into the river by a local tug.

Dec 24 11am. The brigantine *Rupert* of Faversham was struck by heavy seas when between the piers and began to settle down aft. Three or four of the crew took to the rigging. The alarm guns were fired onshore. The next seas capsized the vessel and she foundered inside the Tyne Piers with all hands lost. The *James Young* and *Tom Perry* launched but could not save any of the crew. Tynemouth Volunteer Life Brigade mustered on shore in readiness with the rocket apparatus. The capsized hull of the *Rupert* came ashore on the Black Middens.

4pm. SS *Vildosala* of London was struck by a succession of heavy seas and nearly drove against the north side of the South Pier. She afterwards recovered and proceeded safely into the river. South Shields Volunteer Life Brigade on bad weather watch.

The *James Young* and *Tom Perry* launched to the schooner *Union,* SS *Eccles* and SS *Chipchase*, which were in danger when entering the harbour.

1896

Dec 31 5am. SS *Obedient* of Sunderland struck the Groyne while entering the river. She was assisted off by tugs. South Shields Volunteer Life Brigade on bad weather watch.

1897

Jan 8 8.15pm. SSE gale and heavy seas. Following a steerage failure when entering the harbour, the SS *Wandsworth* came ashore on the Black Middens. Tynemouth Volunteer Life Brigade rescued the 22 crew. The *Bedford* and *James Young* launched to assist.

Jan 22 The *James Young* launched to the schooner *Halls* of Sunderland in danger at the South Pier end. The North Pier was breached by the same storm.

1898

Mar 26 9am. The *Bedford* and *James Young* launched to the barque *Diamant* of Sandefjord, ashore on the Spanish Battery rocks. The crew of eight was landed in eleven minutes by Tynemouth Volunteer Life Brigade.

Apr 15 The *Bedford* and *James Young* launched to the Norwegian barque *Berry Bungis*, which was waterlogged and attempting to enter the harbour. The lifeboats escorted the vessel over the bar.

Jul.14 SS *Ryhope* of London sunk off the South Pier following a collision with SS *Edwin*.

1899

Jan 3 6.30pm. *Forester* launched to SS *Marie* of Kiel. Services not required. This was

Newcastle Libraries

The rescue of the crew of the Diamant, March 26, 1898. Despite the relative shelter of the piers, an easterly gale can still produce heavy seas within the confines of the harbour. Without the protection of the piers, the conditions experienced by the crews of the local lifeboats when they attempted to cross the exposed Tynemouth Bar to reach vessels ashore on the Herd Sands and Black Midden rocks can only be imagined.

the last service launch of this lifeboat at Tynemouth. The *James Young* and *Tom Perry* launched but their services were not required.

Jan 24 11.15pm. SS *Holderness* of Hull got into difficulties inside the harbour, dropped her anchor, but grounded on the Groyne. South Shields Volunteer Life Brigade mustered and set up the rocket apparatus, but their services were not required. The vessel was later towed off by tugs.

Jun 12 The tug *Quickstep* of Shields foundered off Souter Point after a collision.

Sept 30 The *Bedford* and *James Young* launched to the SS *Poplar* of London, in danger when entering the harbour.

Nov 6 The *Bedford* and *James Young* launched to the SS *Snefjord* of Norway, grounded on rocks at Sharpness Point, Tynemouth. The Volunteer Life Brigade mustered, but their services were not required. The vessel was refloated two days later.

Nov 8 The *Bedford* and *James Young* launched to the SS *Anna Eugenie* of France. She later refloated.

Dec 7 SE gale. 10.30am. The SS *Maltby* came ashore on the Black Middens. She was laden with coal, bunkers and stores for the Boer War and bound for HM Naval Base, Simonstown, South Africa. Tynemouth Volunteer Life Brigade fired five rockets, but the distance was too great. The 24 crew were rescued by the *James Young,* with the *Bedford* standing off to assist if required.

Dec 8 Midday. The SS *Craigneuk*, outward bound at high water, drifted onto the Black Middens, some 200 yards to the east of the *Maltby*. She had hit the North Pier three

SS Craigneuk.

times due to her propeller being fouled by a rope. Some of the crew, plus the captain's wife and son, were rescued by Tynemouth Volunteer Life Brigade. The remainder stayed on board until the vessel was refloated. The *Bedford* and *James Young* launched, but their services were not required.

Dec 10 The SS *Onyx* came ashore on the Black Middens. The *Bedford* and *James Young* launched, but their services were not required. The steamship was later towed off by tugs on the rising tide.

1900

Jan 4 The SS *Hispania*, outward bound, struck the South Pier. The *Bedford* and *James Young* launched, but their services were not required.

Feb 7 *Arddan Chan* wrecked off Souter Point.

Feb 15 SE gale. The Spanish steamer, *Lebeito,* in ballast, was driven onto the Black Middens, a little to the west of the *Craigneuk.* The 26 crew, and two pilots, were rescued by Tynemouth Volunteer Life Brigade. The *Bedford* and *James Young* launched, but their services were not required.

May 10 Midnight. The SS *Galtee* of Goole developed a steering fault when leaving the harbour and stranded on the Black Middens. The alarm guns were fired, and Tynemouth Volunteer Life Brigade, after three attempts, got a line on board. As the whip lines began to be hauled out to the vessel, the *Bedford* rowed under the leeside of the *Galtee* and rescued the 13 crew, plus the captain's wife and baby.

May 30 The tug *Conquest* of North Shields foundered off the Tyne.

Aug 20 SS *Greenwood* of Newcastle sunk off the South Pier after a collision with the SS *Bulysses.*

Nov 16 The *Bedford* launched to signals of distress. Nothing found – false alarm.

1901

Mar 29 *Bedford* launched to SS *Astral* of Sweden in difficulties on Black Middens. Assistance not required and the ship was later relocated.

Jun 21 The trawler *Rover* of North Shields wrecked near Souter Point.

1901

Oct 1 *Bedford* went to the assistance of SS *Edenmore* ashore on the Black Middens. Services not required.

Oct 26 1.15am. The *Bedford* launched to SS *Elemore* of Newcastle, ashore on Black Middens in dense fog. Assistance not required. *Forester* stood by. Tynemouth Volunteer Life Brigade got lines aboard. Ship refloated on tide.

South Tyneside Libraries

The wreck of the Constance Ellen.

Nov 12 6pm. *Constance Ellen* of Littlehampton went ashore on Herd Sands to the south of the South Pier. After three hours, seven crew were landed by South Shields Volunteer Life Brigade.

8pm. The *Bedford* and *James Young* launched to the fishing boat *Golden Lily*, grounded on the Groyne. Services not required. Crew of eight rescued by South Shields Volunteer Life Brigade

8pm. *Christiani* of Norway grounded on the Groyne. Eight crew landed by a detachment of South Shields Volunteer Life Brigade. The *Bedford, James Young* and *Forester* stood by.

9pm. The *Bedford* and the *James Young* launched to two trawlers seen in difficulties at harbour entrance. Both lifeboats stood by.

9.30pm. *Lord Dufferin* of London came ashore on Herd Sand to south of South Pier. Five crew landed by South Shields Volunteer Life Brigade. *James Young* launched but services not required.

Nov 13 4am. The barque *Inga* of Christiansand hit the rocks at the northern end of Tynemouth Long Sands. Fifteen crew lost, only one survivor.

7am Unknown vessel foundered outside piers, all crew lost. South Shields Volunteer Life Brigade on bad weather watch.

South Tyneside Libraries

The ketch Lord Dufferin came ashore during the great gale of 12 November 1901. The ferocity of the gale was such that she was driven, on successive tides, so far up the beach that she came to rest on the seaward side of Sea Road, opposite the main entrance to the South Marine Park, South Shields. The South Beach lifeboat house can be seen under the bowsprit.

8am. The Russian ketch *Journeeks* of Riga, anchored half a mile off Sharpness Point to ride out the storm, capsized in heavy seas. Members of Tynemouth Volunteer Life Brigade entered the surf to rescue one of the crew. The remaining three crew perished.

Nov 24 6.30am. The *Bedford* and *James Young* launched to the SS *Dorothy,* ashore on rocks under Tynemouth Castle in heavy fog. Tynemouth Volunteer Life Brigade got a line onboard, but the crew remained. Towed off by the tug *Hercules*, but sank between the piers when entering the harbour. The crew of five was rescued by the *Tom Perry*.

Dec 4 SS *Nordfarer* of Copenhagen came ashore at Trow Rocks in fog. Vessel towed off. The *Tom Perry* and *James Young* launched. South Shields Volunteer Life Brigade on bad weather watch.

Dec 23 The *Tom Perry* and *James Young* launched to SS *Hemlund* of Sweden, ashore on Black Middens. Services not required.

1902

Feb 14 The tug *Champion* of South Shields foundered off Tyne Bar.

Feb 23 *Rotha* of Newcastle foundered off Souter Point after collision with the Danish steamer *Skjold*.

Apr 23 The Norwegian steamer *Hekla* sunk off the Tyne after collision with the *Dilkera*. Seven lives lost.

Nov 20 The SS *Knud* of Denmark sank in the harbour following a collision with SS *Swaledale*, with the loss of eight crew. The *Bedford*, *James Young* and *Forester* all launched. Tynemouth Volunteer Life Brigade set up the rocket apparatus, but the vessel sank so suddenly that no rescue attempt could be made.

Nov 24 The *Tom Perry* and *James Young* launched to signals of distress. Nothing found – false alarm.

Dec 3 The schooner *Schalbe* of Bremen in danger at the harbour entrance. The *Bedford* launched to assist.

1903

Jan 16 SS *Montreal* stranded on the Black Middens. The *Bedford* and *James Young* launched. Services not required. The crew remained onboard.

Apr 4 11.25am. *Renziana* of Groningen drifted against the pier while sailing into the harbour. Towed off.

Apr 21 10.30am. The brig *Celine*, of Malmo was being towed out of harbour when the tow rope broke and she struck the north side of the South Pier, breaking up in few minutes. Seven crew were landed by South Shields Volunteer Life Brigade, and the captain was saved by the *Bedford,* the *James Young* assisting.

July 30 The *Bedford* launched to a Yarmouth fishing boat in danger near the South Pier.

Aug 20 The outward-bound collier *Eastwood* in collision with the inward-bound iron ore carrier *Madeline*. The *Bedford* launched, services not required.

1904

Dec 10 The *James Young* launched to the SS *Grainer* of Norway, in difficulties north of the North Pier.

1905

May 22 12.20am. NNE gale. The SS *Vauxhall,* outward bound, collided with the oil tanker *Broadmayne* at the pier ends. The *Vauxhall* sank between the Groyne and South Pier. The *James Young* and *Bedford* launched, both boats rescuing the 17 crew of the

Vauxhall. Tynemouth motor lifeboat *J. McConnell Hussey* launched for the first time, but her services were not required. She returned to her moorings at 1.05am.

1907

Dec 28 10am. The collier *Pelaw* grounded on the Black Middens. The *Tom Perry, James Young* and *J. McConnell Hussey* all launched. Services not required. The *Pelaw* was later towed off by tugs.

1908

Jan 8 11am. SE gale and heavy seas. The Norwegian steamer SS *Norfolk* and SS *Burham* of London put in the Tyne for shelter and ran onto the Black Middens. Tynemouth Volunteer Life Brigade got a line onboard the *Norfolk*, but there was no response from the crew. The *Tom Perry* and *James Young* launched. Both boats were towed to the wreck by tugs. The *Tom Perry* rescued 13 crew and the *James Young*, four crew. The *Burham* was later refloated by tugs. The *J. McConnell Hussey* was delayed in launching because there was no readily available boarding boat, and then, once the crew got aboard, a frozen engine.

The *Tom Perry* launched to the SS *Denewood* and a trawler in danger near the South Pier.

Mar 21 The SS *Eastwood* and SS *Trader* collided near to the Herd Buoy. The *Tom Perry* launched to their assistance.

July 11 12.30am. SS *Fairy* of Lynn collided with SS *Mar Negro* and then ran on shore. The *Fairy*, holed and taking onboard water, was deliberately beached on the Herd Sand. South Shields Volunteer Life Brigade fired a line over her, but their services were not required and the vessel was later refloated.

1909

Jan 25 8.10pm. The SS *Elleray* and SS *Tees* collided in dense fog. The *J. McConnell Hussey, Tom Perry* and *James Young* all launched, but their services were not required.

Feb 5 A sudden NE gale caught out local fishing cobles. With so many of the lifeboat crew at sea in their cobles, Cullercoats lifeboat was unable to launch. The *J. McConnell Hussey* launched at 6am and escorted one coble over Tynemouth Bar and the remainder back to Cullercoats Harbour.

Mar 3 The *Tom Perry* launched to an incident that turned out to be a false alarm.

June 30 NE gale and heavy seas prevented two fishing cobles from South Shields, with six people on board, crossing the Bar. The Tynemouth motor lifeboat *J. McConnell Hussey* launched at 3pm and towed both boats back to their moorings.

July 3 The *James Young* launched to the fishing boat *Nellie*, observed to be in danger.

South Tyneside Libraries

South Tyneside Libraries

The Norfolk, wrecked 8 January, 1908.

Aug 31 9am. In a freshening NE breeze, the *J. McConnell Hussey* launched to a fishing coble, with a crew of two, which had been salmon fishing and had lost its oars. She towed the boat into the harbour.

Oct 25 The *Tom Perry* launched to a Hopper Barge in danger of stranding on the South Pier.

1910

Jan 28 8.30pm. *Alphonse* of Christiania went ashore on Herd Sands near Trow Rocks. South Shields Volunteer Life Brigade got a line on board, but they were not used. Twenty-nine crew rescued by the *Willie Wouldhave*. The *J. McConnell Hussey* was delayed in launching due to a frozen engine, and did not reach the wreck until 10.30pm, after the crew had been rescued. Due to shallow water, she could not get alongside.

May 16 HMS *Viking* rammed the tug *Triton* abreast the Black Middens in fog. The *Tom Perry* launched, but her services were not required, HMS *Viking* picked up the crew of the *Triton*.

Dec 6 *Tom Perry* launched to the hopper barge *Dromedary*, which had lost its tow at the pier ends. Tow reconnected and services not required.

South Tyneside Libraries

The Alphonse.

1911

Oct 5 NE gale. Swedish steamer *Anna Greta* hit the North Pier entering the harbour, and became disabled between the Black Middens and Herd Sand. The *James Young* launched, but as she came alongside the steamer got underway, and the services of the lifeboat were not required.

Nov 27 Norwegian barque *Trosvik* ran onto the Black Middens. *Bedford* launched but her services not required. The new Tynemouth motor lifeboat *Henry Vernon* launched at 10.30am and stood by until the barque was refloated and taken in tow by tugs.

1912

Jan 18 8.30am. During a severe gale and heavy seas, the Tynemouth motor lifeboat *Henry Vernon* launched to the brigantine, *Maggie A* of Poole, in difficulties outside the piers and escorted her into the harbour.

July 19 5.30pm. N gale. The *Henry Vernon* escorted five fishing cobles into harbour, four from Cullercoats and one from Sunderland.

Sept 30 Midnight. NE gale and heavy seas. SS *Cape Colonna* stranded on the Black Middens. Tynemouth Volunteer Life Brigade succeeded in getting a line onboard, but the crew remained on board to get the vessel refloated. With the weather moderating, but with heavy seas in the harbour, the *Bedford,* with the *James Young* standing off, took off 12 of the crew, and the *Henry Vernon* landed 12 men. The ship was refloated at 4pm but began to sink and was beached on the Herd Sand at South Shields.

Oct 1 10.30am. ENE gale. The *Henry Vernon* launched to search for the missing coble *Unity* of North Shields. The lifeboat found the coble one mile offshore and escorted her into harbour.

Oct 28 6.25am. SSE gale and rough seas. The schooner *Auguste* ran onto the Black Middens. Tynemouth Volunteer Life Brigade assembled and the *Tom Perry* launched, but their services were not required. Tynemouth motor lifeboat *Henry Vernon* stood by while tugs towed the schooner off the rocks.

Nov 16 10am. SS *Jan Blocke* of Rotterdam ran ashore onto Herd Sand in fog and smooth sea. South Shields Volunteer Life Brigade rigged breeches buoy apparatus, but it was not required.

Nov 18 9pm. In a dense fog, the Spanish steamer *Juneo* collided with the Dutch steamer *Dordrecht* in the harbour. The *Tom Perry* launched but her services were not required.

1913

Jan 13 SS *Dunelm* of Sunderland wrecked on Blyth Pier in severe SSE gale and heavy

South Tyneside Libraries

The Cape Colonna.

seas. With the Blyth rowing lifeboat unable to reach the casualty in the conditions, the *Henry Vernon* launched. Taking 75 minutes to travel the ten miles to the wreck, the lifeboat arrived just as the last person had been rescued by Blyth Volunteer Life Brigade. Some of the lifeboat crew had refused to go, so the motor lifeboat crew was reduced to seven. Superintendent Captain Burton took full responsibility of for launching the boat in the best interests of the RNLI to prove the seaworthiness and reliability of the motor.

Nov 5 9pm. In a dense fog, the outward bound collier *Horden* collided with the inward bound collier *Burnley*. The *Tom Perry* launched, but her services were not required.

1914

Jan 9 6pm. Moderate SSE breeze and rough seas. The trawler *Limeswold* stranded on the Black Middens. The *Tom Perry* launched but her services were not required. The *Henry Vernon* launched and ran out an anchor for the trawler, which later refloated under her own steam.

Mar 12 Training ship *Wellesley* on fire at North Shields. The *Tom Perry* transferred 30 boys to the adjacent RNR training ship *Satellite*.

Sept 30 The *James Young* launched to the Spanish steamer *Zolute Mendi,* which had hit the South Pier end.

Oct 30 8.30.am. Ketch *William* broached to trying to enter harbour in heavy seas and struck the South Pier. Two crew hauled ashore with heaving lines by South Shields Volunteer Life Brigade and soldiers stationed in town. The *Bedford*, *James Young* and *Henry Vernon* launched but could not assist due to shoal water.

Nov 1 *Henry Vernon* rescued 50 crew from the Hospital Ship SS *Rohilla,* aground south of Whitby.

The ketch William.

Nov 16 SSE gale. SS *Kenilworth* driven onto the Black Middens. Eleven crew taken off by the *James Young* and 13 crew by the *Bedford*. The Tynemouth Volunteer Life Brigade got a line onboard but with the prompt arrival of the lifeboats the crew did not use the breeches buoy apparatus.

1915

Jan 17 4.30pm. Severe N gale. The schooner *Monitor* of Riga was driven against the South Pier by heavy seas, scraping along and eventually grounding on the pier stones. The crew assisted off by South Shields Volunteer Life Brigade from the end of the jib boom. The *Tom Perry* and *Henry Vernon* both launched, but their services were not required.

Jan 31 5.30am. SS *Perth* of Glasgow sprung a leak and ran ashore for safety on the Herd Sand between the Groyne and South Pier. The *James Young* launched, soon followed by the *Henry Vernon*, but their services were not required. South Shields Volunteer Life Brigade fired a line over the ship, but the crew elected to stay onboard. The vessel was later refloated.

Feb 6 *Bedford* and *Tom Perry* launched to the sloop *Enfield*, in danger of sinking outside the piers. The *Henry Vernon* launched and stood by.

Feb 11 *Tom Perry* launched to the SS *Firth*, in danger of sinking in the harbour. The steamer was successfully beached on the Herd Sand.

Feb 23 SE gale. Belgian salvage steamer *Remier* ran onto the Black Middens. The *Bedford* and *James Young* launched and stood by for three hours. *Henry Vernon* also stood by. No lifeboat services were required.

Mar 12 The *Tom Perry* launched to the assistance of the SS *Storm King* outside the piers.

1916
Jul 2 11.50pm. Torpedo Boat Destroyer *Ness* stranded on Trow Rocks in thick fog. After standing by for three hours, the services of South Shields Volunteer Life Brigade were not required and the vessel refloated on the high tide.

Nov 19 8.30am. SE gale. The Norwegian mail steamer *Bessheim* was driven onto the Black Middens after suffering engine failure. The *Bedford*, *Tom Perry* and *Henry Vernon* all launched. With the *Bedford* standing off, the *Tom Perry* took off 16 crew and the *Henry Vernon* 102 crew and passengers. Tynemouth Volunteer Life Brigade rescued three crew using the breeches buoy.

Nov 20 7.30am. SE gale. SS *Muristan*, ashore in Blyth Bay. Due to the atrocious conditions, Blyth lifeboat was unable to launch and Blyth Volunteer Life Brigade was unsuccessful in getting lines onboard. The *Henry Vernon* launched and found no signs of life on the wreck. Leaving the scene the lifeboat was swamped, which stopped the engine, and she put into the Blyth under sail, where the engine was repaired. On 21 November, the coastguard reported sightings of the crew, and the *Henry Vernon* returned to the *Muristan,* and saved 16 lives.

Dec 19 6.55pm. HM Submarine *C8* aground at Whitley Bay. The *Henry Vernon* launched, but the engine stalled due to a frozen throttle. The lifeboat was towed back into the river by a pilot boat. The 18 crew of the submarine were saved by Cullercoats lifeboat *Co-Operator No.1*.

1917
Oct 25 The *Henry Vernon* launched to assist in a wreck service at Whitby. Recalled off Sunderland.

Dec 17 5.15pm. SS *Butetown* came ashore in heavy seas and strong southerly wind near Cullercoats. Fourteen, plus ten crew found 1.5 miles offshore in the ship's two lifeboats, by the *Co-Operator No.1*. The *Henry Vernon* launched to assist in the search.

1918
Jan 7 The *Bedford* launched to the *Tyne Examination* vessel, ashore on the Herd Sand.

The crew of nine was rescued by South Shields Volunteer Life Brigade. The *Henry Vernon* could not launch due to a frozen engine.

Feb 1 The *Henry Vernon* launched to assist in the search for a ship ashore near Blyth.

Feb 13 5pm. HM Minesweeper *Viola II* ran ashore in dense fog onto Cullercoats rocks. The *Co-Operator No. 1* and *Henry Vernon* launched to assist in refloating the vessel.

1919

July19 Midnight. NE gale. The *Bedford* launched to the assistance of the Danish schooner *William* ashore on the Herd Sand, in between the Groyne and South Pier. Crew came ashore in the ship's boat and were taken to the South Shields Volunteer Life Brigade Watch House.

Nov 19 6pm. E gale. SS *Linerton* driven onto the Herd Sand to the south of the South Pier. 45 crew were rescued by the *Willie Wouldhave*. The force of the gale prevented rockets fired by South Shields Volunteer Life Brigade from reaching the wreck. The new Tynemouth motor lifeboat *Henry Frederick Swan* was put on standby but did not launch.

1920

Dec 30 11.45pm. The North Shields steam trawler *Current* ran onto the Black Middens, following steering gear failure. The *Henry Frederick Swan* launched and assisted in the refloating of the vessel.

1923

Feb 6 Foyboat in difficulty off the Tyne entrance. The *Henry Frederick Swan* launched and escorted the boat into harbour.

South Tyneside Libraries

The wreck of the Linerton.

1925

Nov 25 7.30am. NE gale. The Admiralty 'Q'-ship *PC71* lost her tow and came ashore at Target Rock, to the south of Trow Rocks. Crew of two rescued by South Shields Volunteer Life Brigade. The *Henry Frederick Swan* launched but could not assist.

1931

Feb 13 1pm. NE gale and heavy seas. The *Henry Frederick Swan* launched to three cobles in difficulties off Souter Lighthouse. The cobles arrived safely at Sunderland, soon followed by the lifeboat.

Aug 22 NE gale. The *Henry Frederick Swan* launched to search for missing boat off Marsden. At sea for six hours.

Sept 1 8.50am. The Lowestoft drifter *Fortis* went ashore on the end of the South Pier. The *Henry Frederick Swan* launched and assisted in the refloating of the vessel. South Shields Volunteer Life Brigade mustered on the pier.

1932

Jan 4 Strong NW breeze. Two boys adrift in small boat,three miles ESE of Marsden Coastguard Look-out. *Henry Frederick Swan* launched and found the boat behind the South pier.

1933

Feb 25 9.30am. SE gale. The SS *Eilande*, coal laden, took shelter on the northern side of the South Pier to repair her steering gear, but was driven onto the Black Middens.

South Tyneside Libraries

South Tyneside Libraries

The wreck of the PC71.

Tynemouth Volunteer Life Brigade put a line over her, but the eight crew were taken off by the *Henry Frederick Swan*.

Mar 10 11.30am. SS *Ellind* ran onto the Black Middens. The *Tom Perry* launched. Services not required.

May 1 *Henry Frederick Swan* launched to search for a motor launch off Briar Dene, Whitley Bay.

Dec 27 The trawler *Tartar* ran ashore on the Black Middens. The *Henry Frederick Swan* launched and Tynemouth Volunteer Life Brigade stood by while the vessel was refloated.

1935

Apr 15 7.45pm. SS *Ensign*, laden with coal for Gibraltar, stranded in fog on the South Pier. South Shields Volunteer Life Brigade and the *Henry Frederick Swan* stood by until the vessel was refloated at midnight.

Apr 21 3pm. Strengthening SE breeze. The *Henry Frederick Swan* launched to three boats sheltering off the North Pier.

May 14 6.20pm. The *Henry Frederick Swan* launched to the trawler *Lolist,* in difficulties a half mile east of the Tyne Piers, and escorted her into the Tyne.

Jun 5 12.15am. Moderate NE breeze. SS *Lightfoot* stranded at Seaton Sluice. The *Henry Frederick Swan* launched and stood by until the vessel had refloated, returning to station at 4.30am.

Jul 26 Motor launch in difficulties off Frenchman's Bay. The *Henry Frederick Swan* launched and escorted the boat into harbour.

Sept 23 9am. Moderate NE breeze. The *Henry Frederick Swan* launched and escorted two cobles into Cullercoats Harbour. The Cullercoats lifeboat was off service that day.

1937

Feb 13 Vessel reported ashore at St Mary's Island, Whitley Bay. The *Bedford* launched. When she arrived the vessel had already refloated.

Nov 17 8.40pm. SE gale. Norwegian vessel *Toborg I* driven into Tynemouth (Prior's) Haven, and schooner *Orion* driven onto the Black Middens. The *Bedford*, *Henry Frederick Swan* and the Tynemouth Volunteer Life Brigade stood by while both vessels were refloated.

Appendix 4 – Coxswains

Coxswains were experienced pilots who had progressed from being crewmembers to second coxswain or bowman and operated the steering oar in the bow of the lifeboat, before being promoted to cox.

With a large pool of experienced coxswains, boats, especially in the latter years of the service could be commanded by a number of coxswains. The following list, taken from service records, names known Coxswains with, unfortunately, many gaps to be filled.

Tyne – South Shields

1845 – Jacob Harrison, Joseph Smith 2nd Cox

1851 – Joseph Smith

1854 – Jacob Harrison

1861 – Jacob Burn, Jacob Harrison, John Milburn

1861-1870 – Andrew Harrison

1863-1870 – George Smith

1865 – Joseph Smith

1882 – Andrew Purvis

Providence – South Shields

1849 – Launcelot Burn

1861 – Joseph Smith

1870 – Jacob Burn

Northumberland – North Shields

1861 – Gilbert Young, Matthew Lawson, Andrew Harrison

1870 – Gilbert Young

1872 – H. Sadler

Tom Perry – South Shields

1872 – James Stewart

1883-1895 – John Landers Burn

1883 – Arthur Landers Burn

1881-1888 – Andrew Harrison

1907-1914 – Richard Harrison

1910-1915 – John Whale

1915 – J.L. Carr

1915 – J. Marshall

Willie Wouldhave – South Shields

1882 – Andrew Burn
1884 – William Marshall
1892 – Andrew Purvis
1910 – Richard Harrison

James Young – North Shields

1884-1892 – William O. Thurlbeck
1887 – John Landers Burn
1892-1895 – James Turnbull
1899-1911 – Thomas Wilson
1914-1916 – James Marvin

Bedford – South Shields

1887-1897 – John Landers Burn
1889-1905 – William Marshall
1889 – Andrew Purvis
1892 – John Chambers
1892 – Thomas Bone
1897 – Thomas Gibson
1899 – Thomas Young
1901 – Richard Harrison
1912-1937 – John Whale

Other Coxswains

Henry Appleby
Robert Armour
Anthony Emmerson
John Phillips
Robert Pickering
George W. Purvis
James Purvis
George Smith
John Wells
Mathew Young

Appendix 5 – Lifeboat Site Locations Today

The *Tyne* and the Lifeboat Memorial, South Shields

The *Tyne* is on display next to the Lifeboat Memorial, Pier Head South Shields.

Author's collection

The *Bedford,* Eyemouth

The *Bedford* is stored, awaiting restoration and display as part of the Scottish Small Craft Association plans to develop a maritime museum at Eyemouth Harbour. In October 1968 she went to the Exeter Maritime Museum, where she was displayed for many years. With the demise of that museum, the International Small Craft Association moved the *Bedford* to Lowestoft, where plans to develop this site as a museum did not come to fruition, and in 2003, with the majority of the small boats collection of ISCA, she was transferred to Eyemouth.

Author's collection

The Lawe House, South Shields

The Lawe House was demolished in 1972, and the site redeveloped with a four-storey apartment block.

The *Original's* Boathouse, South Shields

In this photograph, taken from above North Shields Fish Quay, the block of flats that now occupies the site of the Lawe House can be seen to the right of the picture. The boathouse is likely to have been located where the Harbour View housing development is today. This land had formed part of the tidal sandy banks of the river.

Author's collection

Coble Landing, South Shields

The Coble Landing boathouses, adjacent houses, quayside buildings and businesses were demolished in 1937 as part of a comprehensive slum clearance and riverside re-development programme. All evidence of the Coble Landing was lost when the river quay walls were built up and a large factory erected on the site.

Author's collection

The South Beach Boathouses, South Shields

The site of the first South Beach lifeboat house on the Herd Sands now forms part of the Ocean Beach Amusement Park and is occupied by a ghost train ride. The site of the second South Beach boathouse was on the grassed area in front of the South Shields Volunteer Life Brigade Watch House. In the foreground, the site of the second South Beach boathouse with the South Shields Volunteer Life Brigade Watch House in the background. Before the construction of the piers, this area formed part of the tidal Herd Sands. Subsequent development and the raising of land levels have radically altered the appearance of the foreshore since the days of the lifeboat.

Author's collection

The Pilot Jetty, South Shields

The Pilot Jetty boathouse and slipway, near to the site of the *Original's* boathouse, was demolished in 1990, with the reclamation and redevelopment of the former Velva Liquids Oil Depot into the Harbour View housing estate. All that remains of the lifeboat station are the slipway abutment walls in the stone quayside, and three supporting timber piles of the slipway that can be seen at low water.

This photograph indicates the close proximity of the former RNLI and Tyne Lifeboat Institution boathouses. On the opposite bank, at North Shields, the Tynemouth Lifeboat Station can be seen midway between the first North Shields lifeboat house, adjacent the seaward side of the Low Lighthouse. Downstream, the boathouses of the Tyne Lifeboat Institution and RNLI that were at the top of the beach and upstream of the former Lloyds Hailing Station jetty.

Author's collection

Trinity Towers Lookout, Lawe Top, South Shields

After the Tyne Pilotage Authority vacated the tower, moving to a new lookout closer to the Pilot Jetty, the South Shields Marine School took over the building as a radar training school until May 1968. The building was demolished in 1971. A stone memorial and plaque now mark the location of this building.

Author's collection

Henry Greathead and Willie Wouldhave's houses

Housing and river-related commercial premises, confined to the narrow lanes that ran parallel to the river, developed during the industrial revolution – period of prolonged prosperity in the town as a result of its seafaring, shipbuilding and coal industries. It was in these streets that Greathead and Wouldhave lived. The majority of houses were badly built, overcrowded and without proper ventilation, sanitation or drainage. This created severe health problems such as high infant mortality and tuberculosis.

In 1933 the Borough Council embarked on a three-year comprehensive programme of slum clearance, involving over 2,000 dwellings and 8,000 residents. As a result of this programme the Coble Landing boathouses and the houses of Greathead and Wouldhave were demolished.

Greathead lived in a terraced house on Wellington Street, on the western fringes of the Lawe Top, midway between St Stephen's Church and the River Tyne, within a short distance of his boatbuilding yard. The last known residence of Willie Wouldhave was a cottage on Nelson's Bank, a narrow lane connecting Commercial Road with the Customs House and Mill Dam. Today it is a car park for the Customs House theatre.

The site of Wellington Street was redeveloped in the 1950s with residential flats along River Drive.

Willie Wouldhave's Grave, St Hilda's Church

Inside St Hilda's Church, at South Shields Market Place, there are a number of lifeboat-related artefacts. Wouldhave's original gravestone and George Tindale's (drowned in the 1849 lifeboat disaster) headstone are on display, together with a small model of Stephen Laverick's lifeboat.

Southern Wavetrap

The South Shields Sailing Club is now based at the Southern Wavetrap. The proposed lifeboat house would have been located at the top of the beach. The Pilot Jetty boathouse was to the right of the single-storey flat-roofed building, the Foyboatman's Lookout. The block of flats on the skyline occupies the site of the Lawe House.

Author's collection

North Shields Low Lighthouse

Nothing remains of the North Shields lifeboat houses that were located next to the Low Light House.

Northern Wavetrap, East Fish Quay, North Shields

The lifeboat houses of the Tyne Lifeboat Institution and RNLI were located at the head of the Northern

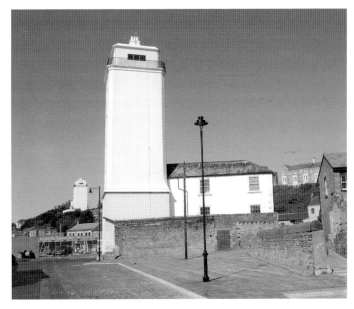

Author's collection

Wavetrap. All references to the presence of lifeboat stations on this site have now disappeared.

Prior's Haven, Tynemouth

The former Tynemouth No. 1 Station boathouse was built to house the lifeboat *Constance* in 1862, following the re-establishment of this station by the RNLI. It was built on the same site as the earlier Coastguard boathouse also used by the Tyne Lifeboat Institution.

Author's collection

Sources, bibliography and artefacts

Source materials and bibliography

The Admiralty, *Duke of Northumberland Competition, Report of the Committee appointed to examine the Lifeboat Models to compete for the Premium offered by His Grace, the Duke of Northumberland*, 1851.

Kenneth Bond, *The Pilots of the Tyne*, 1961, South Tyneside Local History Library.

Tom Cunliffe and Adrian Osler, *Pilots-2. Schooners and Open Boats of the European Pilots and Watermen,* 2002, Chatham Publishing.

Clayton Evans, *Rescue at Sea*, 2003, Conway Maritime Press

Henry Greathead, *The Report of the Evidence, and other Proceedings in Parliament respecting the Invention of the Lifeboat,* 4 June 1803

W.A. Hails, *An Enquiry concerning the Invention of the Lifeboat including Remarks on Mr Greathead's Report of the Evidence and other Proceedings in Parliament,* 1806.

George B. Hodgson, *The Borough of South Shields*, 1903, South Tyneside Libraries

John Cameron Lamb, *The Lifeboat and its Work,* 1911, W. Clowes and Sons

Chris Lambert, *List of Shipwreck Incidents on the North East Coast,* Tynemouth Volunteer Life Brigade, 1997

Nicholas Leach, *A Century of Motor Lifeboats*, 2005, Landmark Publishing Ltd.

Nicholas Leach and Paul Russell, *Cromer Lifeboats*, 2004, Tempus Publishing

The Lifeboat, editions 1862, 1863, 1865 – RNLI

James Mather, *Description and Recommendations of a Life-boat*, 1827 (copy in British Library).

Eric McKee, *Working Boats of Britain.*

Noel T. Methley, *The Lifeboat and its Story,* 1912, Sidgwick & Jackson

David R. Moir, *The Birth and History of Trinity House, Newcastle upon Tyne,* 1960

Jeff Morris, *The History of Cullercoats Lifeboats,* 1994, Lifeboat Enthusiasts' Society

Jeff Morris, *The History of Tynemouth Lifeboats,* 1995, Lifeboat Enthusiasts' Society

Jeff Morris and Graham Farr, *List of British Lifeboats,* 1992, Lifeboat Enthusiasts' Society

Adrian G Osler, *Mr Greathead's Lifeboats,* 1990, Tyne & Wear Archives & Museums

Port of Tyne Authority – River Charts and Construction Records

The Port of Tyne Pilot and Durham and Northumberland Advertiser 1839-1842

Raymond Porter, B.S.C., M.I.C.E., M.I.Mech.E, *The Building of the Tyne Piers,* 1958, Chairman's Address, the Institution of Civil Engineers, Northern Counties Association.

Jean Robinson, *The Tyne Pilots*, May 1982, South Tyneside Local History Library.

Ralph Shanks, Wick York, *The U.S. Life-Saving Service,* 2003 edition, Costano Books, Petaluma, California.

South Shields Gazette, *History of the Lifeboat,* 1889

SSVLB, *South Shields Volunteer Life Brigade Coast Rescue Unit,* 2001, SSVLB and North East Museums Service – Tomorrow's History Project

South Tyneside Local History Library – Extracts from the South Shields Gazette, Photographic Records and Maps, Lifeboat and VLB 'Cuttings Book'

Bill Stephenson, *The Stephenson Pilots of South Shields*, South Tyneside Local History Library.

Robert Surtees, *The History and Antiquities of the County Palatine of Durham,* 1820, J. Nichols and Sons, London.

Tyne & Wear Archives & Museums, Tyne Lifeboat Society Committee Minutes and Rescue Logs 1861-1910. Articles of Association 1905, Companies Act 1862

Tyne Improvement Commission, Annual Reports and Committee Meeting Minutes, 1882-83, 1883-84, 1884-85, 1885-86, 1887-88, 1893-94, 1898-99, 1904-05.

Tynemouth RNLI Lifeboat Station, Service Launch Records

TVLB, *Tynemouth Volunteer Life Brigade 1864-1994 A Chronicle*, 1995, TVLB

James Walker, F.R.S.E., M. Inst. C.E. *The Tyne as a Navigable River,* 1905, Presidential Address, Institution of Civil Engineers

Boswell Whitaker, *South Shields Volunteer Life Brigade*, 1980, South Tyneside Libraries

Boswell Whitaker, *Tynemouth Volunteer Life Brigade*, 1980, South Tyneside Libraries

Boswell Whitaker, *Skuetender Lifeboat,* 1979, South Tyneside Libraries

Barbara and Reginald Yorke, *Britain's First Lifeboat Station,* Alt Press, 1992

Tyne Lifeboat Artefacts

South Shields Museum – original models of Wouldhave's tin lifeboat and the Tyne Lifeboat *Willie Wouldhave*, the bust of Willie Wouldhave and paintings depicting the development of the Shields Lifeboats.

South Shields Volunteer Life Brigade, South Pier – displays of early shipwrecks, rescue equipment and Tyne Lifeboat Institution display and lifeboat model.

Tynemouth Volunteer Life Brigade, Spanish Battery, Tynemouth – displays of early shipwrecks, rescue equipment and model of the second *Northumberland* lifeboat and local lifeboat competition boats.

Discovery Museum, Newcastle – model of the Tyne lifeboat *Willie Wouldhave*, and, in storage, models of various Tyne Institution lifeboats together with models from the national and local lifeboat competitions,

St Hilda's Church, Market Place, South Shields – Wouldhave's original and replacement gravestones, George Tindle's gravestone, a model of a Greathead lifeboat built by one of his apprentices, Stephen Laverick.

Preston Cemetery, North Shields – Gilbert Young's gravestone.

Scottish Small Craft Association, Eyemouth – the Tyne Lifeboat *Bedford*.

RNLI Museum, Redcar – Greathead's 1801 lifeboat *Zetland*.

North East Maritime Trust, Fishermen's Workshops, Wapping Street, South Shields – the former Tynemouth RNLI 40ft. motor lifeboat *Henry Frederick Swan*.

National Maritime Museum, Greenwich, London – Models of Greathead lifeboats.

Science Museum, London – Model of the *Bedford* lifeboat.

Author's Acknowledgements

Until 1841, there were no formal records of the work of the Tyne lifeboats, and those made after that date had either been destroyed or lost, with the exception of two official service record books, correspondence books and accounts ledger all held by the Tyne and Wear Archive Service. The information and research on which this book has been based have been obtained from a number of sources and I am deeply indebted to the following people and organisations. I apologise to anyone I might inadvertently have omitted.

In addition to the Archive Service, I drew heavily on the records of the Local History Library at South Shields, with particular thanks to Keith Bardwell, Anne Sharp and Hildred Whale for their invaluable help and assistance. Thanks also go to Ian Whitehead, Alisdair Wilson, Victoria Rogers and Adam Bell of the Tyne and Wear Museums for access to the many lifeboat models and paintings held by the Museum Service.

Special thanks goes to Barry Cox, Honorary Librarian, RNLI archives in Poole, who, in addition to responding to my telephone queries and correspondence, assisted me when searching through the Management Committee Meeting minute books, the

Grahame Farr Archive and the Station Minute books for Tynemouth Lifeboat Station.

Thanks also go to Michael Nugent, Coxswain of Tynemouth Lifeboat, for his help and knowledge of the local tides and currents in gaining a better understanding surrounding the circumstances of the 1849 lifeboat disaster, and to Kevin Mole, Station Mechanic, regarding access to the service records held at the station. Chris Lambert, a Deputy Launching Authority at Tynemouth Lifeboat Station and archivist at Tynemouth Volunteer Life Brigade provided access to the lifeboat displays in the VLB Watch House and to his own historical research on the Tyne Lifeboat Institution.

Thanks also to Frank Taylor, Lifeboat Operations Manager at Cullercoats Lifeboat Station; to Dave Robertson, Keeper of the Records at South Shields Volunteer Life Brigade; and to Janis Blower of the Shields Gazette.

Research was also undertaken at North Tyneside Local History Library; the Durham County Records Office; Trinity House, Newcastle; and the British Library, London. Thanks also go to the Port of Tyne Authority for allowing access to their archive. Thanks go to Ridley Youngman at the Scottish International Sailing Craft Association, Eyemouth, for access to the *Bedford*, and to John Lightfoot MBE, Vice-Chairman, and Chris May, Company Secretary, of the Tyne Lifeboat Society, for outlining the current activities of the Society. I must not forget the other authors whose books have cast light on this subject, and without which my task would have been much harder, in particular, Adrian Osler's *Mr Greathead's Lifeboats,* and the late Boswell Whitaker's *Skuetender Lifeboat*, the only other known publications about the work of the Tyne Lifeboat Institution. Whitaker's notes and stories about his grandfather and uncles, who were crewmembers of the Tyne Lifeboat Institution boats, gave a fascinating insight into the men who manned the Shields lifeboats.

Finally, thanks to Anna Flowers, and Vanessa Histon at Tyne Bridge Publishing for their help and constructive advice during this project.

Index of ships

Index of people